PYTHON FOR DATA SCIENCE

T0093629

# PYTHON FOR DATA SCIENCE

## A Hands-On Introduction

by Yuli Vasiliev

**no starch press®**

San Francisco

Printed in the United States of America

Second printing

27 26 25 24 23    2 3 4 5 6 7

ISBN-13: 978-1-7185-0220-8 (print)
ISBN-13: 978-1-7185-0221-5 (ebook)

 Published by No Starch Press®, Inc.
245 8th Street, San Francisco, CA 94103
phone: +1.415.863.9900
www.nostarch.com; info@nostarch.com

Publisher: William Pollock
Managing Editor: Jill Franklin
Production Manager: Rachel Monaghan
Production Editor: Jennifer Kepler
Developmental Editor: Nathan Heidelberger
Cover Illustrator: Gina Redman
Interior Design: Octopod Studios
Technical Reviewer: Daniel Zingaro
Copyeditor: Rachel Head
Compositor: Jeff Lytle, Happenstance Type-O-Rama
Proofreader: Jamie Lauer

*Library of Congress Cataloging-in-Publication Data*

Names: Vasiliev, Yuli, author.
Title: Python for data science : a hands-on introduction / Yuli Vasiliev.
Description: San Francisco : No Starch Press, [2022] | Includes index.
Identifiers: LCCN 2022002116 (print) | LCCN 2022002117 (ebook) | ISBN
    9781718502208 (print) | ISBN 9781718502215 (ebook)
Subjects: LCSH: Python (Computer program language) | Electronic data
    processing. | Data mining.
Classification: LCC QA76.73.P98 V37 2022  (print) | LCC QA76.73.P98
    (ebook) | DDC 005.13/3--dc23/eng/20220325
LC record available at https://lccn.loc.gov/2022002116
LC ebook record available at https://lccn.loc.gov/2022002117

For customer service inquiries, please contact info@nostarch.com. For information on distribution, bulk sales, corporate sales, or translations: sales@nostarch.com. For permission to translate this work: rights@nostarch.com. To report counterfeit copies or piracy: counterfeit@nostarch.com.

[S]

## About the Author

Yuli Vasiliev is a programmer, writer, and consultant specializing in open source development, building data structures and models, and implementing database backends. He is the author of *Natural Language Processing with Python and spaCy* (No Starch Press, 2020).

## About the Technical Reviewer

Dr. Daniel Zingaro is an associate teaching professor of computer science and award-winning teacher at the University of Toronto. His research focuses on understanding and enhancing student learning of computer science. He is the author of two recent No Starch Press books: *Algorithmic Thinking* (2020), a no-nonsense, no-math guide to algorithms and data structures; and *Learn to Code by Solving Problems* (2021), a primer for learning Python and computational thinking.

# BRIEF CONTENTS

# CONTENTS IN DETAIL

## 5
## WORKING WITH DATABASES 73

## 6
## AGGREGATING DATA 95

## 7
## COMBINING DATASETS 109

## 8
## CREATING VISUALIZATIONS 127

# INTRODUCTION

We live in a world of information technology (IT), where computer systems collect enormous quantities of data, process it, and extract useful information from it. This data-driven reality affects not only the way modern businesses operate but our daily lives too. Without the numerous devices and systems that employ data-focused technologies, it would be hard for many of us to maintain contact with society. Mobile maps and navigation, online shopping, and smart home devices are some common examples of data-focused technology for everyday life.

In the business world, companies often use IT systems to make decisions by extracting actionable information from large volumes of data. The data may arrive from various sources, in different formats, and may require transformation before it's ready for analysis. For example, many companies that do business online use data analytics to drive customer acquisition and retention, collecting and measuring everything they can to model and understand their users' behavior. They often combine and analyze both quantitative and qualitative user data from many different sources, such as user profiles, social media, and company websites. And in many cases, they accomplish all these tasks using the Python programming language.

This book will introduce you to the Pythonic world of working with data, without the taint of academic jargon or excessive complexity. You'll learn to use Python for data-oriented applications, writing code to power a ride-sharing service, generate product recommendations, predict stock market trends, and more. Through real-world examples such as these, you'll gain practical, hands-on experience with the key Python data science libraries.

## Using Python for Data Science

The easy-on-the-brain Python programming language is an ideal choice for accessing, manipulating, and gaining insight from data of any kind. It has both a rich set of built-in data structures for basic operations and a robust ecosystem of open source libraries for data analysis and manipulation of any level of complexity. We'll explore many such libraries in this book, including NumPy, pandas, scikit-learn, Matplotlib, and more.

With Python, you can write concise and intuitive code with minimal time and effort, expressing most concepts in just a few lines of code. In fact, Python's agile syntax allows you to implement several data operations with a single line of code. For example, you can write a one-liner that filters, transforms, and aggregates data all at once.

As a general-purpose language, Python is suitable for a wide variety of tasks. When you work with Python, you can seamlessly integrate data science with other tasks to create fully functional, well-rounded applications. For example, you could build a bot application that makes stock market predictions in response to natural language requests from users. To create such an application, you'd need a bot API, a machine learning model to make predictions, and a natural language processing (NLP) tool to interact with users. There are powerful Python libraries for all of these.

## Who Should Read This Book?

This book is for developers looking to gain a better understanding of Python's data processing and analysis capabilities. Perhaps you work for a company that wants to use data to improve business processes, make better decisions, and target more customers. Or maybe you want to develop your own data-driven applications, or simply expand your knowledge of Python into the realm of data science.

The book assumes you have some basic experience with Python and that you're comfortable following instructions to perform tasks such as installing a database or obtaining an API key. However, the book covers Python data science concepts from the bottom up, through hands-on examples that are all thoroughly explained. You'll learn by doing, with no prior data experience necessary.

# What's in the Book?

The book begins with a conceptual introduction to data processing and analysis, explaining a typical data processing pipeline. Then we'll cover Python's built-in data structures and some of the third-party Python libraries that are widely used for data science applications. Next, we'll explore increasingly sophisticated techniques for obtaining, combining, aggregating, grouping, analyzing, and visualizing datasets of different sizes and data types. As the book goes on, we'll apply Python data science techniques to real use cases from the world of business management, marketing, and finance. Along the way, each chapter contains "Exercise" sections so you can practice and reinforce what you've just learned.

Here's an overview of what you'll find in each chapter:

**Chapter 1: The Basics of Data**   Provides the necessary background for understanding the essentials of working with data. You'll learn that there are different categories of data, including structured, unstructured, and semistructured data. Then you'll walk through the steps involved in a typical data analysis process.

**Chapter 2: Python Data Structures**   Introduces four data structures that are built into Python: lists, dictionaries, tuples, and sets. You'll see how to use each structure and how to combine them into more complex structures that can represent real-world objects.

**Chapter 3: Python Data Science Libraries**   Discusses Python's robust ecosystem of third-party libraries for data analysis and manipulation. You'll meet the pandas library and its primary data structures, the Series and DataFrame, which have become the de facto standard for data-oriented Python applications. You'll also learn about NumPy and scikit-learn, two other libraries often used for data science.

**Chapter 4: Accessing Data from Files and APIs**   Dives into the details of obtaining data and loading it into your scripts. You'll learn to load data from different sources, such as files and APIs, into data structures in your Python scripts for further processing.

**Chapter 5: Working with Databases**   Continues the discussion of importing data into Python, covering how to work with database data. You'll look at examples of accessing and manipulating data stored in databases of different types, including relational databases like MySQL and NoSQL databases like MongoDB.

**Chapter 6: Aggregating Data**   Approaches the problem of summarizing data by sorting it into groups and performing aggregate calculations. You'll learn to use pandas to group data and produce subtotals, totals, and other aggregations.

**Chapter 7: Combining Datasets**   Covers how to combine data from different sources into a single dataset. You'll learn techniques that SQL developers use to join database tables and apply them to built-in Python data structures, NumPy arrays, and pandas DataFrames.

**Chapter 8: Creating Visualizations** Discusses visualizations as the most natural way to bring to light hidden patterns in data. You'll learn about different types of visualizations, such as line graphs, bar graphs, and histograms, and you'll see how to create them with Matplotlib, the leading Python library for plotting. You'll also use the Cartopy library to generate maps.

**Chapter 9: Analyzing Location Data** Explains how to work with location data using the geopy and Shapely libraries. You'll learn ways to get and use GPS coordinates for both stationary and moving objects, and you'll explore the real-world example of how a ride-sharing service can identify the best car for a given pick-up.

**Chapter 10: Analyzing Time Series Data** Presents some analysis techniques that you can apply to time series data to extract meaningful statistics from it. In particular, the examples in this chapter illustrate how time series data analysis can be applied to stock market data.

**Chapter 11: Gaining Insights from Data** Explores strategies for gaining insight from data in order to make informed decisions. As an example, you'll learn how to discover associations between products sold at a supermarket so you can determine what groups of items are frequently bought together in a single transaction (useful for recommendations and promotions).

**Chapter 12: Machine Learning for Data Analysis** Covers the use of scikit-learn for advanced data analysis tasks. You'll train machine learning models to classify product reviews according to their star ratings and to predict trends in a stock's price.

# 1

## THE BASICS OF DATA

*Data* means different things to different people: a stock trader might think of data as real-time stock quotes, while a NASA engineer might associate data with signals coming from a Mars rover. When it comes to data processing and analysis, however, the same or similar approaches and techniques can be applied to a variety of datasets, regardless of their origin. All that matters is how the data is structured.

This chapter provides a conceptual introduction to data processing and analysis. We'll first look at the main categories of data you may have to deal with, then touch on common data sources. Next, we'll consider the steps in a typical data processing pipeline (that is, the actual process of obtaining, preparing, and analyzing data). Finally, we'll examine Python's unique advantages as a data science tool.

# Categories of Data

Programmers divide data into three main categories: unstructured, structured, and semistructured. In a data processing pipeline, the source data is typically unstructured; from this, you form structured or semistructured datasets for further processing. Some pipelines, however, use structured data from the start. For example, an application processing geographical locations might receive structured data directly from GPS sensors. The following sections explore the three main categories of data as well as time series data, a special type of data that can be structured or semistructured.

## Unstructured Data

Unstructured data is data with no predefined organizational system, or schema. This is the most widespread form of data, with common examples including images, videos, audio, and natural language text. To illustrate, consider the following financial statement from a pharmaceutical company:

```
GoodComp shares soared as much as 8.2% on 2021-01-07 after the company announced positive
early-stage trial results for its vaccine.
```

This text is considered unstructured data because the information found in it isn't organized with a predefined schema. Instead, the information is randomly scattered within the statement. You could rewrite this statement in any number of ways while still conveying the same information. For example:

```
Following the January 7, 2021, release of positive results from its vaccine trial, which is
still in its early stages, shares in GoodComp rose by 8.2%.
```

Despite its lack of structure, unstructured data may contain important information, which you can extract and convert to structured or semistructured data through appropriate transformation and analysis steps. For example, image recognition tools first convert the collection of pixels within an image into a dataset of a predefined format and then analyze this data to identify content in the image. Similarly, the following section will show a few ways in which the data extracted from our financial statement could be structured.

## Structured Data

Structured data has a predefined format that specifies how the data is organized. Such data is usually stored in a repository like a relational database or just a *.csv* (comma-separated values) file. The data fed into such a repository is called a *record*, and the information in it is organized in *fields* that must arrive in a sequence matching the expected structure. Within a database, records of the same structure are logically grouped in a container called a *table*. A database may contain various tables, with each table having a set structure of fields.

There are two basic types of structured data: numerical and categorical. *Categorical data* is that which can be categorized on the basis of similar characteristics; cars, for example, might be categorized by make and model. *Numerical data*, on the other hand, expresses information in numerical form, allowing you to perform mathematical operations on it.

Keep in mind that categorical data can sometimes take on numerical values. For example, consider ZIP codes or phone numbers. Although they are expressed with numbers, it wouldn't make any sense to perform math operations on them, such as finding the median ZIP code or average phone number.

How can we organize the text sample introduced in the previous section into structured data? We're interested in specific information in this text, such as company names, dates, and stock prices. We want to present that information in fields in the following format, ready for insertion into a database:

```
Company:    ABC
Date:       yyyy-mm-dd
Stock:      nnnnn
```

Using techniques of *natural language processing (NLP)*, a discipline that trains machines to understand human-readable text, we can extract information appropriate for these fields. For example, we look for a company name by recognizing a categorical data variable that can only be one of many preset values, such as Google, Apple, or GoodComp. Likewise, we can recognize a date by matching its explicit ordering to one of a set of explicit ordering formats, such as *yyyy-mm-dd*. In our example, we recognize, extract, and present our data in the predefined format like this:

```
Company:    GoodComp
Date:       2021-01-07
Stock:      +8.2%
```

To store this record in a database, it's better to present it as a row-like sequence of fields. We therefore might reorganize the record as a rectangular data object, or a 2D matrix:

```
Company  | Date       | Stock
-------------------------------
GoodComp |2021-01-07  | +8.2%
```

The information you choose to extract from the same unstructured data source depends on your requirements. Our example statement not only contains the change in GoodComp's stock value for a certain date but also indicates the reason for that change, in the phrase "the company announced positive early-stage trial results for its vaccine." Taking the statement from this angle, you might create a record with these fields:

```
Company:    GoodComp
Date:       2021-01-07
Product:    vaccine
Stage:      early-stage trial
```

Compare this to the first record we extracted:

| | |
|---|---|
| Company: | GoodComp |
| Date: | 2021-01-07 |
| Stock: | +8.2% |

Notice that these two records contain different fields and therefore have different structures. As a result, they must be stored in two different database tables.

## Semistructured Data

In cases where the structural identity of the information doesn't conform to stringent formatting requirements, we may need to process semistructured data formats, which let us have records of different structures within the same container (database table or document). Like unstructured data, semistructured data isn't tied to a predefined organizational schema; unlike unstructured data, however, samples of semistructured data do exhibit some degree of structure, usually in the form of self-describing tags or other markers.

The most common semistructured data formats include XML and JSON. This is what our financial statement might look like in JSON format:

```
{
  "Company": "GoodComp",
  "Date":    "2021-01-07",
  "Stock":   8.2,
  "Details": "the company announced positive early-stage trial results for its vaccine."
}
```

Here you can recognize the key information that we previously extracted from the statement. Each piece of information is paired with a descriptive tag, such as "Company" or "Date". Thanks to the tags, the information is organized similarly to how it appeared in the previous section, but now we have a fourth tag, "Details", paired with an entire fragment of the original statement, which looks unstructured. This example shows how semistructured data formats can accommodate both structured and unstructured pieces of data within a single record.

Moreover, you can put multiple records of unequal structure into the same container. Here, we store the two different records derived from our example financial statement in the same JSON document:

```
[
  {
    "Company": "GoodComp",
    "Date":    "2021-01-07",
    "Stock":   8.2
  },
```

```
{
    "Company": "GoodComp",
    "Date":    "2021-01-07",
    "Product": "vaccine",
    "Stage":   "early-stage trial"
  }
]
```

Recall from the discussion in the previous section that a relational database, being a rigidly structured data repository, cannot accommodate records of varying structures in the same table.

## Time Series Data

A time series is a set of data points indexed or listed in time order. Many financial datasets are stored as a time series due to the fact that financial data typically consists of observations at a specific time.

Time series data can be either structured or semistructured. Imagine you're receiving location data in records from a taxi's GPS tracking device at regular time intervals. The data might arrive in the following format:

```
[
  {
    "cab": "cab_238",
    "coord": (43.602508,39.715685),
    "tm": "14:47",
    "state": "available"
  },
  {
    "cab": "cab_238",
    "coord": (43.613744,39.705718),
    "tm": "14:48",
    "state": "available"
  }
  ...
]
```

A new data record arrives every minute that includes the latest location coordinates (latitude/longitude) from cab_238. Each record has the same sequence of fields, and each field has a consistent structure from one record to the next, allowing you to store this time series data in a relational database table as regular structured data.

Now suppose the data comes at unequal intervals, which is often the case in practice, and that you receive more than one set of coordinates in one minute. The incoming structure might look like this:

```
[
  {
    "cab": "cab_238",
    "coord": [(43.602508,39.715685),(43.602402,39.709672)],
    "tm": "14:47",
    "state": "available"
```

```
    },
    {
      "cab": "cab_238",
      "coord": (43.613744,39.705718),
      "tm": "14:48",
      "state": "available"
    }
]
```

Note that the first coord field includes two sets of coordinates and is thus not consistent with the second coord field. This data is semistructured.

## Sources of Data

Now that you know what the main categories of data are, what are the sources from which you might receive such data? Generally speaking, data may come from many different sources, including texts, videos, images, and device sensors, among others. From the standpoint of Python scripts that you'll write, however, the most common data sources are:

- An application programming interface (API)
- A web page
- A database
- A file

This list isn't intended to be comprehensive or restrictive; there are many other sources of data. In Chapter 9, for example, you'll see how to use a smartphone as a GPS data provider for your data processing pipeline, specifically by using a bot application as a go-between connecting the smartphone and your Python script.

Technically, all of the options listed here require you to use a corresponding Python library. For example, before you can obtain data from an API, you'll need to install a Python wrapper for the API or use the Requests Python library to make HTTP requests to the API directly. Likewise, in order to access data from a database, you'll need to install a connector from within your Python code that enables you to access databases of that particular type.

While many of these libraries must be downloaded and installed, some libraries used to load data are distributed with Python by default. For example, to load data from a JSON file, you can take advantage of Python's built-in json package.

In Chapters 4 and 5, we'll take up the data sourcing discussion in greater detail. In particular, you'll learn how to load specific data from different sources into data structures in your Python script for further processing. For now, we'll take a brief look at each of the common source types mentioned in the preceding list.

## APIs

Perhaps the most common way of acquiring data today is via an API (a software intermediary that enables two applications to interact with each other). As mentioned, to take advantage of an API in Python, you may need to install a wrapper for that API in the form of a Python library. The most common way to do this nowadays is via the `pip` command.

Not all APIs have their own Python wrapper, but this doesn't necessarily mean you can't make calls to them from Python. If an API serves HTTP requests, you can interact with that API from Python using the Requests library. This opens you up to thousands of APIs that you can use in your Python code to request datasets for further processing.

When choosing an API for a particular task, you should take the following into account:

**Functionality**   Many APIs provide similar functionalities, so you need to understand your precise requirements. For example, many APIs let you conduct a web search from within your Python script, but only some allow you to narrow down your search results by date of publication.

**Cost**   Many APIs allow you to use a so-called *developer key*, which is usually provided for free but with certain limitations, such as a limited number of calls per day.

**Stability**   Thanks to the Python Package Index (PyPI) repository (*https://pypi.org*), anyone can pack an API into a `pip` package and make it publicly available. As a result, there's an API (or several) for virtually any task you can imagine, but not all of these are completely reliable. Fortunately, the PyPI repository tracks the performance and usage of packages.

**Documentation**   Popular APIs usually have a corresponding documentation website, allowing you to see all of the API commands with sample usages. As a good model, look at the documentation page for the Nasdaq Data Link (aka Quandl) API (*https://docs.data.nasdaq.com/docs/python-time-series*), where you'll find examples of making different time series calls.

Many APIs return results in one of the following three formats: JSON, XML, or CSV. Data in any of these formats can easily be translated into data structures that are either built into or commonly used with Python. For example, the Yahoo Finance API retrieves and analyzes stock data, then returns the information already translated into a pandas DataFrame, a widely used structure we'll discuss in Chapter 3.

## Web Pages

Web pages can be static or generated on the fly in response to a user's interaction, in which case they may contain information from many different sources. In either case, a program can read a web page and extract parts of it. Called *web scraping*, this is quite legal as long as the page is publicly available.

A typical scraping scenario in Python involves two libraries: Requests and BeautifulSoup. Requests fetches the source code of the page, and then BeautifulSoup creates a *parse tree* for the page, which is a hierarchical representation of the page's content. You can search the parse tree and extract data from it using Pythonic idioms. For example, the following fragment of a parse tree:

```
[<td title="03/01/2020 00:00:00"><a href="Download.aspx?ID=630751" id="lnkDownload630751"
 target="_blank">03/01/2020</a></td>,
<td title="03/01/2020 00:00:00"><a href="Download.aspx?ID=630753" id="lnkDownload630753"
 target="_blank">03/01/2020</a></td>,
<td title="03/01/2020 00:00:00"><a href="Download.aspx?ID=630755" id="lnkDownload630755"
 target="_blank">03/01/2020</a></td>]
```

can be easily transformed into the following list of items within a for loop in your Python script:

```
[
    {'Document_Reference': '630751', 'Document_Date': '03/01/2020',
     'link': 'http://www.dummy.com/Download.aspx?ID=630751'}
    {'Document_Reference': '630753', 'Document_Date': '03/01/2020',
     'link': 'http://www.dummy.com/Download.aspx?ID=630753'}
    {'Document_Reference': '630755', 'Document_Date': '03/01/2020',
     'link': 'http://www.dummy.com/Download.aspx?ID=630755'}
]
```

This is an example of transforming semistructured data into structured data.

## Databases

Another common source of data is a relational database, a structure that provides a mechanism to efficiently store, access, and manipulate your structured data. You fetch from or send a portion of data to tables in the database using a Structured Query Language (SQL) request. For instance, the following request issued to an employees table in the database retrieves the list of only those programmers who work in the IT department, making it unnecessary to fetch the entire table:

```
SELECT first_name, last_name FROM employees WHERE department = 'IT' and title = 'programmer'
```

Python has a built-in database engine, SQLite. Alternatively, you can employ any other available database. Before you can access a database, you'll need to install the database client software in your environment.

In addition to the conventional rigidly structured databases, there's been an ever-increasing need in recent years for the ability to store heterogeneous and unstructured data in database-like containers. This has led to the rise of so-called *NoSQL* (*non-SQL* or *not only SQL*) databases. NoSQL databases use flexible data models, allowing you to store large volumes of unstructured data using the *key-value* method, where each piece of data can be accessed using an associated key. Here's what our earlier sample financial statement might look like if stored in a NoSQL database:

```
key   value
---   -----
...
26    GoodComp shares soared as much as 8.2% on 2021-01-07 after the company announced ...
```

The entire statement is paired with an identifying key, 26. It might seem odd to store the entire statement in a database. Recall, however, that several possible records can be extracted from a single statement. Storing the whole statement gives us the flexibility to extract different pieces of information at a later time.

### Files

Files may contain structured, semistructured, and unstructured data. Python's built-in open() function allows you to open a file so you can use its data within your script. However, depending on the format of the data (for example, CSV, JSON, or XML), you may need to import a corresponding library to be able to perform read, write, and/or append operations on it.

Plaintext files don't require a library to be further processed and are simply considered as sequences of lines in Python. As an example, look at the following message that a Cisco router might send to a logfile:

```
dat= 'Jul 19 10:30:37'
host='sm1-prt-highw157'
syslogtag='%SYS-1-CPURISINGTHRESHOLD:'
msg=' Threshold: Total CPU Utilization(Total/Intr): 17%/1%,
            Top 3 processes(Pid/Util):  85/9%, 146/4%, 80/1%'
```

You'll be able to read this line by line, looking for the required information. Thus, if your task is to find messages that include information about CPU utilization and extract particular figures from it, your script should recognize the last line in the snippet as a message to be selected. In Chapter 2, you'll see an example of how to extract specific information from text data using text processing techniques.

## The Data Processing Pipeline

In this section, we'll take a conceptual look at the steps involved in data processing, also known as the data processing pipeline. The usual steps applied to the data are:

1. Acquisition
2. Cleansing
3. Transformation
4. Analysis
5. Storage

As you'll see, these steps aren't always clear-cut. In some applications you'll be able to combine multiple steps into one or omit some steps altogether.

## Acquisition

Before you can do anything with data, you need to acquire it. That's why data acquisition is the first step in any data processing pipeline. In the previous section, you learned about the most common types of data sources. Some of those sources allow you to load only the required portion of the data in accordance with your request.

For example, a request to the Yahoo Finance API requires you to specify the ticker of a company and a period of time over which to retrieve stock prices for that company. Similarly, the News API, which allows you to retrieve news articles, can process a number of parameters to narrow down the list of articles being requested, including the source and date of publication. Despite these qualifying parameters, however, the retrieved list may still need to be filtered further. That is, the data may require cleansing.

## Cleansing

Data cleansing is the process of detecting and correcting corrupt or inaccurate data, or removing unnecessary data. In some cases, this step isn't required, and the data being obtained is immediately ready for analysis. For example, the yfinance library (a Python wrapper for Yahoo Finance API) returns stock data as a readily usable pandas DataFrame object. This usually allows you to skip the cleansing and transformation steps and move straight to data analysis.

However, if your acquisition tool is a web scraper, the data certainly will need cleansing because fragments of HTML markup will probably be included along with the payload data, as shown here:

```
6.\tThe development shall comply with the requirements of DCCâ\x80\x99s Drainage Division as
follows\r\n\r\n
```

After cleansing, this text fragment should look like this:

```
6. The development shall comply with the requirements of DCC's Drainage Division as follows
```

Besides the HTML markup, the scraped text may include other unwanted text, as in the following example, where the phrase *A View full text* is simply hyperlink text. You might need to open this link to access the text within it:

```
Permission for proposed amendments to planning permission received on the 30th A View full text
```

You can also use a data cleansing step to filter out specific entities. After requesting a set of articles from the News API, for example, you may need to select only those articles in the specified period where the titles include a money or percent phrase. This filter can be considered a data cleansing operation because the goal is to remove unnecessary data and prepare for the data transformation and data analysis operations.

## *Transformation*

Data transformation is the process of changing the format or structure of data in preparation for analysis. For example, to extract the information from our GoodComp unstructured text data as we did in "Structured Data," you might shred it into individual words or *tokens* so that a named entity recognition (NER) tool can look for the desired information. In information extraction, a *named entity* typically represents a real-world object, such as a person, an organization, or a product, that can be identified by a proper noun. There are also named entities that represent dates, percentages, financial terms, and more.

Many NLP tools can handle this kind of transformation for you automatically. After such a transformation, the shredded GoodComp data would look like this:

```
['GoodComp', 'shares', 'soared', 'as', 'much', 'as', '8.2%', 'on',
 '2021-01-07', 'after', 'the', 'company', 'announced', 'positive',
 'early-stage', 'trial', 'results', 'for', 'its', 'vaccine']
```

Other forms of data transformation are deeper, with text data being converted into numerical data. For example, if we've gathered a collection of news articles, we might transform them by performing *sentiment analysis*, a text processing technique that generates a number representing the emotions expressed within a text.

Sentiment analysis can be implemented with tools like SentimentAnalyzer, which can be found in the `nltk.sentiment` package. A typical analysis output might look like this:

```
Sentiment  URL
---------  -------------------------------------------------------------
0.9313     https://mashable.com/uk/shopping/amazon-face-mask-store-july-28/
0.9387     https://skillet.lifehacker.com/save-those-crustacean-shells-to
              -make-a-sauce-base-1844520024
```

Each entry in our dataset now includes a number, such as `0.9313`, representing the sentiment expressed within the corresponding article. With the sentiment of each article expressed numerically, we can calculate the average sentiment of the entire dataset, allowing us to determine the overall sentiment toward an object of interest, such as a certain company or product.

## *Analysis*

Analysis is the key step in the data processing pipeline. Here you interpret the raw data, enabling you to draw conclusions that aren't immediately apparent.

Continuing with our sentiment analysis example, you might want to study the sentiment toward a company over a specified period in relation to that company's stock price. Or you might compare stock market index figures, such as those on the S&P 500, with the sentiment expressed in a broad sampling of news articles for this same period. The following fragment illustrates what the dataset might look like, with S&P 500 data shown alongside the overall sentiment of that day's news:

```
Date          News_sentiment   S&P_500
---------------------------------------
2021-04-16    0.281074         4185.47
2021-04-19    0.284052         4163.26
2021-04-20    0.262421         4134.94
```

Since both the sentiment figures and stock figures are expressed in numbers, you might plot two corresponding graphs on the same plot for visual analysis, as illustrated in Figure 1-1.

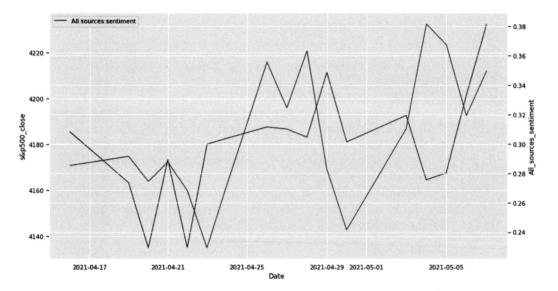

*Figure 1-1: An example of visual data analysis*

Visual analysis is one of the most commonly used and efficient methods for interpreting data. We'll discuss visual analysis in greater detail in Chapter 8.

## Storage

In most cases, you'll need to store the results generated during the data analysis process to make them available for later use. Your storage options typically include files and databases. The latter is preferable if you anticipate frequent reuse of your data.

# The Pythonic Way

When doing data science with Python, your code is expected to be written in a *Pythonic* way, meaning it should be concise and efficient. Pythonic code is often associated with the use of *list comprehensions*, which are ways to implement useful data processing functionality with a single line of code.

We'll cover list comprehensions in more detail in Chapter 2, but for now, the following quick example illustrates how the Pythonic concept works in practice. Say you need to process this multisentence fragment of text:

```
txt = ''' Eight dollars a week or a million a year - what is the difference? A mathematician or
a wit would give you the wrong answer. The magi brought valuable gifts, but that was not among
them. - The Gift of the Magi, O'Henry'''
```

Specifically, you need to split the text by sentences, creating a list of individual words for each sentence, excluding punctuation symbols. Thanks to Python's list comprehension feature, all of this can be implemented in a single line of code, a so-called *one-liner*:

```
word_lists = [[w.replace(',','') ❶ for w in line.split() if w not in ['-']]
              ❷ for line in txt.replace('?','.').split('.')]
```

The `for line in txt` loop ❷ splits the text into sentences and stores those sentences in a list. Then the `for w in line` loop ❶ splits each sentence into individuals words and stores the words in a list within the larger list. As a result, you get the following list of lists:

```
[['Eight', 'dollars', 'a', 'week', 'or', 'a', 'million', 'a', 'year', 'what',
  'is', 'the', 'difference'], ['A', 'mathematician', 'or', 'a', 'wit',
  'would', 'give', 'you', 'the', 'wrong', 'answer'], ['The', 'magi',
  'brought', 'valuable', 'gifts', 'but', 'that', 'was', 'not', 'among',
  'them'], ['The', 'Gift', 'of', 'the', 'Magi', "O'Henry"]]
```

Here you've managed to accomplish two steps of the data processing pipeline within a single line of code: cleansing and transformation. You've cleansed the data by removing punctuation symbols from the text, and you've transformed it by separating the words from each other to form a word list for each sentence.

If you've come to Python from another programming language, try implementing this task with that language. How many lines of code does it take?

# Summary

After reading this chapter, you should have a cursory understanding of the main categories of data, where data comes from, and how a typical data processing pipeline is organized.

As you've seen, there are three major categories of data: unstructured, structured, and semistructured. The raw input material in a data processing pipeline is typically unstructured data, which is passed through cleansing and transformation steps to turn it into structured or semistructured data that is ready for analysis. You also learned about data processing pipelines that use structured or semistructured data from the start, acquired from an API or a relational database.

# 2

## PYTHON DATA STRUCTURES

Data structures organize and store data, making it easier to access the data. Python ships with four data structures: lists, tuples, dictionaries, and sets. These structures are easy to work with, yet they can be used to tackle complex data operations, making Python one of the most popular languages for data analysis.

This chapter will cover Python's four built-in data structures, with an emphasis on the features that allow you to easily build functional data-centric applications with minimal coding. You'll also learn how to combine the basic structures into more complex structures, such as a list of dictionaries, to more accurately represent real-world objects. You'll apply this knowledge to the field of natural language processing and in a short introduction to processing photographs.

# Lists

A Python *list* is an ordered collection of objects. The elements in a list are separated by commas, and the entire list is enclosed in square brackets, as shown here:

```
[2,4,7]
['Bob', 'John', 'Will']
```

Lists are mutable, meaning you can add, remove, and modify a list's elements. Unlike sets, which we'll discuss later in the chapter, lists can have duplicate elements.

Lists contain elements that represent series of usually related, similar things that can be logically grouped together. A typical list contains only elements belonging to a single category (that is, homogeneous data, such as people's names, article titles, or participant numbers). Understanding this point is essential when it comes to choosing the right tool for the task at hand. If you need a structure to include objects with different properties, consider using a tuple or a dictionary.

**NOTE** *Although lists are generally understood to be homogeneous, Python does allow you to have elements of different data types in the same list. This list, for example, includes both strings and integers:*

```
['Ford', 'Mustang', 1964]
```

## Creating a List

To create a basic list, simply place a sequence of elements inside square brackets and assign the sequence to a variable name:

```
regions = ['Asia', 'America', 'Europe']
```

In practice, however, lists are commonly populated dynamically from scratch, often using a loop that calculates one item per iteration. In such cases, your first step is to create an empty list, as illustrated here:

```
regions = []
```

Once you've created a list, you can add, remove, and sort items in that list as needed. You can perform these and other tasks using Python's various list object methods.

## Using Common List Object Methods

List object methods are functions that implement particular behaviors within lists. In this section we'll look at some common list object methods, including append(), index(), insert(), and count(). To practice using them, start by creating a blank list. You'll build it into a to-do list as you go along, filling it with chores and organizing it:

```
my_list = []
```

Perhaps the most common list object method is append(). It adds an item to the end of the list. You can use append() to add some chores to your to-do list, as shown here:

```
my_list.append('Pay bills')
my_list.append('Tidy up')
my_list.append('Walk the dog')
my_list.append('Cook dinner')
```

The list now contains four items, in the order in which they were appended:

```
['Pay bills', 'Tidy up', 'Walk the dog', 'Cook dinner']
```

Each item in a list has a numeric key known as an *index*. This feature enables a list to keep its items in a specified order. Python uses zero-based indexing, meaning the initial item of a sequence is assigned the index 0.

To access an individual item from a list, specify the name of the list, followed by the index of the desired item in square brackets. For example, here's how to print just the first item of your to-do list:

```
print(my_list[0])
```

The print() function yields the following output:

```
Pay bills
```

You can use a list's indices not only to access a required item but also to insert a new item at a certain position in the list. Say you want to add a new chore to your to-do list between walking the dog and cooking dinner. To make this insertion, you first use the index() method to determine the index of the item before which you want to insert the new item. Here, you'll store it in the variable i:

```
i = my_list.index('Cook dinner')
```

This will become the index for the new chore, which you can now add using the insert() method, as shown here:

```
my_list.insert(i, 'Go to the pharmacy')
```

The new chore is added to the list at the specified index, shifting all subsequent chores down by one. This is what the updated list looks like:

```
['Pay bills', 'Tidy up', 'Walk the dog', 'Go to the pharmacy', 'Cook dinner']
```

Because lists allow for duplicate items, you may need to check how many times a certain item appears in a list. This can be done with the count() method, as illustrated in the following example:

```
print(my_list.count('Tidy up'))
```

The print() function reveals only one instance of 'Tidy up' in the list, but it might be a good idea to include this item in your daily list more than once!

**NOTE** *The entire list of list object methods can be found in the Python documentation at https://docs.python.org/3/tutorial/datastructures.html.*

### Using Slice Notation

It's possible to access a range of items from a sequential data type such as a list by using *slice notation*. To take a slice of a list, specify the index of the starting position and the index of the ending position plus 1. Separate the two indices with a colon, and enclose them in square brackets. For example, you can print the first three items from your to-do list as follows:

```
print(my_list[0:3])
```

The result is a list of the items with indices 0 through 2:

```
['Pay bills', 'Tidy up', 'Walk the dog']
```

Both the start and end indices in a slice are optional. If you omit the start index, the slice will start at the beginning of the list. This means that the slice in the preceding example can be safely changed to:

```
print(my_list[:3])
```

If you omit the end index, the slice will continue through the end of the list. Here's how to print the items with indices of 3 and higher:

```
print(my_list[3:])
```

The result is the last two items in your to-do list:

```
['Go to the pharmacy', 'Cook dinner']
```

Finally, you can omit both indices, in which case you'll get a copy of the whole list:

```
print(my_list[:])
```

The result is:

```
['Pay bills', 'Tidy up', 'Walk the dog', 'Go to the pharmacy', 'Cook dinner']
```

Slice notation is not limited to extracting a subsequence from a list. You can also use it instead of the append() and insert() methods to populate a list with data. Here, for example, you add two items to the end of your list:

```
my_list[len(my_list):] = ['Mow the lawn', 'Water plants']
```

The `len()` function returns the number of items in the list, which is also the index of the first unused position outside the list. You can safely add new items starting from this index. Here's how the list looks now:

```
['Pay bills', 'Tidy up', 'Walk the dog', 'Go to the pharmacy', 'Cook dinner',
 'Mow the lawn', 'Water plants']
```

Similarly, you can remove items using the `del` command and slicing as follows:

```
del my_list[5:]
```

This removes the items with indices 5 and above, thus returning the list to its previous form:

```
['Pay bills', 'Tidy up', 'Walk the dog', 'Go to the pharmacy', 'Cook dinner']
```

### Using a List as a Queue

A *queue* is an abstract data type that can be implemented using the list data structure. One end of a queue is always used to insert items (*enqueue*), and the other is used to remove them (*dequeue*), thus following the *first-in, first-out (FIFO)* methodology. In practice, the FIFO methodology is often used in warehousing: the first products that arrive at the warehouse are the first products to leave. Organizing the sale of goods in this way can help prevent product expiration by ensuring that the older products are the first to be sold.

It's easy to turn a Python list into a queue using Python's deque object (short for *double-ended queue*). In this section, we'll explore how this works using your to-do list. For a list to function as a queue, completed tasks should drop off the beginning while new tasks appear at the end of the list, as illustrated in Figure 2-1.

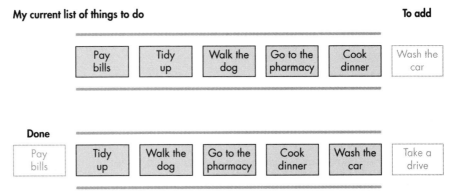

Figure 2-1: An example of using a list as a queue

Here's how to implement the process shown in the figure:

```
from collections import deque
queue = deque(my_list)
```

```
queue.append('Wash the car')
print(queue.popleft(), ' - Done!')
my_list_upd = list(queue)
```

In this script, you first turn the my_list object from the previous examples into a deque object, which is part of Python's collections module. The deque() object constructor adds a set of methods to the list object being passed into it, making it easier to use that list as a queue. In this particular example, you add a new element to the right side of the queue with the append() method, then you remove an item from the left side of the queue using the popleft() method. This method not only removes the leftmost item but also returns it, thus feeding it into your printed message. You should see the following message as a result:

```
Pay bills - Done!
```

After being converted back from a deque object to a list in the last line of the script, the updated to-do list appears as follows:

```
['Tidy up', 'Walk the dog', 'Go to the pharmacy', 'Cook dinner', 'Wash the car']
```

As you can see, the first item has been pushed out of the list, while a new one has been appended.

### Using a List as a Stack

Like a queue, a *stack* is an abstract data structure that you can organize on top of a list. A stack implements the *last-in, first-out (LIFO)* methodology, where the last item added is the first item retrieved. For your to-do list to function as a stack, you would complete the tasks in reverse order, starting with the rightmost task. Here's how to implement this concept in Python:

```
my_list = ['Pay bills', 'Tidy up', 'Walk the dog', 'Go to the pharmacy', 'Cook dinner']
stack = []
for task in my_list:
  stack.append(task)
while stack:
  print(stack.pop(), ' - Done!'))
print('\nThe stack is empty')
```

In the for loop, you push the tasks from the to-do list into a stack defined as another list, starting from the first task. This is an example of using append() in a loop to dynamically populate an empty list. Then, in the while loop, you remove the tasks from the stack, starting from the last one. You do this with the pop() method, which removes the last item from a list and returns the removed item. The stack's output will look like this:

```
Cook dinner - Done!
Go to the pharmacy - Done!
```

```
Walk the dog - Done!
Tidy up - Done!
Pay bills - Done!

The stack is empty
```

## Using Lists and Stacks for Natural Language Processing

Lists and stacks have many real-world applications, including in the field of NLP. For example, you can use lists and stacks to extract all the noun chunks from a text. A noun chunk consists of a noun and its left syntactic children (that is, all those words to the noun's left that are syntactically dependent on the noun, such as adjectives or determiners). Thus, to extract the noun chunks from a text, you'll need to search the text for all the nouns and the nouns' left syntactic children. This can be implemented with a stack-based algorithm, as illustrated in Figure 2-2.

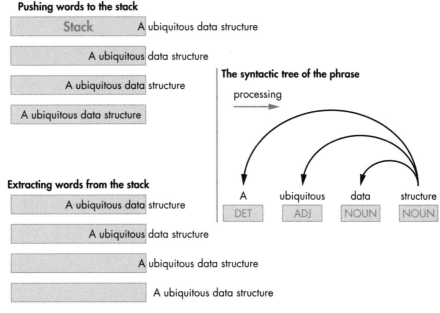

Figure 2-2: An example of using a list as a stack

The figure uses a single noun chunk as an example, *A ubiquitous data structure*. The arrows in the syntactic tree on the right illustrate how the words *A*, *ubiquitous*, and *data* are syntactic children of the noun *structure*, which is known as the *head* of those syntactic children. The algorithm analyzes the text from left to right, one word at a time, pushing the word to the stack if it's a noun or the left syntactic child of a noun. When the algorithm encounters a word that doesn't fit that description, or if there are no words left in the text, an entire noun chunk has been found, and the chunk is extracted from the stack.

To implement this stack-based algorithm for noun chunk extraction, you'll need to install spaCy, the leading open source Python library for natural language processing, as well as one of its English models. Use these commands:

```
$ pip install -U spacy
$ python -m spacy download en_core_web_sm
```

The following script uses spaCy to implement the leading open source Python library for natural language processing:

```
import spacy
txt = 'List is a ubiquitous data structure in the Python programming language.'

nlp = spacy.load('en_core_web_sm')
doc = nlp(txt)
stk = []
for w in doc:
  if w.pos_ == 'NOUN' or w.pos_ == 'PROPN': ❶
    stk.append(w.text)
  elif (w.head.pos_ == 'NOUN' or w.head.pos_ == 'PROPN') and (w in w.head.lefts): ❷
    stk.append(w.text)
  elif stk: ❸
    chunk = ''
    while stk:
      chunk = stk.pop() + ' ' + chunk ❹
    print(chunk.strip())
```

The first few lines of the script go through the standard setup process for analyzing a text phrase with spaCy. You import the spaCy library, define a sentence to be processed, and load spaCy's English model. After that, you apply the nlp pipeline to the sentence, instructing spaCy to generate the sentence's syntactic structure, which is needed for tasks like noun chunk extraction.

**NOTE**    *For more information about spaCy, refer to the documentation at* https://spacy.io.

Next, you implement the algorithm described previously, iterating through each word of the text. If you find either a noun ❶ or one of its left syntactic children ❷, you send it to the stack using the append() operation. You make these determinations using spaCy's built-in properties, such as w.head.lefts, which allow you to navigate across the sentence's syntactic structure and find desired words in it. Thus, with w in w.head.lefts, you look up the head of a word (w.head), then look up the left syntactic children of that head (.lefts) and determine whether the word in question is one of them. To illustrate, when evaluating the word *ubiquitous*, w.head would yield *structure*, the syntactic head of *ubiquitous*, and .lefts of *structure* would yield the words *a*, *ubiquitous*, and *data*, demonstrating that *ubiquitous* is indeed a left child of *structure*.

Finishing up the algorithm, once you determine that the next word in the text isn't part of the noun chunk at hand (neither a noun nor a left child of a noun) ❸, you have a complete noun chunk, and you extract the words from the stack ❹. This script finds and outputs the following three noun chunks:

```
List
a ubiquitous data structure
the Python programming language.
```

## Making Improvements with List Comprehensions

In Chapter 1, you saw an example of creating a list using the list comprehension feature. In this section, we'll use list comprehensions to improve our noun chunk extraction algorithm. Improving the functionality of a solution often requires you to make significant enhancements to existing code. In this case, however, since list comprehensions are involved, the enhancements to be made will be quite compact.

Looking at the syntactic dependency tree shown in Figure 2-2, you may notice that each element of the phrase depicted there is directly related by a syntactic arc to the noun *structure*. However, a noun chunk can also follow another pattern, where some words are not connected to the phrase's noun by a direct syntactic relationship. Figure 2-3 illustrates what the dependency tree of such a phrase might look like. Notice that the adverb *most* is the child of the adjective *useful*, not the noun *type*, yet it's still part of the noun chunk that has *type* as its head.

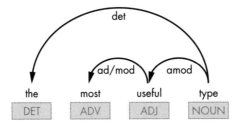

det: determiner
ad/mod: adverbial modifier
amod: adjectival modifier

*Figure 2-3: The syntactic dependency tree of a more complex noun chunk*

We need to improve the script from the previous section so that it can also extract noun chunks like the one shown in Figure 2-3, where some words in a chunk are not connected to the phrase's noun directly. To refine our algorithm, let's first compare the syntactic dependency trees depicted in Figures 2-2 and 2-3 to find what they have in common. The important similarity is that in both trees, the head of each word that is dependent in a noun chunk can be found to the right of the word. However, the noun that forms the phrase may not follow this pattern. For example, in the sentence "List is a ubiquitous data structure in the Python programming language," the word *structure* is the head of a noun chunk, but its own head, the verb *is*, is located to its left. To make sure it is so, you can run the following script that outputs the head for each word in the sentence:

```
txt = 'List is a ubiquitous data structure in the Python programming language.'
import spacy
nlp = spacy.load('en')
doc = nlp(txt)
for t in doc:
  print(t.text, t.head.text)
```

Our new algorithm needs to scan a text looking for words whose heads are to their right, thus indicating potential noun chunks. The idea is to create a kind of matrix for a sentence that indicates whether the head of a word is to its right or not. For readability, the words whose heads are on the right could be included in the matrix as they are in the sentence, while all the others could be replaced with zeros. Thus, for the following sentence:

```
List is arguably the most useful type in the Python programming language.
```

you would have the following matrix:

```
['List', 0, 0, 'the', 'most', 'useful', 0, 0, 'the', 'Python', 'programming', 0, 0]
```

You can create this matrix using a list comprehension:

```
  txt = 'List is arguably the most useful type in the Python
                                       programming language.'
  import spacy
  nlp = spacy.load('en')
  doc = nlp(txt)
❶ head_lefts = [t.text if t in t.head.lefts else 0 for t in doc]
  print(head_lefts)
```

Here, you iterate over the words of the submitted sentence in the loop within the list comprehension, substituting zeros for those words whose heads are not to the right ❶.

The generated list looks as follows:

```
['List', 0, 0, 'the', 'most', 'useful', 0, 0, 'the', 'Python', 'programming', 0, 0]
```

You may notice that the list contains one more element than there are words in the sentence. This is because spaCy actually breaks the text up into tokens, which may be words or punctuation marks. The final 0 in the list represents the period at the end of the sentence.

Now you need a way to move through this list in order to find and extract noun chunks. You'll need to create a series of text fragments, where each fragment starts at a certain position and continues until the end of the text. In the following snippet, you move word by word from the start through the rest of the text, generating a matrix of the sides of the heads in each iteration:

```
for w in doc:
    head_lefts = [t.text if t in t.head.lefts else 0 for t in ❶ doc[w.i:]]
    print(head_lefts)
```

You use slice notation in the doc object to get the fragment that is needed ❶. This mechanism allows you to shift the leftmost position of the resulting slice one word to the right at each iteration of the for loop. The code generates the following set of matrices:

```
['List', 0, 0, 'the', 'most', 'useful', 0, 0, 'the', 'Python', 'programming', 0, 0]
[0, 0, 'the', 'most', 'useful', 0, 0, 'the', 'Python', 'programming', 0, 0]
[0, 'the', 'most', 'useful', 0, 0, 'the', 'Python', 'programming', 0, 0]
['the', 'most', 'useful', 0, 0, 'the', 'Python', 'programming', 0, 0]
['most', 'useful', 0, 0, 'the', 'Python', 'programming', 0, 0]
['useful', 0, 0, 'the', 'Python', 'programming', 0, 0]
[0, 0, 'the', 'Python', 'programming', 0, 0]
[0, 'the', 'Python', 'programming', 0, 0]
['the', 'Python', 'programming', 0, 0]
['Python', 'programming', 0, 0]
['programming', 0, 0]
[0, 0]
[0]
```

You must analyze each fragment next, looking for the first zero. The words up to and including that zero could potentially be a noun chunk. Here's the code for this:

```
for w in doc:
    head_lefts = [t.text if t in t.head.lefts else 0 for t in doc[w.i:]]
❶ i0 = head_lefts.index(0)
    if i0 > 0:
    ❷ noun = [1 if t.pos_ == 'NOUN' or t.pos_ == 'PROPN' else 0 for t in
                    reversed(doc[w.i:w.i+i0 +1])]
        try:
        ❸ i1 = noun.index(1)+1
        except ValueError:
            pass
        print(head_lefts[:i0 +1])
    ❹ print(doc[w.i+i0 +1-i1])
```

You set i0 equal to head_lefts.index(0) to find the index of the first zero in the fragment ❶. If there are multiple zero elements, head_lefts.index(0) returns the index of the first element. Then, you check whether i0 > 0 to weed out fragments that don't start with a head-left element.

You then use another list comprehension to process the elements of the noun chunks to be sent to the stack. In this second list comprehension, you look for a noun or a proper noun within each fragment that could potentially be a noun chunk. You loop over the fragment in reverse order to first pick up the noun or proper noun that forms the chunk and which, therefore, is supposed to appear in the last position of the fragment ❷. What you actually send to the list when any noun or proper noun is found is a 1, and you send a 0 for every other element. Thus, the first 1 found in the list indicates the position of the main noun in the fragment relative to the fragment's end ❸. You'll need it when calculating the slice of the text representing the noun chunk ❹.

For now, you simply output the generated fragments along with the nouns found within them. You will see the following output:

```
['List', 0]
List
['the', 'most', 'useful', 0]
type
['most', 'useful', 0]
type
['useful', 0]
type
['the', 'Python', 'programming', 0]
language
['Python', 'programming', 0]
language
['programming', 0]
language
```

Now you can incorporate the new code into the solution introduced in the previous section. Putting it all together, you arrive at the following script:

```
txt = 'List is arguably the most useful type in the Python
                                programming language.'
import spacy
nlp = spacy.load('en')
doc = nlp(txt)
stk = []
❶ for w in doc:
❷   head_lefts = [1 if t in t.head.lefts else 0 for t in doc[w.i:]]
    i0 = 0
    try: i0 = head_lefts.index(0)
    except ValueError: pass
    i1 = 0
    if i0 > 0:
      noun = [1 if t.pos_ == 'NOUN' or t.pos_ == 'PROPN' else 0 for t in
                    reversed(doc[w.i:w.i+i0 +1])]
      try: i1 = noun.index(1)+1
      except ValueError: pass
    if w.pos_ == 'NOUN' or w.pos_ == 'PROPN':
❸     stk.append(w.text)
    elif (i1 > 0):
❹     stk.append(w.text)
    elif stk:
      chunk = ''
      while stk:
```

```
❺ chunk = stk.pop() + ' ' + chunk
  print(chunk.strip())
```

You iterate over the tokens in the submitted sentence ❶, generating a
head_lefts list in each iteration ❷. Recall that this list is a matrix containing
zeros for those words in the sentence whose syntactic heads are to their left.
These matrices are used to identify noun chunks. For each chunk you identify, you send each noun or proper noun to the stack ❸, as well as any other
word that belongs to the chunk but is not a noun ❹. Once you reach the end
of the chunk, you extract the tokens from the stack, forming a phrase ❺.

The script will produce the following output:

```
List
the most useful type
the Python programming language
```

NOTE     *If you want to learn more about natural language processing, check out my book*
         Natural Language Processing with Python and spaCy, *also from No Starch*
         *Press (https://nostarch.com/NLPPython).*

# Tuples

Like a list, a *tuple* is an ordered collection of objects. Unlike lists, however,
tuples are immutable. Once a tuple is created, it cannot be changed. The
items in a tuple are separated by commas and can optionally be enclosed in
parentheses, as shown here:

```
('Ford', 'Mustang', 1964)
```

Tuples are typically used to store collections of heterogeneous data;
that is, data of different types, such as the make, model, and year of a car.
As this example illustrates, they are especially useful when you need a structure to hold the properties of a real-world object.

## A List of Tuples

It's common to nest Python data structures inside each other. For example,
you can have a list where each element is a tuple, which lets you assign more
than one attribute to each element in the list. Say you want to assign a start
time to each task in the to-do list you created earlier in the chapter. Each
item in the list will become a data structure unto itself, consisting of two
elements: the description of a task and its scheduled start time.

To implement such a structure, tuples are an ideal choice, since they
are intended to collect heterogeneous data in a single structure. Your list of
tuples might look as follows:

```
[('8:00','Pay bills'), ('8:30','Tidy up'), ('9:30','Walk the dog'),
 ('10:00','Go to the pharmacy'), ('10:30','Cook dinner')]
```

You can build this list of tuples from the following two simple lists:

```
task_list = ['Pay bills', 'Tidy up', 'Walk the dog', 'Go to the pharmacy', 'Cook dinner']
tm_list = ['8:00', '8:30', '9:30', '10:00', '10:30']
```

As you can see, the first list is the original my_list, and the second one is a list containing the corresponding start times. The easiest way to combine them into a list of tuples is to use a list comprehension, as shown here:

```
sched_list = [(tm, task) for tm, task in zip(tm_list, task_list)]
```

Within the list comprehension, you use Python's zip() function, which iterates over the two simple lists simultaneously, combining the corresponding times and tasks into tuples.

Just as with lists, to access an item in a tuple you specify the item's index enclosed in square brackets following the name of the tuple. Note, however, that tuples nested within a list are not assigned names. To access an item in a nested tuple, you first need to specify the name of the list, then the index of the tuple in the list, and finally the index of the item in the tuple. For example, to see the time assigned to the second task in your to-do list, you would use the following syntax:

```
print(sched_list[1][0])
```

This generates the following output:

```
8:30
```

## Immutability

An important thing to remember about tuples is that they're immutable. That is, you can't modify them. For example, if you try to change the start time for one of your chores:

```
sched_list[1][0] = '9:00'
```

you'll get the following error:

```
TypeError: 'tuple' object does not support item assignment
```

Because they're immutable, tuples are not suitable for holding data values that need to be updated periodically.

## Dictionaries

The *dictionary* is another widely used built-in data structure in Python. Dictionaries are mutable, unordered collections of *key-value pairs*, where each *key* is a unique name that identifies an item of data, the *value*. A dictionary is delimited by curly brackets. Each key is separated from its value by a colon, and key-value pairs are separated by commas, as shown here:

```
{'Make': 'Ford', 'Model': 'Mustang', 'Year': 1964}
```

Dictionaries, like tuples, are useful for storing heterogeneous data about real-world objects. As this example illustrates, dictionaries have the added benefit of assigning a label to each item of data.

## A List of Dictionaries

Like other data structures, dictionaries can be nested inside other structures. Your to-do list, when implemented as a list of dictionaries, might look like this:

```
dict_list = [
  {'time': '8:00', 'name': 'Pay bills'},
  {'time': '8:30', 'name': 'Tidy up'},
  {'time': '9:30', 'name': 'Walk the dog'},
  {'time': '10:00', 'name': 'Go to the pharmacy'},
  {'time': '10:30', 'name': 'Cook dinner'}
]
```

Unlike tuples, dictionaries are mutable, which means that you can easily change the value in a key-value pair:

```
dict_list[1]['time'] = '9:00'
```

This example also illustrates how to access values in a dictionary: unlike with lists and tuples, you use key names rather than numeric indices.

## Adding to a Dictionary with setdefault()

The setdefault() method provides a convenient way to add new data to a dictionary. It takes a key-value pair as its parameter. If the specified key already exists, the method simply returns the current value of that key. If the key doesn't exist, setdefault() inserts the key with the specified value. To see an example, first create a dictionary called car where the model is Jetta:

```
car = {
  "brand": "Volkswagen",
  "style": "Sedan",
  "model": "Jetta"
}
```

Now try adding a new model key with a value of Passat using setdefault():

```
print(car.setdefault("model", "Passat"))
```

This produces the following output, showing that the value of the model key has remained the same:

```
Jetta
```

However, if you specify a new key, setdefault() inserts the key-value pair and returns the value:

```
print(car.setdefault("year", 2022))
```

The output will be as follows:

```
2022
```

If you now print the entire dictionary:

```
print(car)
```

this is what you see:

```
{
  "brand": "Volkswagen",
  "style": "Sedan",
  "model": "Jetta",
  "year": 2022
}
```

As you can see, the setdefault() method relieves you from having to manually check whether the key in the key-value pair you want to insert is already in the dictionary. You can safely try to insert a key-value pair into a dictionary without the risk of overwriting the value of a key that already exists.

Now that you know how setdefault() works, let's look at a practical example. Counting the number of occurrences of each word in a text phrase is a common task in NLP. The following example demonstrates how this can be accomplished, with the help of a dictionary, using the setdefault() method. Here's the text that you'll process:

```
txt = '''Python is one of the most promising programming languages today. Due to the
simplicity of Python syntax, many researchers and scientists prefer Python over many other
languages.'''
```

The first step is to remove the punctuation from the text. Without this step, 'languages' and 'languages.' would count as two separate words. Here, you remove the periods and commas:

```
txt = txt.replace('.', '').replace(',', '')
```

Next, you split the text into words, putting them into a list:

```
lst = txt.split()
print(lst)
```

The generated list of words is as follows:

```
['Python', 'is', 'one', 'of', 'the', 'most', 'promising', 'programming',
 'languages', 'today', 'Due', 'to', 'the', 'simplicity', 'of', 'Python',
 'syntax', 'many', 'researchers', 'and', 'scientists', 'prefer', 'Python',
 'over', 'many', 'other', 'languages']
```

Now you can count the occurrences of each word in the list. This can be implemented with a dictionary using the `setdefault()` method as follows:

```
dct = {}
for w in lst:
  c = dct.setdefault(w,0)
  dct[w] += 1
```

First, you create an empty dictionary. Then you add key-value pairs to it, using the words from the list as the keys. The setdefault() method sets the initial value for each key to 0. The value is then increased by 1 for the first occurrence of each word, yielding a count of 1. On subsequent occurrences of that word, setdefault() will leave the previous count value intact, but the count value will be incremented by 1 with the += operator, producing an accurate count.

Before outputting the dictionary, you might want to sort the words by number of occurrences:

```
dct_sorted = dict(sorted(dct.items(), key=lambda x: x[1], reverse=True))
print(dct_sorted)
```

Using the dictionary's `items()` method, you can convert this dictionary into a list of tuples, where each tuple contains a key and its value. Thus, when you specify x[1] in lambda for the key parameter of the sorted() function, you're sorting according to the items in the tuples with index 1—that is, the values (word counts) from the original dictionary. The resulting dictionary appears as follows:

```
{'Python': 3, 'of': 2, 'the': 2, 'languages': 2, 'many': 2, 'is': 1, 'one': 1,
 'most': 1, 'promising': 1, 'programming': 1, 'today': 1, 'Due': 1, 'to': 1,
 'simplicity': 1, 'syntax': 1, 'researchers': 1, 'and': 1, 'scientists': 1,
 'prefer': 1, 'over': 1, 'other': 1}
```

## Loading JSON into a Dictionary

With the help of dictionaries, you can easily convert Python data structures into JSON strings and vice versa. Here's how to load a string representing a JSON document into a dictionary using only the assignment operator:

```
d = { "PONumber"              : 2608,
      "ShippingInstructions" : {"name"    : "John Silver",
                      "Address": {  "street"   : "426 Light Street",
                                    "city"     : "South San Francisco",
                                    "state"    : "CA",
                                    "zipCode" : 99237,
                                    "country" : "United States of America" },
                          "Phone" : [ { "type" : "Office", "number" : "809-123-9309" },
                                      { "type" : "Mobile", "number" : "417-123-4567" }
                                    ]
                      }
    }
```

As you might notice, this dictionary has a complex structure. The value of the ShippingInstructions key is itself a dictionary, in which the value of the Address key is yet another dictionary and the value of the Phone key is a list of dictionaries.

You can save the dictionary directly to a JSON file with Python's json module using the json.dump() method:

```
import json
with open("po.json", "w") as outfile:
  json.dump(d, outfile)
```

Similarly, you can use the json.load() method to load the contents of a JSON file directly into a Python dictionary:

```
with open("po.json",) as fp:
    d = json.load(fp)
```

As a result, you get the same dictionary that was shown at the beginning of this section. We'll discuss working with files in more detail in Chapter 4.

# Sets

A Python *set* is an unordered collection of unique items. Duplicate items are not allowed in a set. A set is defined with curly brackets containing items separated by commas, as illustrated here:

```
{'London', 'New York', 'Paris'}
```

## Removing Duplicates from Sequences

Since members of a set must be unique, sets are useful when you need to remove duplicate items from a list or a tuple. Suppose a business wants to see a list of its customers. You might obtain such a list by deriving customers' names from the orders they've placed. Since a customer may have placed more than one order, the list may have duplicate names. The duplicates can be removed with the help of a set as follows:

```
lst = ['John Silver', 'Tim Jemison', 'John Silver', 'Maya Smith']
lst = list(set(lst))
print(lst)
```

You simply convert the original list to a set and then back to a list. The set constructor automatically deletes the duplicates. The updated list looks something like this:

```
['Maya Smith', 'Tim Jemison', 'John Silver']
```

A drawback of this approach is that it does not preserve the initial order of elements. This is due to the fact that a set is an unordered collection of items. Indeed, if you run the preceding code two or three times, the order of the output might be different each time.

To perform the same operation without losing the initial order, use Python's sorted() function, as shown here:

```
lst = ['John Silver', 'Tim Jemison', 'John Silver', 'Maya Smith']
lst = list(sorted(set(lst), key=lst.index))
```

This sorts the set by the indices of the original list, thus preserving the order. The updated list is as follows:

```
['John Silver', 'Tim Jemison', 'Maya Smith']
```

## Performing Common Set Operations

Set objects come with methods for performing common math operations on sequences, like unions and intersections. These methods let you easily combine sets or extract the elements shared by multiple sets.

Imagine that you need to classify a huge number of photos into groups based on what's in the photos. To automate this task, you might start with a visual recognition tool like Clarifai API that will generate a set of descriptive tags for each photo. The sets of tags can then be compared with each other using the intersection() method. This method compares two sets and creates a new set containing all of the elements that are in both. In this particular case, the more tags that there are in both sets, the more similar the two images are with respect to their theme.

For simplicity, the following example uses just two photos. Using their corresponding sets of descriptive tags, you can determine the extent to which the subject matter of the two photos coincides:

```
photo1_tags = {'coffee', 'breakfast', 'drink', 'table', 'tableware', 'cup', 'food'}
photo2_tags = {'food', 'dish', 'meat', 'meal', 'tableware', 'dinner', 'vegetable'}
intersection = photo1_tags.intersection(photo2_tags)
if len(intersection) >= 2:
  print("The photos contain similar objects.")
```

In this code, you perform the intersection operation to find the items shared by both sets. If the number of the items that the sets have in common is equal to or greater than two, you can conclude that the photos have a similar theme and, therefore, can be grouped together.

## EXERCISE #1: IMPROVED PHOTO TAG ANALYSIS

This section encourages you to practice what you've learned in this chapter. While continuing with the example using sets from the previous section, you'll also need to use dictionaries and lists.

In the previous example, you compared the descriptive tags of just two photos, determining their common tags by intersection. Let's enhance the functionality of the code so that it can process an arbitrary number of photos, grouping them into categories generated on the fly based on intersecting tags.

As the input, suppose you have the following list of dictionaries, where each dictionary represents a photo (of course, you might create your own list containing many more items). The list of dictionaries used here is available for download from the GitHub repository accompanying this book, at *https://github.com/pythondatabook/sources/blob/main/ch2/list_of_dicts.txt*:

```python
l = [
{
  "name": "photo1.jpg",
  "tags": {'coffee', 'breakfast', 'drink', 'table', 'tableware', 'cup', 'food'}
},
{
  "name": "photo2.jpg",
  "tags": {'food', 'dish', 'meat', 'meal', 'tableware', 'dinner', 'vegetable'}
},
{
  "name": "photo3.jpg",
  "tags": {'city', 'skyline', 'cityscape', 'skyscraper', 'architecture', 'building',
          'travel'}
},
{
  "name": "photo4.jpg",
  "tags": {'drink', 'juice', 'glass', 'meal', 'fruit', 'food', 'grapes'}
}
]
```

Your task is to group photos with intersecting tags, saving the results to a dictionary:

```python
photo_groups = {}
```

To accomplish this task, you'll need to iterate over all possible pairs of photos presented in the list. This can be implemented with a nested pair of for loops, organized as follows:

```python
for i in range(1, len(l)):
  for j in range(i+1,len(l)+1):
    print(f"Intersecting photo {i} with photo {j}")
    # Implement intersection here, saving results to photo_groups
```

You'll need to implement the body of the inner loop on your own so that it performs the intersection between l[i]['tags'] and l[j]['tags'] and creates a new key-value pair in the photo_groups dictionary if the result of the intersection is not empty. The key can be composed of the names of the intersecting tags, while the value is a list with the names of corresponding files. If the key already exists for a certain set of intersecting tags, you just need to append the names of the corresponding files to the value's list. To implement this functionality, you can take advantage of the setdefault() method.

If you use the preceding list of photos, you'll end up with the following groups:

```
{
  'tableware_food': ['photo1.jpg', 'photo2.jpg'],
  'drink_food': ['photo1.jpg', 'photo4.jpg'],
  'meal_food': ['photo2.jpg', 'photo4.jpg']
}
```

If you're using your own set of photos with more items, you may see more keys and more files associated with each key in the resulting dictionary.

The solution for this and all other exercises in this book can be found in the GitHub repository accompanying this book.

## Summary

This chapter has covered Python's four built-in data structures: lists, tuples, dictionaries, and sets. You saw a wide range of examples showing how these structures can represent real-world objects, and you learned how they can be combined into nested structures, including a list of tuples, a list of dictionaries, and a dictionary whose values are lists.

The chapter also explored features that allow you to easily build functional data analysis applications in Python. For example, you learned how to use list comprehensions to create new lists from existing ones and how to use the setdefault() method to efficiently access and manipulate the data in a dictionary. Through examples, you saw how these features are transferable to common challenges like text processing and photo analysis.

# 3

## PYTHON DATA SCIENCE LIBRARIES

Python provides access to a robust ecosystem of third-party libraries that you'll find useful for data analysis and manipulation. This chapter introduces you to three of the more popular data science libraries: NumPy, pandas, and scikit-learn. As you'll see, many data analysis applications use these libraries extensively, either explicitly or implicitly.

## NumPy

NumPy, or the Numeric Python library, is useful for working with *arrays*, which are data structures that store values of the same data type. Many other Python libraries that perform numerical computations rely on NumPy.

The NumPy array, a grid of elements of the same type, is the key component of the NumPy library. The elements in a NumPy array are indexed by a tuple of nonnegative integers. NumPy arrays are similar to Python lists except that they require less memory and are usually faster because they use optimized, precompiled C code.

NumPy arrays support *element-wise operations*, which allow you to perform basic arithmetic on entire arrays using compact and readable code. An element-wise operation is an operation on two arrays of the same dimensions that produces another array of the same dimensions, where each element $i, j$ is the result of a calculation performed on elements $i, j$ of the original two arrays. Figure 3-1 illustrates an element-wise operation performed against two NumPy arrays.

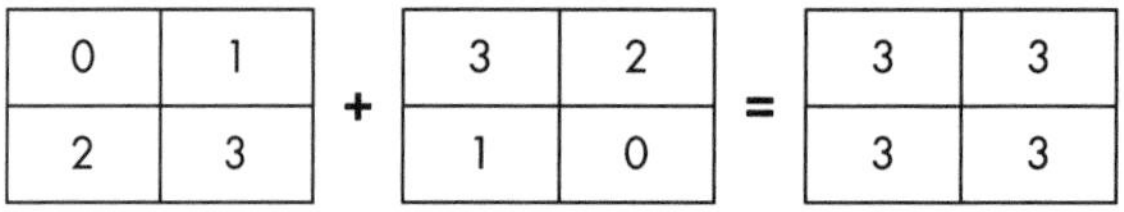

| 0 | 1 |   | 3 | 2 |   | 3 | 3 |
|---|---|---|---|---|---|---|---|
| 2 | 3 | **+** | 1 | 0 | **=** | 3 | 3 |

Figure 3-1: Adding two NumPy arrays

As you can see, the resulting array has the same dimensions as the original two arrays, and each new element is the sum of the corresponding elements in the original arrays.

## Installing NumPy

NumPy is a third-party library, meaning it's not part of Python's standard library. The simplest way to install it is with this command:

```
$ pip install NumPy
```

Python considers NumPy a module, so you'll need to import it into your script before you can use it.

## Creating a NumPy Array

You can create a NumPy array from the data in one or more Python lists. Suppose you have a list for each employee at a company containing that employee's base salary payments over the past three months. You can use code like the following to get all the salary information into one data structure:

```
❶ import numpy as np
❷ jeff_salary = [2700,3000,3000]
  nick_salary = [2600,2800,2800]
  tom_salary = [2300,2500,2500]
❸ base_salary = np.array([jeff_salary, nick_salary, tom_salary])
  print(base_salary)
```

You start by importing the NumPy library ❶. Then you define a set of lists, where each list contains the base salary data of an employee over the past three months ❷. Finally, you combine these lists into a NumPy array ❸. The array looks like this:

```
[[2700 3000 3000]
 [2600 2800 2800]
 [2300 2500 2500]]
```

This is a 2D array. It has two axes, which are indexed by integers, starting with 0. Axis 0 runs vertically downward across the array's rows, while axis 1 runs horizontally across the columns.

You can follow the same process to create an array containing the employees' monthly bonuses:

```
jeff_bonus = [500,400,400]
nick_bonus = [600,300,400]
tom_bonus = [200,500,400]
bonus = np.array([jeff_bonus, nick_bonus, tom_bonus])
```

## Performing Element-Wise Operations

It's easy to perform element-wise operations on multiple NumPy arrays of the same dimensions. For example, you can add the base_salary and bonus arrays together to determine the total amount paid each month to each employee:

```
❶ salary_bonus = base_salary + bonus
print(type(salary_bonus))
print(salary_bonus)
```

As you can see, the addition operation is a one-liner ❶. The resulting dataset is a NumPy array too, in which each element is the sum of the corresponding elements in the base_salary and bonus arrays:

```
<class 'NumPy.ndarray'>
[[3200 3400 3400]
 [3200 3100 3200]
 [2500 3000 2900]]
```

## Using NumPy Statistical Functions

NumPy's statistical functions allow you to analyze the contents of an array. For example, you can find the maximum value of an entire array or the maximum value of an array along a given axis.

Let's say you want to find the maximum value in the salary_bonus array you created in the previous section. You can do this with the NumPy array's max() function:

```
print(salary_bonus.max())
```

The function returns the maximum amount paid in the past three months to any employee in the dataset:

```
3400
```

NumPy can also find the maximum value of an array along a given axis. If you want to determine the maximum amount paid to each employee in the past three months, you can use NumPy's amax() function, as shown here:

```
print(np.amax(salary_bonus, axis = 1))
```

By specifying axis = 1, you instruct amax() to search horizontally across the columns for a maximum in the salary_bonus array, thus applying the function across each row. This calculates the maximum monthly amount paid to each employee in the past three months:

```
[3400 3200 3000]
```

Similarly, you can calculate the maximum amount paid each month to any employee by changing the axis parameter to 0:

```
print(np.amax(salary_bonus, axis = 0))
```

The results are as follows:

```
[3200 3400 3400]
```

**NOTE** *For the entire list of statistical functions supported by NumPy, refer to the NumPy documentation at* https://NumPy.org/doc/stable/reference/routines .statistics.html.

---

**EXERCISE #2: USING NUMPY STATISTICAL FUNCTIONS**

Each result set returned by np.amax() in the previous examples is itself a NumPy array. That means you can pass the retrieved result set into the amax() function again if you want to find the maximum value in the result set. Likewise, you can pass the result set to any other NumPy statistical function, such as np.median() or np.average(). Give it a try. For example, try to find the average of the maximum amounts paid each month to all employees.

---

## pandas

The pandas library is the de facto standard for data-oriented Python applications. (In case you're wondering, the name is somehow derived from Python Data Analysis Library.) The library includes two data structures: the *Series*, which is 1D, and the *DataFrame*, which is 2D. While the DataFrame is the primary pandas data structure, a DataFrame is actually a collection of Series objects. Therefore, it's important to understand Series as well as DataFrames.

## pandas Installation

The standard Python distribution does not ship with the pandas module. You can install pandas with this command:

```
$ pip install pandas
```

The `pip` command also resolves the library's dependencies, installing the NumPy, pytz, and python-dateutil packages implicitly.

Just like with NumPy, you'll need to import the pandas module into your script before you can use it.

## pandas Series

A pandas Series is a 1D labeled array. By default, elements in a Series are labeled with integers according to their position, like in a Python list. However, you can specify custom labels instead. These labels need not be unique, but they must be of a hashable type, such as integers, floats, strings, or tuples.

The elements of a Series can be of any type (integers, strings, floats, Python objects, and so on), but a Series works best if all its elements are of the same type. Ultimately, a Series may become one column in a larger DataFrame, and it's unlikely you'll want to store different kinds of data in the same column.

### Creating a Series

There are several ways to create a Series. In most cases, you feed it some kind of 1D dataset. Here's how you create a Series from a Python list:

```
❶ import pandas as pd
❷ data = ['Jeff Russell','Jane Boorman','Tom Heints']
❸ emps_names = pd.Series(data)
  print(emps_names)
```

You start by importing the pandas library and aliasing it as `pd` ❶. Then you create a list of items to be used as the data for the Series ❷. Finally, you create the Series, passing the list in to the `Series` constructor method ❸.

This gives you a single list with numeric indices set by default, starting from 0:

```
0    Jeff Russell
1    Jane Boorman
2     Tom Heints
dtype: object
```

The `dtype` attribute indicates the type of the underlying data for the given Series. By default, pandas uses the data type `object` to store strings.

You can create a Series with user-defined indices as follows:

```
data = ['Jeff Russell','Jane Boorman','Tom Heints']
emps_names = pd.Series(data,index=[9001,9002,9003])
print(emps_names)
```

This time the data in the emps_names Series object appears as follows:

```
9001    Jeff Russell
9002    Jane Boorman
9003       Tom Heints
dtype: object
```

## Accessing Data in a Series

To access an element in a Series, specify the Series name followed by the element's index within square brackets, as shown here:

```
print(emps_names[9001])
```

This outputs the element corresponding to index 9001:

```
Jeff Russell
```

Alternatively, you can use the loc property of the Series object:

```
print(emps_names.loc[9001])
```

Although you're using custom indices in this Series object, you can still access its elements by position (that is, use integer location–based indexing) via the iloc property. Here, for example, you print the first element in the Series:

```
print(emps_names.iloc[0])
```

You can access multiple elements by their indices with a slice operation, as discussed in Chapter 2:

```
print(emps_names.loc[9001:9002])
```

This produces the following output:

```
9001    Jeff Russell
9002    Jane Boorman
```

Notice that slicing with loc includes the right endpoint (in this case, index 9002), whereas usually Python slice syntax does not.

You can also use slicing to define the range of elements by position rather than by index. For instance, the preceding results could instead be generated by the following code:

```
print(emps_names.iloc[0:2])
```

or simply as follows:

```
print(emps_names[0:2])
```

As you can see, unlike slicing with loc, slicing with [] or iloc works the same as usual Python slicing: the start position is included but the stop is not. Thus, [0:2] leaves out the element in position 2 and returns only the first two elements.

### Combining Series into a DataFrame

Multiple Series can be combined to form a DataFrame. Let's try this by creating another Series and combining it with the emps_names Series:

```
  data = ['jeff.russell','jane.boorman','tom.heints']
❶ emps_emails = pd.Series(data,index=[9001,9002,9003], name = 'emails')
❷ emps_names.name = 'names'
❸ df = pd.concat([emps_names,emps_emails], axis=1)
  print(df)
```

To create the new Series, you call the Series() constructor ❶, passing the following arguments: the list to be converted to a Series, the indices of the Series, and the name of the Series.

You need to name Series before concatenating them into a DataFrame, because their names will become the names of the corresponding DataFrame columns. Since you didn't name the emps_names Series when you created it earlier, you name it here by setting its name property to 'names' ❷. After that, you can concatenate it with the emps_emails Series ❸. You specify axis=1 in order to concatenate along the columns.

The resulting DataFrame looks like this:

```
           names        emails
9001  Jeff Russell  jeff.russell
9002  Jane Boorman  jane.boorman
9003    Tom Heints    tom.heints
```

---

**EXERCISE #3: COMBINING THREE SERIES**

In the previous section, you created a DataFrame by concatenating two Series. Using this same approach, try to create a DataFrame from three Series. In order to do this, you'll need to create one more Series (say, emps_phones).

---

## pandas DataFrames

A pandas DataFrame is a 2D labeled data structure with columns that can be of different types. A DataFrame can be thought of as a dictionary-like container for Series objects, where each key in the dictionary is a column label and each value is a Series.

If you are familiar with relational databases, you'll notice that a pandas DataFrame is similar to a regular SQL table. Figure 3-2 illustrates an example of a pandas DataFrame.

Index column

| | Date | Open | High | Low | Close | Volume |
|---|---|---|---|---|---|---|
| 0 | 2020-08-26 | 412.00 | 433.20 | 410.73 | 430.63 | 71197000 |
| 1 | 2020-08-27 | 436.09 | 459.12 | 428.50 | 447.75 | 118465000 |
| 2 | 2020-08-28 | 459.02 | 463.70 | 437.30 | 442.68 | 20081200 |
| 3 | 2020-08-31 | 444.61 | 500.14 | 440.11 | 498.32 | 117841900 |
| 4 | 2020-09-01 | 502.14 | 502.49 | 470.51 | 493.43 | 43843641 |

*Figure 3-2: An example of a pandas DataFrame*

Notice that the DataFrame includes an index column. Like with Series, pandas uses zero-based numeric indexing for DataFrames by default. However, you can replace the default index with one or more existing columns. Figure 3-3 shows the same DataFrame but with the Date column set as the index.

Index column

| | Open | High | Low | Close | Volume |
|---|---|---|---|---|---|
| **Date** | | | | | |
| **2020-08-26** | 412.00 | 433.20 | 410.73 | 430.63 | 71197000 |
| **2020-08-27** | 436.09 | 459.12 | 428.50 | 447.75 | 118465000 |
| **2020-08-28** | 459.02 | 463.70 | 437.30 | 442.68 | 20081200 |
| **2020-08-31** | 444.61 | 500.14 | 440.11 | 498.32 | 117841900 |
| **2020-09-01** | 502.14 | 502.49 | 470.51 | 494.28 | 45409943 |

*Figure 3-3: A pandas DataFrame that uses a column as the index*

In this particular example, the index is a column of type date. In fact, pandas allows you to have DataFrame indexes of any type. The most commonly used index types are integers and strings. However, you are not limited to using only simple types. You might define an index of a sequence type, such as List or Tuple, or even use an object type that is not built into Python; this could be a third-party type or even your own object type.

## Creating a pandas DataFrame

You've seen how you can create a pandas DataFrame by combining multiple Series objects. You can also create a DataFrame by loading data from a database, a CSV file, an API request, or another external source using one of the pandas library's *reader* methods. Readers allow you to read different types of data, like JSON and Excel, into a DataFrame.

Consider the DataFrame shown in Figure 3-2. It might have been created as the result of a request to the Yahoo Finance API via the yfinance library. To create the DataFrame for yourself, first install yfinance with pip as follows:

```
$ pip install yfinance
```

Then request the stock data, as shown here:

```
import yfinance as yf
❶ tkr = yf.Ticker('TSLA')
❷ hist = tkr.history(period="5d")
❸ hist = hist.drop("Dividends", axis = 1)
  hist = hist.drop("Stock Splits", axis = 1)
❹ hist = hist.reset_index()
```

In this script, you send a request to the API for stock price data for a given ticker ❶ and use yfinance's history() method to specify that you want data for a five-day period ❷. The resulting data, stored in the variable hist, is already in the form of a pandas DataFrame. You don't need to create the DataFrame explicitly; yfinance does this for you behind the scenes. After obtaining the DataFrame, you remove some of its columns ❸ and switch to numeric indexing ❹, yielding the structure that was shown in Figure 3-2.

To set the index to the Date column, as was shown in Figure 3-3, you'll need to execute the following line of code:

```
hist = hist.set_index('Date')
```

**NOTE**    *yfinance automatically indexes DataFrames by the Date column. In the preceding examples, we changed to numeric indexing and back to indexing by date to illustrate the reset_index() and set_index() methods.*

Let's now try converting a JSON document to a pandas object. The sample dataset used here contains the monthly salary data of three employees identified by their IDs in the Empno column:

```
import json
import pandas as pd
data = [
  {"Empno":9001,"Salary":3000},
  {"Empno":9002,"Salary":2800},
  {"Empno":9003,"Salary":2500}
]
```

```
❶ json_data = json.dumps(data)
❷ salary = pd.read_json(json_data)
❸ salary = salary.set_index('Empno')
  print(salary)
```

You use the pandas read_json() reader method to pass a JSON string into a DataFrame ❷. For simplicity, this example uses a JSON string converted from a list by json.dumps() ❶. Alternatively, you could pass a path object into the reader that points to a JSON file of interest or a URL to an HTTP API that publishes data in JSON format. Finally, you set the Empno column as the DataFrame index ❸, thus replacing the default numeric index.

The resulting DataFrame will look like this:

```
       Salary
Empno
9001    3000
9002    2800
9003    2500
```

Another common practice is to create pandas DataFrames from the standard Python data structures introduced in the previous chapter. For example, here's how to create a DataFrame from a list of lists:

```
  import pandas as pd
❶ data = [['9001','Jeff Russell', 'sales'],
          ['9002','Jane Boorman', 'sales'],
          ['9003','Tom Heints', 'sales']]
❷ emps = pd.DataFrame(data, columns = ['Empno', 'Name', 'Job'])
❸ column_types = {'Empno': int, 'Name': str, 'Job': str}
  emps = emps.astype(column_types)
❹ emps = emps.set_index('Empno')
  print(emps)
```

First, you initialize a list of lists with the data to be sent to the DataFrame ❶. Each nested list will become a row in the DataFrame. Then you explicitly create the DataFrame, defining the columns to be used ❷. Next, you use a dictionary, column_types, to change the data types set for the columns by default ❸. This step is optional, but it can be crucial if you're planning to join the DataFrame to another one. This is because you can join two DataFrames only on columns of the same data type. Finally, you set the Empno column as the DataFrame index ❹. The resulting DataFrame will look like this:

```
             Name      Job
Empno
9001    Jeff Russell    sales
9002    Jane Boorman    sales
9003      Tom Heints    sales
```

Notice that the emps and salary DataFrames both use Empno as the index column to uniquely identify each row. In both cases, you set this column as the DataFrame index to simplify the process of merging the two DataFrames into a single one, which we'll discuss in the next section.

## Combining DataFrames

pandas allows you to merge (or join) DataFrames together, in the same way that you can join different tables in a relational database. This lets you gather together data for analysis. DataFrames support database-style join operations through two methods: `merge()` and `join()`. Although these methods come with some different parameters, you can more or less use them interchangeably.

To begin, let's join the `emps` and `salary` DataFrames defined in the previous section. This is an example of a *one-to-one join* since one row in one DataFrame is associated with a single row in the other DataFrame. Figure 3-4 illustrates how this works.

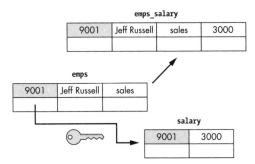

*Figure 3-4: Joining two DataFrames connected with a one-to-one relationship*

Here we see an entry from the `emps` DataFrame and one from the `salary` DataFrame. The entries share the same index value, `9001`, so they can be joined into a single entry in the new `emps_salary` DataFrame. In relational database terminology, the columns through which tables are related are known as *key columns*. Although pandas uses the term *index* for such columns, Figure 3-4 uses the key icon for visual association.

With the help of the `join()` method, the implementation is quite straightforward:

```
emps_salary = emps.join(salary)
print(emps_salary)
```

The `join()` method is designed to easily join DataFrames based on their indexes. In this particular example, you didn't even need to provide any additional parameters to join these two DataFrames; joining them index-on-index is the default behavior.

The resulting dataset looks as follows:

```
              Name     Job  Salary
Empno
9001   Jeff Russell   sales    3000
9002   Jane Boorman   sales    2800
9003    Tom Heints    sales    2500
```

In practice, you may need to join two DataFrames even if one of them has rows with no matches in the other DataFrame. Suppose you have one more row in the emps DataFrame and that there is no corresponding row in the salary DataFrame:

```
new_emp = pd.Series({'Name': 'John Hardy', 'Job': 'sales'}, name = 9004)
emps = emps.append(new_emp)
print(emps)
```

Here you create a pandas Series object and then add it to the emps DataFrame using the append() method. This is a common way to add new rows to a DataFrame.

The updated emps DataFrame will be as follows:

```
            Name       Job
Empno
9001    Jeff Russell   sales
9002    Jane Boorman   sales
9003    Tom Heints     sales
9004    John Hardy     sales
```

If you now apply the join operation again:

```
emps_salary = emps.join(salary)
print(emps_salary)
```

the result is the following DataFrame:

```
            Name       Job   Salary
Empno
9001    Jeff Russell   sales  3000.0
9002    Jane Boorman   sales  2800.0
9003    Tom Heints     sales  2500.0
9004    John Hardy     sales     NaN
```

Note that the row added to the emps DataFrame appears in the resulting dataset even though it doesn't have a related row in the salary DataFrame. The NaN entry in the Salary field of the last row denotes that the salary value is missing. In some cases you may want to allow incomplete rows like this, but in other cases you may want to exclude the rows that don't have a related row in the other DataFrame.

By default, the join() method uses the index of the calling DataFrame in the resulting joined DataFrame, thus performing a *left join*. In this example, the calling DataFrame is emps. It's considered to be the left DataFrame in the join operation, and therefore all the rows from it are included in the resulting dataset. You can change this default behavior by passing the how parameter in to the join() method. This parameter takes the following values:

**left** Uses the index of the calling DataFrame (or another column if the on parameter is specified), returning all rows from the calling (left) DataFrame and only the matching rows from the other (right) DataFrame

**right** Uses the other (right) DataFrame's index, returning all rows from that DataFrame and only the matching rows from the calling (left) DataFrame

**outer** Forms the combination of the calling DataFrame's index (or another column if the on parameter is specified) and the other DataFrame's index, returning all rows from both DataFrames

**inner** Forms the intersection of the calling DataFrame's index (or another column if the on parameter is specified) with the other DataFrame's index, returning only those rows whose indexes appear in both DataFrames

Figure 3-5 illustrates each type of join.

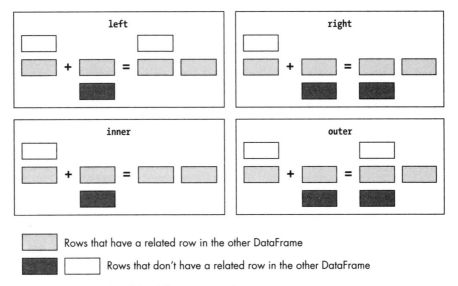

Figure 3-5: The results of the different types of joins

If you want the resulting DataFrame to include only those rows from emps that have a related row in the salary DataFrame, set the how parameter of join() to inner:

```
emps_salary = emps.join(salary, how = 'inner')
print(emps_salary)
```

The resulting DataFrame looks like this:

```
              Name    Job  Salary
Empno
9001   Jeff Russell  sales    3000
9002   Jane Boorman  sales    2800
9003    Tom Heints   sales    2500
```

Another way to get this result is to pass right in as the how parameter. In this case, join() returns all the rows from the salary DataFrame, attaching to them the fields of the matched rows from the emps DataFrame. It's important to realize, however, that a right join will not be equal to an inner join in many other cases. For example, if you add a row to the salary DataFrame with no match in the emps DataFrame, the right join will include this row along with the rows that have matches in emps.

**NOTE** *For further details on joining DataFrames, refer to the pandas documentation at* https://pandas.pydata.org/pandas-docs/stable/reference/frame.html# *combining-comparing-joining-merging.*

---

### EXERCISE #4: USING DIFFERENT JOINS

It's important to understand how different values of the how parameter passed to the join() method affect the resulting DataFrame.

Add a new row to the salary DataFrame so that the value of Empno in this row cannot be found in the emps DataFrame. (In the previous section, you saw how to add a row to a DataFrame using a Series object.) After that, join the emps DataFrame with the salary DataFrame so that the new DataFrame includes only those rows from emps that have matches in the salary DataFrame. Then, join emps with salary again so that the new DataFrame includes all rows from both DataFrames.

---

### One-to-Many Joins

In a *one-to-many join*, a row from one DataFrame can match multiple rows from the other DataFrame. Consider the situation where each salesperson in the emps DataFrame has processed a number of orders. This might be reflected in an orders DataFrame as follows:

```
import pandas as pd
data = [[2608, 9001,35], [2617, 9001,35], [2620, 9001,139],
        [2621, 9002,95], [2626, 9002,218]]
orders = pd.DataFrame(data, columns = ['Pono', 'Empno', 'Total'])
print(orders)
```

Here's how the orders DataFrame will look:

```
   Pono  Empno  Total
0  2608   9001     35
1  2617   9001     35
2  2620   9001    139
3  2621   9002     95
4  2626   9002    218
```

Now that you have a DataFrame of orders, you can combine it with the DataFrame of employees defined previously. This is a one-to-many join since one employee from the emps DataFrame can be associated with multiple rows in the orders DataFrame:

```
emps_orders = emps.merge(orders, how='inner', left_on='Empno',
                         right_on='Empno').set_index('Pono')
print(emps_orders)
```

In this code, you use the merge() method to define a one-to-many join, combining the data from the emps and orders DataFrames. The merge() method allows you to specify the columns to join on in both DataFrames, using left_on to specify the column in the calling DataFrame and right_on for the column in the other DataFrame. With join(), you can only specify the column to join on for the calling DataFrame. For the other DataFrame, join() uses the index column.

In this example, you use the inner type of join to include only related rows from both DataFrames. The resulting dataset looks as follows:

```
       Empno         Name      Job  Total
Pono
2608    9001  Jeff Russell    sales     35
2617    9001  Jeff Russell    sales     35
2620    9001  Jeff Russell    sales    139
2621    9002  Jane Boorman    sales     95
2626    9002  Jane Boorman    sales    218
```

Figure 3-6 illustrates how this one-to-many join works.

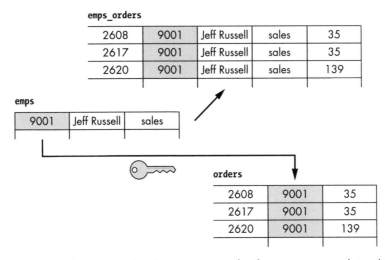

Figure 3-6: Joining two DataFrames connected with a one-to-many relationship

As you can see, the one-to-many join in the figure includes one row for each row in the dataset on the *many* side of the join. Since you're using the inner type of join, no other rows will be included. In the case of a left or outer join, however, the join would also include those rows from the dataset on the *one* side of the join that have no matches on the *many* side.

Apart from one-to-many and one-to-one joins, there are also *many-to-many joins*. As an example of this relationship, consider two datasets: one that lists books and the other that lists authors. Every record in the authors dataset can be linked to one or more records in the books dataset, and every record in the books dataset can be linked to one or more author records. We'll discuss this type of relationship in Chapter 7, which covers concatenating, merging, and joining datasets in greater detail.

### Aggregating Data with groupby()

The pandas groupby() function lets you aggregate data over multiple rows of a DataFrame. For example, it can find the sum of a column or get the mean of a subset of the values in a column.

Imagine that you need to calculate an average total for the orders processed by each employee in the orders DataFrame you created earlier. You can use the groupby() function as follows:

```
print(orders.groupby(['Empno'])['Total'].mean())
```

groupby() returns a GroupBy object that supports several aggregate functions. In this particular example, you use mean() to calculate an average total for the group of orders associated with an employee. To achieve this, you group the rows in the orders DataFrame by the Empno column and then apply the mean() operation to the Total column. The generated dataset is a Series object:

```
Empno
9001    69.666667
9002    156.500000
Name: Total, dtype: float64
```

Now suppose you want to sum up the totals of the orders within the groups. This is where the sum() function of the GroupBy object comes in handy:

```
print(orders.groupby(['Empno'])['Total'].sum())
```

The data in the generated Series object will be as follows:

```
Empno
9001    209
9002    313
Name: Total, dtype: int64
```

NOTE    *To learn more about the functions supported by the GroupBy object, see the pandas API reference at* https://pandas.pydata.org/pandas-docs/stable/reference/groupby.html.

## scikit-learn

scikit-learn is a Python package designed for machine learning applications. Together with NumPy and pandas, it's another core component in the Python data science ecosystem. scikit-learn provides efficient, easy-to-use tools that can be applied to common machine learning problems, including exploratory and predictive data analysis. We'll take a deeper dive into machine learning at the end of the book. For now, this section offers a taste of how Python can be applied in the field of machine learning, particularly for predictive data analysis.

Predictive data analysis is an area of machine learning that relies on classification and regression algorithms. Both classification and regression use past data to make predictions about new data, but classification sorts data into discrete categories, while regression can output a continuous range of numerical values. In this section, we'll look at an example of classification implemented with scikit-learn. We'll build a predictive model that can analyze customer product reviews and sort them into two classes: positive reviews and negative reviews. The model will learn from already classified samples how to predict the class of other samples. Once we have trained the model, we'll show it some new reviews for classification as either positive or negative.

## Installing scikit-learn

Like NumPy and pandas, scikit-learn is a third-party Python library. You can install it as follows:

```
$ pip install sklearn
```

The scikit-learn package has many submodules, each with its own specific functionality. It's therefore common to only import the submodule needed for a particular task (say, `sklearn.model_selection`) rather than the entire module.

## Obtaining a Sample Dataset

In order to be accurate, a predictive model should be trained on a large number of labeled samples, so your first step toward building a model that can classify product reviews is to obtain a set of reviews that are already labeled either positive or negative. This saves you from having to gather reviews yourself and manually label them.

There are several online sources for labeled datasets. One of the best is UC Irvine's Machine Learning Repository, at *https://archive.ics.uci.edu/ml/index.php*. Search the repository using the term "customer product reviews" and you'll find a link to the Sentiment Labelled Sentences Data Set (or alternatively, just point your browser to *https://archive.ics.uci.edu/ml/datasets/Sentiment+Labelled+Sentences*). Download and unpack the *sentiment labelled sentences.zip* file from the dataset's web page.

**NOTE** *The Sentiment Labelled Sentences Data Set was created for the paper "From Group to Individual Labels Using Deep Features," by Dimitrios Kotzias et al.*

The *.zip* file contains reviews from IMDb, Amazon, and Yelp, in three different *.txt* files. The reviews are labeled with positive or negative sentiment

(1 or 0, respectively); there are 500 positive and 500 negative reviews from each source, for a total of 3,000 labeled reviews in the entire dataset. For simplicity, we'll use the instances from Amazon only. They can be found in the *amazon _cells_labelled.txt* file.

### Loading the Sample Dataset into a pandas DataFrame

To simplify further computations, you need to load the reviews from the text file into a more manageable data structure. You can read the data from *amazon_cells_labelled.txt* into a pandas DataFrame as follows:

```
import pandas as pd
df = pd.read_csv('/usr/Downloads/sentiment labelled sentences/amazon_cells_labelled.txt',
                 names=[❶ 'review', ❷ 'sentiment'], ❸ sep='\t')
```

Here, you use the pandas read_csv() reader method to load the data into a DataFrame. You specify two columns: the first one to hold reviews ❶ and the second for the corresponding sentiment scores ❷. Since tabs separate the reviews from their corresponding sentiment scores in the original file, you specify \t as the separator ❸.

### Splitting the Sample Dataset into a Training Set and a Test Set

Now that you've imported your dataset, the next step is to split it into two parts: one to train the predictive model and one to test its accuracy. scikit-learn lets you do this with just a few lines of code:

```
from sklearn.model_selection import train_test_split
reviews = df['review'].values
sentiments = df['sentiment'].values
reviews_train, reviews_test, sentiment_train, sentiment_test = train_test_split(reviews,
                         sentiments, ❶ test_size=0.2, ❷ random_state=500)
```

You split your dataset using the train_test_split() function from the sklearn.model_selection module. The reviews and their corresponding sentiments (the sentiment scores) are passed in to the function as NumPy arrays obtained via the values property of the corresponding Series objects extracted from the DataFrame. You pass the test_size parameter ❶ to control how the dataset is split. The value 0.2 means 20 percent of the reviews will be randomly assigned to the test set. Thus, you follow the 80/20 pattern; the remaining 80 percent of reviews will make up the training set. The random_state parameter ❷ initializes the internal random number generator needed to randomly split up the data.

### Transforming Text into Numerical Feature Vectors

To train and test your model, you need a way to represent the text data numerically. This is where the *bag of words (BoW)* model comes in. This model represents a text as the set (bag) of its words in order to generate numerical data about the text. The most typical numerical feature generated from the BoW model is word frequency, the number of times each word occurs in the text. This simple example shows how the BoW model transforms a text into a numerical feature vector based on word frequency:

```
Text: I know it. You know it too.
BoW: {"I":1,"know":2,"it":2,"You":1,"too":1}
Vector: [1,2,2,1,1]
```

You can use scikit-learn's `CountVectorizer()` function to create a BoW matrix for text data. `CountVectorizer()` converts text data into numerical feature vectors (*n*-dimensional vectors of numerical features representing some object) and performs tokenization (separating a text into individual words and punctuation symbols) using either the default tokenizer or a custom one. A custom tokenizer can be implemented with a natural language processing tool like spaCy, introduced in the previous chapter. In this example, we'll use the default option to keep things simple.

Here's how to convert the reviews into feature vectors:

```
from sklearn.feature_extraction.text import CountVectorizer
vectorizer = CountVectorizer()
vectorizer.fit(reviews)
X_train = vectorizer.transform(reviews_train)
X_test = vectorizer.transform(reviews_test)
```

First, you create a vectorizer object. Then, you apply the vectorizer's `fit()` method to build the vocabulary of tokens found in the `reviews` dataset, which contains all reviews from both the training and test sets. After that, you use the `transform()` method of the vectorizer object to transform the text data in the training and test sets into numerical feature vectors.

## Training and Evaluating the Model

Now that you have the training and test sets in the form of numerical vectors, you're ready to train and test the model. You'll first train scikit-learn's `LogisticRegression()` classifier to predict the sentiment of a review. *Logistic regression* is a basic yet popular algorithm for solving classification problems.

Here, you create a `LogisticRegression()` classifier, then use its `fit()` method to train the model according to the given training data:

```
from sklearn.linear_model import LogisticRegression
classifier = LogisticRegression()
classifier.fit(X_train, sentiment_train)
```

Now you must evaluate how accurately the model can make predictions on new data. You'll need a set of labeled data for this, which is why it's common to split a labeled dataset into a training set and a test set, as you did earlier. Here, you evaluate the model using the test set:

```
accuracy = classifier.score(X_test, sentiment_test)
print("Accuracy:", accuracy)
```

The accuracy rating typically appears as follows:

```
Accuracy: 0.81
```

This means that the model is 81 percent accurate. If you experiment with the random_state parameter in the train_test_split() function, you may get a slightly different value because the instances for the training and test sets are chosen randomly from the original set.

### Making Predictions on New Data

Now that you've trained and tested your model, it's ready to analyze new, unlabeled data. This will give you a more complete picture of how well the model is working. Try it out by feeding your model some new sample reviews:

```
new_reviews = ['Old version of python useless', 'Very good effort, but not
               five stars', 'Clear and concise']
X_new = vectorizer.transform(new_reviews)
print(classifier.predict(X_new))
```

You start by creating a list of new reviews, then you transform that new text into numerical feature vectors. Finally, you predict class sentiments for the new samples. The sentiments are returned as a list:

```
[0, 1, 1]
```

Remember, 0 indicates a negative review and 1 indicates a positive review. As you can see, the model has worked for these sample reviews, showing that the first one is negative and the other two are positive.

## Summary

This chapter introduced you to some of the most popular third-party Python libraries for data science applications. First we explored the NumPy library and its multidimensional array objects, then we looked at the pandas library and its Series and DataFrame data structures. You learned to create NumPy arrays, pandas Series, and pandas DataFrame objects from built-in Python structures such as lists and from data sources stored in standard formats such as JSON. You also saw how to access and manipulate data in those objects. Finally, you used scikit-learn, a popular machine learning Python library, to build a predictive model for classification.

# 4

## ACCESSING DATA FROM FILES AND APIS

Accessing data and getting it into your script is the first step of data analysis. This chapter covers several ways of importing data from files and other sources into your Python application, as well as ways to export data to files. You'll see how to access the content of different types of files, including those stored locally on your machine and others accessible remotely through HTTP requests. You'll also learn how to get data by sending requests to APIs that are accessible via a URL. Finally, you'll learn how to load different types of data into pandas DataFrames.

## Importing Data Using Python's open() Function

Python's built-in open() function opens a file of any type to be processed within a script. The function returns a file object, which comes with methods that allow you to access and manipulate the content found in the file. If the file contains data in certain formats, such as CSV, JSON, or HTML, however, you'll also need to import a corresponding library to access and manipulate the data. Processing plaintext files doesn't require a special library; you can simply rely on the methods of the file object returned by open().

## Text Files

Text files (*.txt*) are perhaps the most common file type you'll encounter. To Python, a text file is a sequence of string objects. Each string object is one line of the text file—that is, a sequence of characters ending in a nondisplayed newline character (\n) or hard return.

**NOTE** *A single line of a text file may display as multiple lines on your screen, depending on the width of the viewing window, but Python will still understand it as one line as long as it isn't broken up by newline characters.*

Python has built-in functions to work with text files, allowing you to perform read, write, and append operations on them. In this section, we'll focus on how to read data from a text file. Start off by typing the following passage into a text editor and saving it as *excerpt.txt*. Be sure to press ENTER twice at the end of the first paragraph to create the blank line between the paragraphs (but don't press ENTER to break up the long lines):

```
Today, robots can talk to humans using natural language, and they're getting smarter. Even so, very few people understand how these robots work or how they might use these technologies in their own projects.

Natural language processing (NLP) - a branch of artificial intelligence that helps machines understand and respond to human language - is the key technology that lies at the heart of any digital assistant product.
```

To humans, the passage consists of two paragraphs that include three sentences total. To Python, however, the passage includes two nonempty lines and one blank line between them. Here's how to read the entire contents of the file into a Python script and print it out:

```
❶ path = "/path/to/excerpt.txt"
with open(❷ path, ❸ "r") as ❹ f:
❺ content = f.read()
print(content)
```

You start by specifying the path to the file ❶. You'll have to replace */path/to/excerpt.txt* with your own file path based on where the file is saved. You pass the path to the open() function as the first parameter ❷. The second parameter controls how the file will be used. The parameter defaults to reading in text mode, meaning the file's contents will be opened for reading only (not editing) and treated as strings. You explicitly specify "r" for *reading* ❸, but this isn't strictly necessary. (Passing "rt" would make text mode explicit along with specifying reading.) The open() function returns a file object in the specified mode ❹. Then, you use the read() method of the file object to read the entire contents of the file ❺.

Using the with keyword with open() ensures that the file object is properly closed when you're done with it even if an exception has been raised. Otherwise, you would need to call f.close() to close the file object and free up the system resources it consumes.

The following snippet reads in the same */path/to/excerpt.txt* file content line by line, printing out only nonempty lines:

```
path = "/path/to/excerpt.txt"
with open(path,"r") as f:
❶ for i, line in enumerate(f):
    ❷ if line.strip():
        print(f"Line {i}: ", line.strip())
```

In this example, you add line numbers to each line with the enumerate() function ❶. Then you filter out empty lines with the strip() method ❷, which removes any whitespace from the start and end of the string object in each line. The blank second line of the text file contains only one character, a newline, which strip() removes. The second line thus becomes an empty string, which the if statement will evaluate as false and skip over. The output appears as follows. As you can see, there's no Line 1:

```
Line 0:  Today, robots can talk to humans using natural language, and they're getting smarter.
Even so, very few people understand how these robots work or how they might use these
technologies in their own projects.
Line 2:  Natural language processing (NLP) - a branch of artificial intelligence that helps
machines understand and respond to human language - is the key technology that lies at the
heart of any digital assistant product.
```

Rather than print the lines, you can send them to a list by using a list comprehension:

```
path = "/path/to/excerpt.txt"
with open(path,"r") as f:
    lst = [line.strip() for line in f if line.strip()]
```

Each nonempty line will be a separate item in the list.

## Tabular Data Files

A *tabular* data file is a file in which the data is structured into rows. Each row typically contains information about someone or something, as shown here:

```
Jeff Russell, jeff.russell, sales
Jane Boorman, jane.boorman, sales
```

This is an example of a *flat file*, the most common type of tabular data file. The name comes from the structure: flat files contain simple-structured (flat) records, meaning the records do not contain nested structures, or subrecords. Typically, a flat file is a plaintext file in CSV or tab-separated values (TSV) format, containing one record per line. In *.csv* files, values in a record are separated by commas, while *.tsv* files use tabs as separators. Both formats are widely supported and are often used in data exchange to move tabular data between different applications.

The following is an example of data in CSV format, where the first line contains headers that describe the content of the lines below it. The header descriptions are used as *keys* to the data in the lines that follow. Copy this data into a text editor and save it as *cars.csv*:

```
Year,Make,Model,Price
1997,Ford,E350,3200.00
1999,Chevy,Venture,4800.00
1996,Jeep,Grand Cherokee,4900.00
```

Python's open() function can open *.csv* files in text mode. Then you can load the data into a Python object using a reader function from the csv module, as illustrated here:

```
import csv
path = "/path/to/cars.csv"
with open(path, "r") as ❶ csv_file:
  csv_reader = ❷ csv.DictReader(csv_file)
  cars = []
  for row in csv_reader:
  ❸ cars.append(dict(row))
print(cars)
```

The open() function returns a file object ❶, which you pass to a reader from the csv module. In this case, you use DictReader() ❷, which maps the data in each row to a dictionary using the corresponding headers from the first line as keys. You append these dictionaries to a list ❸. The resulting list of dictionaries looks like this:

```
[
{'Year': '1997', 'Make': 'Ford', 'Model': 'E350', 'Price': '3200.00'},
{'Year': '1999', 'Make': 'Chevy', 'Model': 'Venture', 'Price': '4800.00'},
{'Year': '1996', 'Make': 'Jeep', 'Model': 'Grand Cherokee', 'Price': '4900.00'}
]
```

Alternatively, you might use the csv module's reader() method to turn the *.csv* file into a list of lists, where each inner list represents a row, including the header row:

```
import csv
path = "cars.csv"
with open(path, "r") as csv_file:
  csv_reader = csv.reader(csv_file)
  cars = []
  for row in csv_reader:
    cars.append(row)
print(cars)
```

Here is the output:

```
[
  ['Year', 'Make', 'Model', 'Price']
  ['1997', 'Ford', 'E350', '3200.00']
  ['1999', 'Chevy', 'Venture', '4800.00']
  ['1996', 'Jeep', 'Grand Cherokee', '4900.00']
]
```

The `csv.DictReader()` and `csv.reader()` methods have an optional `delimiter` parameter, allowing you to specify the character that separates fields in your tabular data file. This parameter defaults to a comma, which is perfect for *.csv* files. However, by setting the parameter to `delimiter = "\t"`, you can read in the tab-separated data of *.tsv* files instead.

### EXERCISE #5: OPENING JSON FILES

You can open JSON files with the open() function in text mode and then use the json module for further processing. Like csv, json is a built-in Python package, so you don't need to install it separately. You saw an example of using the json module in Chapter 3 when converting a JSON document to a pandas object. In this exercise, you'll use the json module to save the following text to a *.json* file:

```
{"cars":
  [{"Year": "1997", "Make": "Ford", "Model": "E350", "Price": "3200.00"},
   {"Year": "1999", "Make": "Chevy", "Model": "Venture", "Price": "4800.00"},
   {"Year": "1996", "Make": "Jeep", "Model": "Grand Cherokee", "Price": "4900.00"}
]}
```

Open the file for reading with the open() function and send the retrieved file object to the json.load() method, which will deserialize the JSON to a Python object. From this object, extract the part that contains the rows of cars. In a loop, iterate over these rows, outputting the values as follows:

```
Year: 1997
Make: Ford
Model: E350
Price: 3200.00

Year: 1999
Make: Chevy
Model: Venture
Price: 4800.00

Year: 1996
Make: Jeep
Model: Grand Cherokee
Price: 4900.00
```

### Binary Files

Text files are not the only types of files you may have to deal with. There are also executable (*.exe*) and image files (*.jpeg*, *.bmp*, and so on), which contain data in binary format, represented as a sequence of bytes. Since these bytes are typically intended to be interpreted as something other than text characters, you can't open a binary file in text mode to access and manipulate its content. Instead, you must use the open() function's binary mode.

The following example shows how to open an image file in binary mode. An attempt to do this in text mode would result in an error. You can run this code with any *.jpg* file on your computer:

```
image = "/path/to/file.jpg"
with open(image, ❶ "rb") as image_file:
  content = ❷ image_file.read()
❸ print(len(content))
```

You instruct the open() function to open a file for reading in binary mode by passing in "rb" as the second parameter ❶. The retrieved object, like an object retrieved in text mode, has the read() method to get the file's content ❷. Here, the content is retrieved as a bytes object. In this example, you simply determine the number of bytes read from the file ❸.

# Exporting Data to Files

After some processing, you may need to store data to a file so that you can use the data during the next execution of the script or import it into other scripts or applications. You may also need to store information in a file so that you or others can view it. For example, you may want to log information about the errors and exceptions generated by your application for later review.

You can create a new file from your Python script and write data to it, or you can write over the data in an existing file. We'll explore an example of the latter here. Returning to the example from "Tabular Data Files," suppose you need to modify a row in the *cars.csv* file, changing the price of a certain car. Recall that the data was read from the *cars.csv* file into a list of dictionaries named cars. To see the values of each dictionary in that list, you can run the following loop:

```
for row in cars:
  print(list(row.values()))
```

In the loop body, you call the values() method on each dictionary in the list, thus converting the dictionary's values into a dict_values object that can be easily converted into a list. Each list represents a row from the original *.csv* file, as shown here:

```
['1997', 'Ford', 'E350', '3200.00']
['1999', 'Chevy', 'Venture', '4800.00']
['1996', 'Jeep', 'Grand Cherokee', '4900.00']
```

Suppose you need to update the Price field in the second row (for the Chevy Venture) and store this change in the original *cars.csv* file. You can make the change as follows:

```
❶ to_update = ['1999', 'Chevy', 'Venture']
❷ new_price = '4500.00'
❸ with open('path/to/cars.csv', 'w') as csvfile:
❹   fieldnames = cars[0].keys()
❺   writer = csv.DictWriter(csvfile, fieldnames=fieldnames)
    writer.writeheader()
❻   for row in cars:
        if set(to_update).issubset(set(row.values())):
            row['Price'] = new_price
        writer.writerow(row)
```

First, you need a way to identify the row to be updated. You create a list called to_update, including enough of the row's fields to uniquely identify the row ❶. Then, you specify the new value for the field to be changed as new_price ❷. Next, you open the file for writing, passing in the 'w' flag to the open() function ❸. The w mode used here will overwrite the existing content of the file. You therefore must define the field names to be sent to the file ❹. These are the names of the keys used in a dictionary representing a car row.

Using the csv.DictWriter() function ❺, you create a writer object that will map the dictionaries from the cars list onto the output rows to be sent to the *cars.csv* file. In a loop over the dictionaries in the cars list ❻, you check if each row matches your specified identifier. If so, you update the row's Price field. Finally, still within the loop, you write each row to the file using the writer.writerow() method.

Here's what you will see in the *cars.csv* file after executing the script:

```
Year,Make,Model,Price
1997,Ford,E350,3200.00
1999,Chevy,Venture,4500.00
1996,Jeep,Grand Cherokee,4900.00
```

As you can see, it looks like the original content, but the value of the Price field in the second row has been changed.

## Accessing Remote Files and APIs

Several third-party Python libraries, including urllib3 and Requests, let you get data from a URL-accessible remote file. You can also use the libraries to send requests to HTTP APIs (those that use HTTP as their transfer protocol), many of which return the requested data in JSON format. Both urllib3 and Requests work by formulating custom HTTP requests based on information you input.

*HTTP (HyperText Transfer Protocol)*, the client/server protocol that forms the foundation of data exchange over the web, is structured as a series of requests and responses. The HTTP messages sent by a client are *requests*, while the answer messages returned by the server are *responses*. For example, whenever you click a link in your browser, the browser, acting as the client, sends an HTTP request to fetch the desired web page from the appropriate web server. You can do the same thing from a Python script. The script, acting as the client, obtains the requested data in the form of a JSON or XML document.

## How HTTP Requests Work

There are several types of HTTP requests. The most common ones include GET, POST, PUT, and DELETE. These are also known as *HTTP request methods*, *HTTP commands*, or just *HTTP verbs*. The HTTP command in any HTTP request defines the action to be performed for a specified resource. For example, a GET request retrieves data from a resource, while a POST request pushes data to a destination.

An HTTP request also includes the request *target*, usually comprising a URL, and *headers*, the latter being fields that pass additional information along with the request. Some requests also include a *body*, which carries actual request data, such as a form submission. POST requests typically include a body, while GET requests don't.

As an example, consider the following HTTP request:

```
❶ GET ❷ /api/books?bibkeys=ISBN%3A1718500521&format=json HTTP/1.1
❸ Host: openlibrary.org
❹ User-Agent: python-requests/2.24.0
❺ Accept-Encoding: gzip, deflate
  Accept: */*
❻ Connection: keep-alive
```

This request uses the GET HTTP command ❶ to retrieve data from the given server (indicated as Host ❸) using the specified URI ❷. The remaining lines include other headers specifying additional information. The User-Agent request header identifies the application making the request and its version ❹. The Accept headers advertise which content types the client is able to understand ❺. The Connection header, set to keep-alive ❻, instructs the server to establish a persistent connection to the client, which allows for subsequent requests to be made.

In Python, you don't have to fully understand the internal structure of HTTP requests to send them and receive responses. As you'll learn in the following sections, libraries like Requests and urllib3 let you manipulate HTTP requests easily and efficiently, just by calling an appropriate method and passing the required parameters in to it.

With the help of the Requests library, the preceding HTTP request can be generated by a simple Python script as follows:

```
import requests
PARAMS = {'bibkeys':'ISBN:1718500521', 'format':'json'}
requests.get('http://openlibrary.org/api/books', params = PARAMS)
```

We'll discuss the Requests library in detail shortly. For now, notice that the library saves you from having to set the headers of a request manually. It sets the default values behind the scenes, automatically generating a fully formatted HTTP request on your behalf based on just a few lines of code.

## The urllib3 Library

urllib3 is a URL-handling library that lets you access and manipulate URL-accessible resources such as HTTP APIs, websites, and files. The library is designed to efficiently manipulate HTTP requests, using thread-safe connection pooling to minimize the resources needed on your server's end. Compared to the Requests library, which we'll discuss next, urllib3 requires more manual work, but it also gives you more direct control over the requests you prepare, which is useful when, for example, you need to customize pool behavior or explicitly decode HTTP responses.

### Installing urllib3

Since urllib3 is a dependency of many popular Python packages, like Requests and pip, chances are you have it already installed in your Python environment. To check this, try to import it in a Python session. If you get a ModuleNotFoundError, you can install it explicitly with this command:

```
$ pip install urllib3
```

### Accessing Files with urllib3

To see how to load data from a URL-accessible file with urllib3, you can use the *excerpt.txt* file you created earlier. To make this file accessible via a URL, you might put it into the document folder of an HTTP server running on your local host. Alternatively, use the following URL to obtain it from the GitHub repository accompanying this book: *https://github.com/pythondatabook/ sources/blob/main/ch4/excerpt.txt*.

Run the following code, replacing the URL if necessary:

```
  import urllib3
❶ http = urllib3.PoolManager()
❷ r = http.request('GET', 'http://localhost/excerpt.txt')
  for i, line in enumerate(❸ r.data.decode('utf-8').split('\n')):
    if line.strip():
    ❹ print("Line %i: " %(i), line.strip())
```

First you create a PoolManager instance ❶, which is how urllib3 makes requests. After that, you make an HTTP request to the specified URL with the request() method of PoolManager ❷. The request() method returns an HTTPResponse object. You access the requested data through the data attribute of this object ❸. Then you output only nonempty lines, enumerating them at the beginning of each line ❹.

## API Requests with urllib3

You can also use urllib3 to make requests to HTTP APIs. In the following example, you make a request to the News API (*https://newsapi.org*), which searches for articles from a wide range of news sources, finding those that are most relevant to your request. Like many other APIs today, it requires you to pass in an API key with each request. You can get a developer API key for free at *https://newsapi.org/register* after filling in a simple registration form. Then use this code to search for articles about the Python programming language:

```
import json
import urllib3
http = urllib3.PoolManager()
r = http.request('GET', 'https://newsapi.org/v2/everything? ❶ q=Python
        programming language& ❷ apiKey=your_api_key_here& ❸ pageSize=5')
❹ articles = json.loads(r.data.decode('utf-8'))
for article in articles['articles']:
  print(article['title'])
  print(article['publishedAt'])
  print(article['url'])
  print()
```

You pass in the search phrase as the q parameter in the request URL ❶. The only other required parameter to specify in the request URL is apiKey ❷, where you pass in your API key. There are also many other optional parameters. For example, you can specify the news sources or blogs you want articles from. In this particular example, you use pageSize to set the number of articles being retrieved to five ❸. The entire list of supported parameters can be found in the News API documentation at *https://newsapi.org/docs*.

The data attribute of the HTTPResponse object returned by request() is a JSON document in the form of a bytes object. You decode it to a string, which you then pass to the json.loads() method to convert it into a dictionary ❹. To see how the data is structured in this dictionary, you might output it, but this step is omitted in this listing. If you looked at the output, you'd see that information about the articles can be found in the list called articles within the returned document, and each record in this list has the fields title, publishedAt, and url.

Using that information, you can print the retrieved list of articles in a more readable format, producing something like this:

```
A Programming Language To Express Programming Frustration
2021-12-15T03:00:05Z
https://hackaday.com/2021/12/14/a-programming-language-to-express-programming-frustration/

Raise Your Business's Potential by Learning Python
2021-12-24T16:30:00Z
https://www.entrepreneur.com/article/403981

TIOBE Announces that the Programming Language of the Year Was Python
2022-01-08T19:34:00Z
https://developers.slashdot.org/story/22/01/08/017203/tiobe-announces-that-the-programming
-language-of-the-year-was-python
```

Python is the TIOBE programming language of 2021 – what does this title even mean?
2022-01-04T12:28:01Z
https://thenextweb.com/news/python-c-tiobe-programming-language-of-the-year-title-analysis

Which programming language or compiler is faster
2021-12-18T02:15:28Z

This example illustrated how to integrate the News API into a Python application using direct HTTP requests via the urllib3 library. An alternative would be to use the unofficial Python client library covered at *https://newsapi.org/docs/client-libraries/python*.

## The Requests Library

Requests is another popular URL-handling library that allows you to easily send HTTP requests. Requests uses urllib3 under the hood and makes it even easier to make requests and retrieve data. You can install the Requests library with the pip command:

```
$ pip install requests
```

HTTP verbs are implemented as the library's methods (for example, requests.get() for an HTTP GET request). Here's how to remotely access *excerpt.txt* with Requests. Replace the URL with the file's GitHub link if necessary:

```
import requests
❶ r = requests.get('http://localhost/excerpt.txt')
for i, line in enumerate(❷ r.text.split('\n')):
  if line.strip():
  ❸ print("Line %i: " %(i), line.strip())
```

You make an HTTP GET request using the requests.get() method, passing the file's URL as the parameter ❶. The method returns a Response object that includes the retrieved content in the text attribute ❷. Requests automatically decodes the retrieved content, making knowledgeable guesses about the encoding, so you don't have to do it manually. Just as in the urllib3 example, you output only nonempty lines, adding a line number at the beginning of each ❸.

---

**EXERCISE #6: ACCESSING AN API WITH REQUESTS**

Like urllib3, the Requests library can interact with HTTP APIs. Try rewriting the code that sends a GET request to the News API so that it uses the Requests library in place of urllib3. Note that with Requests, you don't have to manually add query parameters to the URL passed in. Instead, you can pass parameters as a dictionary of strings.

---

# Moving Data to and from a DataFrame

pandas comes with a range of reader methods, each of which is designed to load data in a certain format and/or from a certain type of source. These methods allow you to load tabular data into a DataFrame with the help of a single call, thus making the imported dataset immediately ready for analysis. pandas also has methods for converting DataFrame data into other formats, such as JSON. This section explores examples of these methods for moving data to or from a DataFrame. We'll also consider the pandas-datareader library, which is helpful for loading data from various online sources into pandas DataFrames.

## Importing Nested JSON Structures

Since JSON has become the de facto standard for data interchange between applications, it's important to have a way to quickly import a JSON document and convert it to a Python data structure. In the previous chapter, you saw an example of loading a simple, non-nested JSON structure into a DataFrame with the pandas read_json() reader. In this section, you'll learn how to load a more complex, nested JSON document, like this one:

```
data = [{"Emp":"Jeff Russell",
  "POs":[{"Pono":2608,"Total":35},
        {"Pono":2617,"Total":35},
        {"Pono":2620,"Total":139}
  ]},
  {"Emp":"Jane Boorman",
  "POs":[{"Pono":2621,"Total":95},
        {"Pono":2626,"Total":218}
  ]
}]
```

As you can see, each entry in the JSON document begins with a simple-structured key-value pair with the key Emp, followed by a nested structure with the key POs. You can convert that hierarchical JSON structure into a tabular pandas DataFrame using the pandas library's json_normalize() reader method, which takes a nested structure and flattens, or *normalizes*, it into a simple table. Here's how:

```
import json
import pandas as pd
df = pd.json_normalize(❶ data, ❷ "POs", ❸ "Emp").set_index([❹ "Emp","Pono"])
print(df)
```

Apart from the JSON sample ❶ to be processed by json_normalize(), you also specify POs as the nested array to be flattened ❷ and Emp as the field to be used as part of the complex index in the resulting table ❸. In the same line of code, you set two columns as the index: Emp and Pono ❹. As a result, you will see the following pandas DataFrame:

```
                      Total
Emp           Pono
Jeff Russell 2608       35
```

```
                    2617     35
                    2620    139
    Jane Boorman 2621     95
                    2626    218
```

**NOTE**   *Using a two-column index simplifies aggregating data within groups. We'll cover*
*DataFrames with multicolumn indexes in more detail in Chapter 6.*

## Converting a DataFrame to JSON

In practice, you may often need to perform the reverse operation, converting a pandas DataFrame into JSON. The following code converts
our DataFrame back to the JSON sample from which it was originally
generated:

```
❶ df = df.reset_index()
   json_doc = (❷ df.groupby(['Emp'], as_index=True)
                  ❸ .apply(lambda x: x[['Pono','Total']].to_dict('records'))
                  ❹ .reset_index()
                  ❺ .rename(columns={0:'POs'})
                  ❻ .to_json(orient='records'))
```

You start by dropping the two-column index of the DataFrame to
make Emp and Pono regular columns ❶. Then, you use a composite one-liner
to convert the DataFrame to a JSON document. First you apply a groupby
operation to the DataFrame, grouping the rows by the Emp column ❷. You
use groupby() in combination with apply() to apply a lambda function to
each record in each group ❸. In the lambda expression, you specify the list
of fields that you want to see in a row of the nested array associated with
each Emp record. You use the DataFrame.to_dict() method with the records
parameter to format the fields in the array as follows: [{*column:value*}, ... ,
{*column:value*}], where each dictionary represents an order associated with a
given employee.

At this point, you have a Series object with the index Emp and a column containing an array of orders associated with an employee. To give
this column a name (in this case, POs), you need to convert the Series to a
DataFrame. One simple way to do this is with reset_index() ❹. In addition
to converting the Series to a DataFrame, reset_index() changes Emp from
an index to a regular column, which will be important when you convert
the DataFrame to JSON format. Finally, you explicitly set the name of the
column containing the nested array (POs) using the DataFrame's rename()
method ❺ and turn the revised DataFrame into JSON ❻.

The content of json_doc looks as follows:

```
[{"Emp": "Jeff Russell",
    "POs": [{"Pono": 2608, "Total": 35},
      {"Pono": 2617, "Total": 35},
      {"Pono": 2620, "Total": 139}
    ]},
  {"Emp": "Jane Boorman",
```

```
        "POs": [{"Pono": 2621, "Total": 95},
           {"Pono": 2626, "Total": 218}
         ]
}]
```

To improve readability, you might print it out using the following command:

```
print(json.dumps(json.loads(json_doc), indent=2))
```

The JSON sample used in the previous section had a single simple-structured field (Emp) in the top level of each record. In a real-world JSON document, there could be more such fields. The entries in this sample have a second simple field, Emp_email, at the top level:

```
data = [{"Emp":"Jeff Russell",
  "Emp_email":"jeff.russell",
  "POs":[{"Pono":2608,"Total":35},
         {"Pono":2617,"Total":35},
         {"Pono":2620,"Total":139}
  ]},
  {"Emp":"Jane Boorman",
  "Emp_email":"jane.boorman",
  "POs":[{"Pono":2621,"Total":95},
         {"Pono":2626,"Total":218}
  ]
}]
```

To load this data into a DataFrame, you need to pass a list of all the top-level simple-structured fields into the third parameter of json_normalize(), as shown here:

```
df = pd.json_normalize(data, "POs", ["Emp","Emp_email"]).set_index(["Emp","Emp
_email","Pono"])
```

The content of the DataFrame will be as follows:

```
                                    Total
Emp            Emp_email    Pono
Jeff Russell   jeff.russell 2608     35
                            2617     35
                            2620     139
Jane Boorman   jane.boorman 2621     95
                            2626     218
```

Try to convert this DataFrame back into the original JSON document by modifying the groupby operation shown in the previous section.

## Loading Online Data into a DataFrame with pandas-datareader

Several third-party libraries come with pandas-compatible reader methods for accessing data from a variety of online sources, such as Quandl (*https://data.nasdaq.com*) and Stooq (*https://stooq.com*). The most popular of these is pandas-datareader. At the time of writing, this library included 70 methods, each designed to load data from a certain source into a pandas DataFrame. Many of the library's methods are wrappers for finance APIs, allowing you to easily get financial data in pandas format.

### Installing pandas-datareader

Enter this command to install pandas-datareader:

```
$ pip install pandas-datareader
```

For descriptions of the library's reader methods, consult the pandas-datareader documentation at *https://pandas-datareader.readthedocs.io/en/latest/remote_data.html*. You can also print a list of the available methods with Python's dir() function:

```
import pandas_datareader.data as pdr
print(dir(pdr))
```

### Obtaining Data from Stooq

In the following example, you use the get_data_stooq() method to obtain S&P 500 index data for a specified period:

```
import pandas_datareader.data as pdr
spx_index = pdr.get_data_stooq('^SPX', '2022-01-03', '2022-01-10')
print(spx_index)
```

The get_data_stooq() method obtains data from Stooq, a free site that provides information on a number of market indexes. Pass in the ticker of the market index you want as the first parameter. The available options can be found at *https://stooq.com/t*.

The obtained S&P 500 index data will typically appear in this format:

|  | Open | High | Low | Close | Volume |
|---|---|---|---|---|---|
| Date |  |  |  |  |  |
| 2022-01-10 | 4655.34 | 4673.02 | 4582.24 | 4670.29 | 2668776356 |
| 2022-01-07 | 4697.66 | 4707.95 | 4662.74 | 4677.03 | 2414328227 |
| 2022-01-06 | 4693.39 | 4725.01 | 4671.26 | 4696.05 | 2389339330 |
| 2022-01-05 | 4787.99 | 4797.70 | 4699.44 | 4700.58 | 2810603586 |
| 2022-01-04 | 4804.51 | 4818.62 | 4774.27 | 4793.54 | 2841121018 |
| 2022-01-03 | 4778.14 | 4796.64 | 4758.17 | 4796.56 | 2241373299 |

The Date column is set as the DataFrame's index by default.

## Summary

In this chapter, you learned how to obtain data from different sources and bring it into your Python scripts for further processing. In particular, you saw how to import data from files using Python's built-in functions, how to send HTTP requests from your Python scripts to online APIs, and how to take advantage of pandas readers to acquire different forms of data from various sources. You also learned how to export data to files and how to convert DataFrame data into JSON.

# 5

## WORKING WITH DATABASES

A *database* is an organized collection of data that can be easily accessed, managed, and updated. Even if there isn't a database in the initial architecture of your project, data that flows through your application will likely touch one or more databases at some point.

Continuing the previous chapter's discussion on importing data into your Python applications, this chapter covers working with database data. The examples here will show you how to access and manipulate data stored in databases of different types, including those that position SQL as the primary tool to work with data and those that don't. You'll explore how to use Python to interface with a variety of popular databases, including MySQL, Regis, and MongoDB.

Databases offer many advantages. For one, with the help of a database, you can persist data between invocations of a script and efficiently share data between different applications. Moreover, database languages can help you systematically organize and answer questions about your data. Additionally, many database systems allow you to implement programming code within the database itself, which can improve the performance, modularity, and reusability of an application. For example, you might store a *trigger* in a database; this is a piece of code that's invoked automatically each time a certain event happens, such as every time you insert a new row into a particular table.

There are two categories of databases: relational databases and non-relational (NoSQL) databases. Relational databases have a rigid structure implemented in the form of a schema for the data being stored. This approach helps ensure the integrity, consistency, and overall accuracy of the data. However, the major drawback of relational databases is that they don't scale well as data volumes increase. In contrast, NoSQL databases don't impose restrictions on the structure of the data being stored, thus allowing for more flexibility, adaptability, and scalability. This chapter will cover storing and retrieving data in both relational and nonrelational databases.

## Relational Databases

*Relational databases*, also known as *row-and-column databases*, are the most common type of database in use today. They provide a structured way of storing data. Just like a list of books on Amazon has a set structure for storing information, with fields for book titles, authors, descriptions, ratings, and so on, the data stored in a relational database must fit a predefined formal schema. Working with a relational database starts with designing that formal schema: you define a collection of tables, each made up of a set of fields or columns, and you specify what type of data each field will store. You also establish the relationships between the tables. Then you can store data to the database, retrieve data from the database, or update the data as needed.

Relational databases are designed to allow the efficient insertion, updating, and/or deleting of small to vast amounts of structured data. There are plenty of applications where this type of database can be put to great use. In particular, relational databases are well suited for *online transaction processing (OLTP)* applications, which process a high volume of transactions for a large number of users.

Some common relational database systems are MySQL, MariaDB, and PostgreSQL. This section will focus on MySQL, arguably the world's most popular open source database, to illustrate how to interact with a database. You'll learn how to set up MySQL, create a new database, define its structure, and write Python scripts to store and retrieve data to and from the database.

## Understanding SQL Statements

*SQL*, or *Structured Query Language*, is the primary tool for interacting with a relational database. Although our focus here is on interfacing with databases using Python, the Python code must itself contain SQL statements to do this. A comprehensive look at SQL is beyond the scope of this book, but a brief introduction to this query language is nonetheless in order.

SQL statements are text commands recognized and executed by a database engine like MySQL. For example, this SQL statement asks a database to retrieve all the rows from a table called orders whose status field is set to Shipped:

```
SELECT * FROM orders WHERE status = 'Shipped';
```

SQL statements typically have three major components: an *operation* to be performed, a *target* for that operation, and a *condition* that narrows the scope of the operation. In the preceding example, SELECT is the SQL operation, meaning we're accessing rows from the database. The orders table is the target for the operation, as defined by the FROM clause, and the condition is specified in the WHERE clause of the statement. All SQL statements must have an operation and a target, but the condition is optional. This statement, for instance, lacks a condition, so it retrieves all the rows from the orders table:

```
SELECT * FROM orders;
```

You can also refine SQL statements to only affect certain columns of a table. Here's how to retrieve only the pono and date columns of all the rows in the orders table:

```
SELECT pono, date FROM orders;
```

By convention, language-reserved words in SQL, such as SELECT and FROM, are written in all caps. However, SQL is a case-insensitive language, so this capitalization isn't strictly necessary. Each SQL statement should end with a semicolon.

SELECT operations like those just shown are examples of *Data Manipulation Language (DML) statements*, a category of SQL statements that you use to access and manipulate database data. Other DML operations include INSERT, UPDATE, and DELETE, which add, change, and remove records from a database, respectively. *Data Definition Language (DDL) statements* are another common category of SQL statements. You use these to actually define the database structure. Typical DDL operations include CREATE to make, ALTER to modify, and DROP to delete data containers, whether that be columns, tables, or whole databases.

## Getting Started with MySQL

MySQL is available on a majority of modern operating systems, including Linux, Unix, Windows, and macOS. Both free and commercial editions are available. For the purposes of this chapter, you can use MySQL Community Edition (*https://www.mysql.com/products/community*), the freely downloadable version of MySQL, which is available under the GPL license. For detailed MySQL installation instructions for your operating system, refer to the reference manual for the latest version of MySQL, available at *https://dev.mysql.com/doc*.

To start the MySQL server after installation, you need to use the command that the installation guide specifies for your operating system. Then you can connect to the MySQL server from a system terminal using the *mysql* client program:

```
$ mysql -uroot -p
```

**NOTE**    *On macOS, you may need to use the entire path to MySQL, such as */usr/local/mysql/bin/mysql -uroot -p.*

You'll be asked to enter your password, which you set during the MySQL server installation process. After that, you'll see the MySQL prompt:

```
mysql>
```

If you like, you can choose a new password for the root user with the following SQL command:

```
mysql> ALTER USER 'root'@'localhost' IDENTIFIED BY 'your_new_pswd';
```

Now you can create the database that you'll need for your application. Enter this command at the mysql> prompt:

```
mysql> CREATE DATABASE sampledb;
Query OK, 1 row affected (0.01 sec)
```

This creates a database called sampledb. Next, you must choose that database for use:

```
mysql> USE sampledb;
Database changed
```

Now any subsequent commands will apply to your sampledb database.

## Defining the Database Structure

A relational database gets its structure from the makeup of its constituent tables and from the connections between those tables. The fields that link different tables are called *keys*. There are two types: *primary keys* and *foreign keys*. A primary key uniquely identifies a record in a table. A foreign key is a field in another table that corresponds to the primary key in the first table. Typically, the primary key and its corresponding foreign key share the same name in both tables.

*The terms* field *and* column *are often used interchangeably. Strictly speaking, a column becomes a field when you refer to it in the context of a single row.*

Now that you've created your `sampledb` database, you're ready to create some tables and define their structure. For demonstration purposes, the tables will have the same structure as some of the pandas DataFrames you worked with in Chapter 3. Here are three tabular data structures to be implemented in your database:

```
emps

empno  empname        job
---------------------------
9001   Jeff Russell   sales
9002   Jane Boorman   sales
9003   Tom Heints     sales


salary

empno     salary
-----------------
9001      3000
9002      2800
9003      2500


orders

pono   empno  total
-------------------
2608   9001   35
2617   9001   35
2620   9001   139
2621   9002   95
2626   9002   218
```

To review what relations can be established between these structures, refer back to Figures 3-4 and 3-6 from Chapter 3. As can be seen in Figure 3-4, the rows in the `emps` and `salary` tables are related with a one-to-one relationship. The relation is established via the `empno` field. The `emps` and `orders` tables are also related via the `empno` field. This is a one-to-many relationship, as depicted in Figure 3-6.

You can add these data structures to your relational database using SQL commands at the `mysql>` prompt. Start by creating the `emps` table:

```
mysql> CREATE TABLE emps (
        empno INT NOT NULL,
        empname VARCHAR(50),
        job VARCHAR(30),
        PRIMARY KEY (empno)
      );
```

You create the table with the CREATE TABLE command, specifying each column along with the type and, optionally, the size of data you can store in it. For example, the empno column is for integers (type INT), and the NOT NULL constraint applied to it guarantees that you won't be able to insert a row with an empty empno field. Meanwhile, the empname column can hold strings (type VARCHAR) up to 50 characters long, while job can hold strings up to 30 characters long. You also specify that empno is the primary key column in the table, meaning it's not supposed to have duplicates across the table.

On successful execution of this command, you'll see the following message:

```
Query OK, 0 rows affected (0.03 sec)
```

Similarly, here's how to create the salary table:

```
mysql> CREATE TABLE salary (
       empno INT NOT NULL,
       salary INT,
       PRIMARY KEY (empno)
       );

Query OK, 0 rows affected (0.05 sec)
```

Next, you'll add a foreign key constraint to the empno column of the salary table, referencing the empno column of the emps table:

```
mysql> ALTER TABLE salary ADD FOREIGN KEY (empno) REFERENCES emps (empno);
```

This command creates the relationship between the salary and empno tables. It establishes that an employee number in the salary table must match an employee number in the emps table. This constraint guarantees that you won't be able to insert a row into the salary table if the table doesn't have a corresponding row in the emps table.

Since the salary table has no rows so far, the ALTER TABLE operation affects no rows, as can be seen from the resulting message:

```
Query OK, 0 rows affected (0.14 sec)
Records: 0  Duplicates: 0  Warnings: 0
```

Finally, create the orders table:

```
mysql> CREATE TABLE orders (
       pono INT NOT NULL,
       empno INT NOT NULL,
       total INT,
       PRIMARY KEY (pono),
       FOREIGN KEY (empno) REFERENCES emps (empno)
       );

Query OK, 0 rows affected (0.13 sec)
```

This time you add a foreign key constraint within the CREATE TABLE command, thus defining the foreign key immediately upon the creation of the table.

## Inserting Data into the Database

Now you're ready to insert rows into your newly created tables. While you could do this using the mysql> prompt, this type of operation is usually performed from an application. You'll interact with the database from your Python code through the MySQL Connector/Python driver. You can install it via pip, as follows:

```
$ pip install mysql-connector-python
```

Run the following script to populate your database tables with data:

```
import mysql.connector

try:
❶ cnx = mysql.connector.connect(user='root', password='your_pswd',
                                host='127.0.0.1',
                                database='sampledb')
❷ cursor = cnx.cursor()
   # defining employee rows
❸ emps = [
     (9001, "Jeff Russell", "sales"),
     (9002, "Jane Boorman", "sales"),
     (9003, "Tom Heints", "sales")
   ]
   # defining the query
❹ query_add_emp = ("""INSERT INTO emps (empno, empname, job)
                      VALUES (%s, %s, %s)""")
   # inserting the employee rows
   for emp in emps:
❺   cursor.execute(query_add_emp, emp)
   # defining and inserting salaries
   salary = [
     (9001, 3000),
     (9002, 2800),
     (9003, 2500)
   ]
   query_add_salary = ("""INSERT INTO salary (empno, salary)
                         VALUES (%s, %s)""")
   for sal in salary:
     cursor.execute(query_add_salary, sal)
   # defining and inserting orders
   orders = [
     (2608, 9001, 35),
     (2617, 9001, 35),
     (2620, 9001, 139),
     (2621, 9002, 95),
     (2626, 9002, 218)
   ]
```

```
      query_add_order = ("""INSERT INTO orders(pono, empno, total)
                             VALUES (%s, %s, %s)""")
      for order in orders:
        cursor.execute(query_add_order, order)
      # making the insertions permanent in the database
  ❻ cnx.commit()
❼ except mysql.connector.Error as err:
    print("Error-Code:", err.errno)
    print("Error-Message: {}".format(err.msg))
❽ finally:
    cursor.close()
    cnx.close()
```

In this script, you import the MySQL Connector/Python driver as
mysql.connector. Then you open a try/except block, which provides a template
for any database-related operations you need to perform within your script.
You write the code for the operation in the try block, and if an error occurs
when the operation is carried out, the execution is transferred to the except
block.

Within the try block, you start by establishing a connection to the database, specifying your username and password, the host IP address (in this
case, your local host), and the database name ❶. Then you obtain a cursor
object related to this connection ❷. The cursor object provides the means
for statement execution as well as the interface for fetching the results.

You define rows for the emps table as a list of tuples ❸. Then, you define
the SQL statement to be executed to insert these rows into the table ❹. In
this INSERT statement, you specify the fields to be filled with data, along with
%s placeholders that map these fields to the members of each tuple. In a
loop, you execute the statement, inserting the rows one at a time with the
cursor.execute() method ❺. Similarly, you then insert rows into the salary
and orders tables. At the end of the try block, you make all the insertions
into the database permanent with the connection's commit() method ❻.

If any database-related operation fails, the rest of the try clause is
skipped and the except clause executes ❼, printing out an error code generated by the MySQL server along with the corresponding error message.

The finally clause is executed in any case ❽. In this clause, you explicitly close the cursor and then close the connection.

## Querying Database Data

Now that you've populated the tables with data, you can query that data for
use in your Python code. Say you want to retrieve all the rows in the emps
table where empno is greater than 9001. To achieve this, use the script from
the previous section as a model, changing only the try block as follows:

```
--snip--
try:
  cnx = mysql.connector.connect(user='root', password='your_pswd',
                                host='127.0.0.1',
                                database='sampledb')
  cursor = cnx.cursor()
```

```
query = ("SELECT ❶ * FROM emps WHERE ❷ empno > %s")
❸ empno = 9001
❹ cursor.execute(query, (empno,))
❺ for (empno, empname, job) in cursor:
    print("{}, {}, {}".format(
      empno, empname, job))
--snip--
```

Unlike the insertion operation, selecting rows doesn't require you to perform multiple `cursor.execute()` operations in a loop, one for each row. Instead, you write a query specifying criteria for the rows you want to select, then get them all at once with a single `cursor.execute()` operation.

In the `SELECT` statement that forms your query, you specify the asterisk symbol (*), which means you want to see all the fields in the retrieved rows ❶. In the `WHERE` clause, you specify the condition that a row must meet in order to be selected. Here, you indicate that rows must have an `empno` greater than the value of the variable bound to the `%s` placeholder ❷. The variable `empno` is bound to the placeholder during execution ❸. When you execute the query with `cursor.execute()`, you pass in the binding variable within a tuple as the second parameter ❹. The `execute()` method requires that binding variables be passed within a tuple or a dictionary even if you only need to pass in a single variable.

You access the retrieved rows via the `cursor` object, iterating over it in a loop. Each row is accessible as a tuple whose items represent the values of the row's fields ❺. Here, you simply print the fields' values, outputting the results row by row, as follows:

```
9002, Jane Boorman, sales
9003, Tom Heints, sales
```

You can also write `SELECT` statements that join rows from different tables together. Joining relational database tables mirrors the process of joining pandas DataFrames, as discussed in Chapter 3. You typically join tables through the foreign key relationship you define when you set up the database.

For example, suppose you want to join the `emps` and `salary` tables while keeping the condition that `empno` be greater than 9001. You do this through their shared `empno` columns, since you defined `empno` in the `salary` table as a foreign key referencing `empno` in the `emps` table. You can implement this join with another modification to the `try` block of your script:

```
--snip--
try:
  cnx = mysql.connector.connect(user='root', password='your_pswd',
                                host='127.0.0.1',
                                database='sampledb')
  cursor = cnx.cursor()
  query = ("""SELECT ❶ e.empno, e.empname, e.job, s.salary
              FROM ❷ emps e JOIN salary s ON ❸ e.empno = s.empno
              WHERE ❹ e.empno > %s""")

  empno = 9001
```

```
cursor.execute(query, (empno,))
for (empno, empname, job, salary) in cursor:
  print("{}, {}, {}, {}".format(
    empno, empname, job, salary))
--snip--
```

This time, query contains a SELECT statement joining the emps and salary tables. In the SELECT list, you specify the columns from both tables that you want to include in the join ❶. In the FROM clause, you specify the two tables, connecting them with the JOIN keyword, along with the aliases e and s, which are needed to differentiate columns with the same name in both tables ❷. In the ON clause, you define the join condition, stating that the values in both tables' empno columns should match ❸. In the WHERE clause, as in the previous example, you use the %s placeholder to set the minimum empno value ❹.

The script outputs the following rows, with each employee's salary joined to their record from the emps table:

```
9002, Jane Boorman, sales, 2800
9003, Tom Heints, sales, 2500
```

### EXERCISE #8: PERFORMING A ONE-TO-MANY JOIN

Modify the code shown in the previous section so that the query is a join of the emps table to the orders table. You may keep the condition that empno should be greater than 9001. Adjust the print() call to output the rows of the modified join.

## Using Database Analytics Tools

When persisting data in MySQL, you can take advantage of the database's built-in analytics tools, such as analytical SQL, to significantly reduce the volume of data sent between your application and the database. *Analytical SQL* is an extra set of SQL commands designed for actually analyzing data stored in a database rather than simply storing, retrieving, and updating data. As an example, say you only want to import stock market data related to those companies whose prices didn't drop more than 1 percent below the previous day's price over a certain period. You can perform this preliminary analysis with analytical SQL, saving you from having to load an entire dataset of stock prices from the database into your Python script.

To see how this works, you'll obtain stock data via the yfinance library introduced in Chapter 3 and store it to a database table. You'll then query the table from a Python script, loading only the portion of the stock data that satisfies the specified condition. To start, you need to create a table in your sampledb database to store the stock data. The table should have three columns: ticker, date, and price. Enter the following command at the mysql> prompt:

```
mysql> CREATE TABLE stocks(
       ticker VARCHAR(10),
       date VARCHAR(10),
       price DECIMAL(15,2)
       );
```

Now use this script to obtain some stock data with yfinance:

```
   import yfinance as yf
❶ data = []
❷ tickers = ['TSLA', 'FB', 'ORCL', 'AMZN']
   for ticker in tickers:
❸    tkr = yf.Ticker(ticker)
     hist = tkr.history(period='5d')
❹     .reset_index()
❺    records = hist[['Date','Close']].to_records(index=False)❻ records =
   list(records)
     records = [(ticker, ❼ str(elem[0])[:10], round(elem[1],2)) for elem in
   records]
❽    data = data + records
```

First, you define an empty list called data that will be populated with stock data ❶. As you saw earlier in the chapter, the cursor.execute() method expects data in the form of a list object when it executes an INSERT statement. Next, you define a list of tickers for which you want to obtain data ❷. Then, in a loop, you pass in each ticker from the tickers list to yfinance's Ticker() function ❸. The function returns a Ticker object, whose history() method provides you with data related to the corresponding ticker. In this example you obtain stock data for each ticker for the last five business days (period='5d').

The history() method returns stock data as a pandas DataFrame with the Date column as the index. Ultimately, you want to convert that DataFrame into a list of tuples for insertion into the database. Since you need to include the Date column in your dataset, you remove it from the index with the DataFrame's reset_index() method, thus turning Date into a regular column ❹. You then take only the Date and Close columns from the retrieved DataFrame, where Close contains stock prices at the end of the day, and convert them to a NumPy record array, an intermediate step in the process of converting the input data ❺. Next, you convert the data to a list of tuples ❻. After that, you still need to reformat each tuple so that it can be inserted into the stocks database table as a row. In particular, each Date field contains a lot of extraneous information (hours, minutes, seconds, and so on). By taking only the first 10 characters of field 0 in each tuple, you extract just the year, month, and day, which is all that you need for your analysis ❼. For example, 2022-01-06T00:00:00.000000000 would become simply 2022-01-06. Finally, still within the loop, you append the tuples related to the ticker to the data list ❽.

As a result, the content of the data list of tuples might look as follows:

```
[
('TSLA', '2022-01-06', 1064.7),
('TSLA', '2022-01-07', 1026.96),
('TSLA', '2022-01-10', 1058.12),
('TSLA', '2022-01-11', 1064.4),
('TSLA', '2022-01-12', 1106.22),
('FB', '2022-01-06', 332.46),
('FB', '2022-01-07', 331.79),
('FB', '2022-01-10', 328.07),
('FB', '2022-01-11', 334.37),
('FB', '2022-01-12', 333.26),
('ORCL', '2022-01-06', 86.34),
('ORCL', '2022-01-07', 87.51),
('ORCL', '2022-01-10', 89.28),
('ORCL', '2022-01-11', 88.48),
('ORCL', '2022-01-12', 88.31),
('AMZN', '2022-01-06', 3265.08),
('AMZN', '2022-01-07', 3251.08),
('AMZN', '2022-01-10', 3229.72),
('AMZN', '2022-01-11', 3307.24),
('AMZN', '2022-01-12', 3304.14)
]
```

To insert this dataset into the stocks table as a set of rows, append the following code to the previous script and re-execute it:

```
import mysql.connector
from mysql.connector import errorcode
try:
  cnx = mysql.connector.connect(user='root', password='your_pswd',
                                host='127.0.0.1',
                                database='sampledb')
  cursor = cnx.cursor()
  # defining the query
  query_add_stocks = ("""INSERT INTO stocks (ticker, date, price)
                         VALUES (%s, %s, %s)""")
  # adding the stock price rows
❶ cursor.executemany(query_add_stocks, data)
  cnx.commit()
except mysql.connector.Error as err:
  print("Error-Code:", err.errno)
  print("Error-Message: {}".format(err.msg))
finally:
  cursor.close()
  cnx.close()
```

The code follows the same model you used earlier to insert data into the database. This time, however, you use the cursor.executemany() method, which allows you to efficiently execute the INSERT statement multiple times, for each tuple in the data list of tuples ❶.

Now that you have the data in the database, you can play with queries against it using analytical SQL, trying to answer questions. For example, to filter out stocks that have dropped more than 1 percent below the previous day's price, as suggested at the beginning of this section, you'll need a query that can analyze prices for the same ticker across multiple days. As a first step, the following query generates a dataset that includes both the current stock price and its price for the previous day within the same row. Try it out at the mysql> prompt:

```
SELECT
  date,
  ticker,
  price,
  LAG(price) OVER(PARTITION BY ticker ORDER BY date) AS prev_price
FROM stocks;
```

The LAG() function in the SELECT list is an analytical SQL function. It lets you access a previous row's data from the current row. The PARTITION BY clause within the OVER clause divides the dataset into groups, one for each ticker. The LAG() function is applied separately within each group, ensuring data won't bleed over from one ticker to the next. The result generated by the query will look something like this:

```
+------------+--------+---------+------------+
| date       | ticker | price   | prev_price |
+------------+--------+---------+------------+

| 2022-01-06 | AMZN   | 3265.08 |       NULL |
| 2022-01-07 | AMZN   | 3251.08 |    3265.08 |
| 2022-01-10 | AMZN   | 3229.72 |    3251.08 |
| 2022-01-11 | AMZN   | 3307.24 |    3229.72 |
| 2022-01-12 | AMZN   | 3304.14 |    3307.24 |
| 2022-01-06 | FB     |  332.46 |       NULL |
| 2022-01-07 | FB     |  331.79 |     332.46 |
| 2022-01-10 | FB     |  328.07 |     331.79 |
| 2022-01-11 | FB     |  334.37 |     328.07 |
| 2022-01-12 | FB     |  333.26 |     334.37 |
| 2022-01-06 | ORCL   |   86.34 |       NULL |
| 2022-01-07 | ORCL   |   87.51 |      86.34 |
| 2022-01-10 | ORCL   |   89.28 |      87.51 |
| 2022-01-11 | ORCL   |   88.48 |      89.28 |
| 2022-01-12 | ORCL   |   88.31 |      88.48 |
| 2022-01-06 | TSLA   | 1064.70 |       NULL |
| 2022-01-07 | TSLA   | 1026.96 |    1064.70 |
| 2022-01-10 | TSLA   | 1058.12 |    1026.96 |
| 2022-01-11 | TSLA   | 1064.40 |    1058.12 |
| 2022-01-12 | TSLA   | 1106.22 |    1064.40 |
+------------+--------+---------+------------+
20 rows in set (0.00 sec)
```

The query generated a new column, prev_price, containing the previous day's stock prices. As you can see, LAG() essentially gives you access to two rows' worth of data in the same row, meaning you can manipulate data from both rows within the same math expression as part of a query.

For example, you can divide one price by the other to calculate the percent change from day to day. With this in mind, here's a query to address the original requirement, selecting the rows of only those tickers whose prices didn't drop more than 1 percent below the previous day's price over the specified period:

```
❶ SELECT s.* FROM stocks AS s
  LEFT JOIN
❷ (SELECT DISTINCT(ticker) FROM
    ❸ (SELECT
        ❹ price/LAG(price) OVER(PARTITION BY ticker ORDER BY date) AS dif,
          ticker
        FROM stocks) AS b
  ❺ WHERE dif <0.99) AS a
❻ ON a.ticker = s.ticker
❼ WHERE a.ticker IS NULL;
```

The SQL statement is a join between two different queries issued against the same table: stocks. The first query of the join retrieves all the rows from the stocks table ❶, while the second query retrieves only the names of those tickers whose prices dropped 1 percent or more below their previous day's price at least once over the period of analysis ❷. This second query of the join has a complex structure: it selects data from a subquery rather than from the stocks table directly. The subquery, which starts at ❸, retrieves those rows from the table whose values in the price field are at least 1 percent lower than in the previous row. You determine this by dividing price by LAG(price) ❹ and checking if the result is less than 0.99 ❺. Then, in the SELECT list of the main query, you apply the DISTINCT() function to the ticker field to eliminate duplicate ticker names from the result set ❷.

You join the queries on the ticker column ❻. In the WHERE clause, you instruct the join to retrieve only the rows where no correspondence is found between the a.ticker field (tickers whose price dropped more than 1 percent) and the s.ticker field (all the tickers) ❼. Since you have a left join, only the matching rows from the first query are retrieved. As a result, the join returns all the rows of the stocks table with a ticker not found among the tickers retrieved by the second query.

Given the stock data shown previously, the result set generated by the query is as follows:

```
+--------+------------+---------+
| ticker | date       | price   |
+--------+------------+---------+

| ORCL   | 2022-01-06 |   86.34 |
| ORCL   | 2022-01-07 |   87.51 |
| ORCL   | 2022-01-10 |   89.28 |
| ORCL   | 2022-01-11 |   88.48 |
| ORCL   | 2022-01-12 |   88.31 |
| AMZN   | 2022-01-06 | 3265.08 |
| AMZN   | 2022-01-07 | 3251.08 |
```

```
| AMZN   | 2022-01-10 | 3229.72 |
| AMZN   | 2022-01-11 | 3307.24 |
| AMZN   | 2022-01-12 | 3304.14 |
+--------+------------+--------+
10 rows in set (0.00 sec)
```

As you can see, not all the rows from the stocks table have been retrieved. In particular, you won't find the rows related to the FB and TSLA tickers. The latter, for example, was excluded due to the following row found in the output generated by the previous query:

```
+------------+--------+---------+------------+
| date       | ticker | price   | prev_price |
+------------+--------+---------+------------+
  ...
2022-01-07 | TSLA   | 1026.96 |    1064.70 |
  ...
```

This row shows a 3.54 percent drop, which exceeds the 1 percent threshold.

In the following script, you issue the same query from within Python code and fetch the results into a pandas DataFrame:

```
import pandas as pd
import mysql.connector
from mysql.connector import errorcode
try:
  cnx = mysql.connector.connect(user='root', password='your_pswd',
                                host='127.0.0.1',
                                database='sampledb')
  query = ("""
    SELECT s.* FROM stocks AS s
    LEFT JOIN
     (SELECT DISTINCT(ticker) FROM
       (SELECT
         price/LAG(price) OVER(PARTITION BY ticker ORDER BY date) AS dif,
         ticker
        FROM stocks) AS b
      WHERE dif <0.99) AS a
    ON a.ticker = s.ticker
    WHERE a.ticker IS NULL""")
❶ df_stocks = pd.read_sql(query, con=cnx)
❷ df_stocks = df_stocks.set_index(['ticker','date'])
except mysql.connector.Error as err:
  print("Error-Code:", err.errno)
  print("Error-Message: {}".format(err.msg))
finally:
  cnx.close()
```

The script looks mostly like the ones shown earlier in the chapter. The key difference is that you load the database data directly into a pandas DataFrame. For that, you use the pandas read_sql() method, which takes a SQL query as a string as the first parameter and a database connection object as the second ❶. Then, you set the ticker and date columns as the DataFrame index ❷.

Given the stock data shown previously, the resulting df_stocks DataFrame will look as follows:

```
                     price
ticker date
ORCL   2022-01-06    86.34
       2022-01-07    87.51
       2022-01-10    89.28
       2022-01-11    88.48
       2022-01-12    88.31
AMZN   2022-01-06  3265.08
       2022-01-07  3251.08
       2022-01-10  3229.72
       2022-01-11  3307.24
       2022-01-12  3304.14
```

Now that you have the data in a DataFrame, you can proceed with further analysis within Python. For example, you might want to calculate the average price of each ticker over a defined period. In the next chapter, you'll see how you can solve such problems, applying an appropriate aggregate function at a group level in a DataFrame.

## NoSQL Databases

*NoSQL databases*, or *nonrelational databases*, don't require a predetermined organizational schema for the data being stored, and they don't support standard relational database operations like joins. Instead, they provide ways to store data with more structural flexibility, making it easier to handle massive volumes of data. For example, key-value stores, one type of NoSQL database, let you store and retrieve data as key-value pairs, such as time-event pairs. Document-oriented databases, another type of NoSQL database, are designed to work with flexibly structured data containers such as JSON documents. This allows you to store all the information related to a given object as a single entry in the database rather than splitting information across multiple tables, as is common in relational databases.

Although NoSQL databases haven't been around as long as their relational counterparts, they've quickly become popular because they allow developers to store data in simple, straightforward formats and don't require advanced expertise to access and manipulate the data. Their flexibility makes them particularly well suited to real-time and big data applications such as Google Gmail or LinkedIn.

**NOTE**    *There's no consensus on the origin of the term* NoSQL. *Some say it stands for* non-SQL, *while others state it stands for* not only SQL. *Both are appropriate: NoSQL databases store data in a format other than relational (SQL) tables, and at the same time, many of these databases support SQL-type queries.*

## Key-Value Stores

A *key-value store* is a database that holds key-value pairs, similar to a Python dictionary. A good example of a key-value store is Redis, which stands for Remote Dictionary Service. Redis supports commands such as GET, SET, and DEL to access and manipulate key-value pairs, as illustrated in this simple example:

```
$ redis-cli
127.0.0.1:6379> SET emp1 "Maya Silver"
OK
127.0.0.1:6379> GET emp1
"Maya Silver"
```

Here, you use the SET command to create the key emp1 with the value Maya Silver, then you use GET to retrieve the value via its key.

### Setting Up Redis

To explore Redis yourself, you'll need to install it. You can find details on the Redis Quick Start page at *https://redis.io/topics/quickstart*. After installing the Redis server in your system, you'll also need to install redis-py, the Python library that lets you interact with Redis from your Python code. You can do this with the pip command:

```
$ pip install redis
```

You then import redis-py into your script with the command import redis.

### Accessing Redis with Python

The following is a simple example of accessing the Redis server from Python via the redis-py library:

```
> import redis
❶ > r = redis.Redis()
❷ > r.mset({"emp1": "Maya Silver", "emp2": "John Jamison"})
  True
❸ > r.get("emp1")
  b'Maya Silver'
```

You use the redis.Redis() method to set a connection to the Redis server ❶. Since the method's parameters are omitted, the default values will be taken, which assume the server is running on your local machine: host='localhost', port=6379, and db=0.

**NOTE** *Redis numbers databases using zero-based indexing. New connections use database 0 by default.*

After establishing a connection, you use the mset() method to set multiple key-value pairs ❷ (*m* is short for *multiple*). The server returns True when data has been stored successfully. You can then get the value of any of your stored keys with the get() method ❸.

Like any other database, Redis allows you to persist the data being inserted, so you'll be able to get a value by its key in another Python session or script. Redis also allows you to set an *expire flag* on a key when you set a key-value pair, specifying how long it should be retained. This can be especially useful in real-time applications where input data becomes irrelevant after a certain period of time. For example, if your application was for a taxi service, you might want to store data about the availability of each individual cab. Since this data would be subject to change often, you'd want it to expire after a short time. Here's how this might work:

```
--snip--
> from datetime import timedelta
> r.setex("cab26", timedelta(minutes=1), value="in the area now")
True
```

You use the setex() method to set a key-value pair that will be automatically removed from the database after a specified period of time. Here, you specify the expiration time as a timedelta object. Alternatively, you could specify it as a number in seconds.

So far we've only looked at simple key-value pairs, but you can also store multiple pieces of information about the same object using Redis, as illustrated here:

```
> cabDict = {"ID": "cab48", "Driver": "Dan Varsky", "Brand": "Volvo"}
> r.hmset("cab48", cabDict)
> r.hgetall("cab48")
{'Cab': 'cab48', 'Driver': 'Dan Varsky', 'Brand': 'Volvo'}
```

You start by defining a Python dictionary that can contain an arbitrary number of key-value pairs. Then, you send the entire dictionary to the database, storing it under the key cab48 using hmset() (*h* is short for *hash*). You then use the hgetall() function to retrieve all the key-value pairs stored under the cab48 key.

## Document-Oriented Databases

A *document-oriented database* stores each record as a separate document. Rather than having to conform to a predefined schema, like the fields of a relational database table, each document in a document-oriented database can have its own structure. This flexibility makes document-oriented databases the most popular category of NoSQL databases, and among document-oriented databases, MongoDB is arguably the leader. MongoDB is designed to manage collections of JSON-like documents. We'll explore how to work with MongoDB in this section.

### Setting Up MongoDB

There are several ways you can try out MongoDB. One is to install the MongoDB database on your system. For details, refer to the MongoDB documentation at *https://docs.mongodb.com/manual/installation*. Another option that requires no installation overhead is to create a free hosted MongoDB database using MongoDB Atlas. You'll need to register at *https://www.mongodb .com/cloud/atlas/register.*

Before you can start interacting with a MongoDB database from Python, you'll need to install PyMongo, the official Python driver for MongoDB. This can be done with the `pip` command:

```
$ pip install pymongo
```

### Accessing MongoDB with Python

The first step to working with MongoDB using Python is to establish a connection to the database server via a PyMongo `MongoClient` object, as shown here:

```
> from pymongo import MongoClient
> client = MongoClient('connection_string')
```

The connection string can be a MongoDB connection URI, such as *mongodb://localhost:27017.* This connection string assumes you have installed MongoDB on your local system. If you're using MongoDB Atlas instead, you'll need to use a connection string provided by Atlas. For further details, refer to the "Connect via Driver" page in the Atlas documentation at *https:// docs.atlas.mongodb.com/driver-connection.* You might also want to check out the "Connection String URI Format" page of the MongoDB documentation at *https://docs.mongodb.com/manual/reference/connection-string.*

Instead of using a connection string, you might specify the host and port as separate parameters of the `MongoClient()` constructor:

```
> client = MongoClient('localhost', 27017)
```

A single MongoDB instance can support multiple databases, so once a connection to the server is established, you need to specify the database you want to work with. MongoDB doesn't provide a separate command to create a database, so you use the same syntax for creating a new database and accessing an existing one. For example, to create a database named `sampledb` (or access it if it already exists), you can use the following dictionary-like syntax:

```
> db = client['sampledb']
```

or use the attribute-access syntax:

```
> db = client.sampledb
```

Unlike relational databases, MongoDB doesn't store data in tables. Instead, documents are grouped into *collections.* Creating or accessing a collection is similar to creating or accessing a database:

```
> emps_collection = db['emps']
```

This command will create the `emps` collection in the `sampledb` database, if it has not already been created. Then, you can use the `insert_one()` method to insert a document into the collection. In this example, you insert an `emp` document formatted as a dictionary:

```
> emp = {"empno": 9001,
...         "empname": "Jeff Russell",
...         "orders": [2608, 2617, 2620]}
> result = emps_collection.insert_one(emp)
```

Upon insertion of the document, an "`_id`" field is automatically added to it. The value of this field is generated to be unique across the collection. You can access the ID via the `inserted_id` field of the object returned by `insert_one()`:

```
> result.inserted_id
ObjectId('69y67385ei0b650d867ef236')
```

Now that you have some data in the database, how can you query it? The most common type of query can be performed with `find_one()`, which returns a single document that matches the search criteria:

```
> emp = emps_collection.find_one({"empno": 9001})
> print(emp)
```

As you can see, `find_one()` doesn't require you to use the document's ID, which was automatically added on insert. Instead, you can query on specific elements, assuming that the resulting document matches them.

The result will look similar to this:

```
{
 u'empno': 9001,
 u'_id': ObjectId('69y67385ei0b650d867ef236'),
 u'empname': u'Jeff Russell',
 u'orders': [2608, 2617, 2620]
}
```

---

**EXERCISE #9: INSERTING AND QUERYING MULTIPLE DOCUMENTS**

In the previous section, you learned to insert or retrieve a single document in a MongoDB database. Continuing with the emps collection created in the sampledb database, try to perform bulk inserts with the insert_many() method, and then query for more than one document using the find() method. For details on how to use these methods, refer to the PyMongo documentation at *https://pymongo.readthedocs.io/en/stable*.

# Summary

In this chapter, you saw examples of moving data to and from databases of different types, including relational and NoSQL databases. You worked with MySQL, one of the most popular relational databases. Then you looked at Redis, a NoSQL solution that allows you to efficiently store and retrieve key-value pairs. You also explored MongoDB, arguably the most popular NoSQL database today, which allows you to work with JSON-like documents in a Python-friendly manner.

# 6

## AGGREGATING DATA

To get the most decision-making value out of your data, you'll often need to generate aggregations of the data. *Aggregation* is a process of collecting data so that it can be presented in summary form, grouped by subtotals, totals, averages, or other statistics. This chapter explores aggregation techniques built into pandas and discusses how you can use them to analyze your data.

Aggregation is an efficient way to get a big-picture overview of a large dataset, allowing you to answer questions about the values in the data. For example, a large retail business might want to determine product performance based on brand or look at the sales totals for different regions. A website owner might want to identify the most attractive resources on the site based on the number of visitors. A climatologist might need to determine the sunniest places in a region based on the average number of sunny days per year.

An aggregation can answer questions like these by collecting specific data values together and presenting them in a summarized format. Since aggregation presents information based on related clusters of data, it implies first grouping the data by one or more attributes. In the case of the large retailer, this might mean grouping the data by brand, or perhaps by both region and date.

In the examples that follow, you'll see how grouping, along with *aggregate functions* applied to each group of rows, can be implemented when using pandas DataFrames. An aggregate function returns a single result row based on an entire group of rows, thus forming a single aggregated summary row for each group.

## Data to Aggregate

To see how aggregation works, we'll create a set of example DataFrames containing sales data for an online outdoor fashion retailer. The data will include values such as order numbers and dates; details about the items purchased in each order, such as price and quantity; the employees who fulfill each order; and the locations of the company's fulfillment warehouses. In a real application, this data would most likely be stored in a database that you could access from your Python code, as described in Chapter 5. For simplicity, we'll instead load the data into the DataFrames from lists of tuples. You can download the lists of tuples from this book's GitHub repository.

Let's start with some sample orders. The list named orders contains several tuples, each of which represents one order. Each tuple has three fields: the order number, the date, and the ID of the employee who fulfilled the order, respectively:

```
orders = [
 (9423517, '2022-02-04', 9001),
 (4626232, '2022-02-04', 9003),
 (9423534, '2022-02-04', 9001),
 (9423679, '2022-02-05', 9002),
 (4626377, '2022-02-05', 9003),
 (4626412, '2022-02-05', 9004),
 (9423783, '2022-02-06', 9002),
 (4626490, '2022-02-06', 9004)
]
```

Import pandas and load the list into a DataFrame like so:

```
import pandas as pd
df_orders = pd.DataFrame(orders, columns =['OrderNo', 'Date', 'Empno'])
```

Order details (also known as *order lines*) are usually stored in another data container. In this case, we have a list of tuples named details that you'll load into another DataFrame. Each tuple represents a line of an order, with fields corresponding to the order number, item name, brand, price, and quantity:

```
details = [
  (9423517, 'Jeans', 'Rip Curl', 87.0, 1),
  (9423517, 'Jacket', 'The North Face', 112.0, 1),
  (4626232, 'Socks', 'Vans', 15.0, 1),
  (4626232, 'Jeans', 'Quiksilver', 82.0, 1),
  (9423534, 'Socks', 'DC', 10.0, 2),
  (9423534, 'Socks', 'Quiksilver', 12.0, 2),
  (9423679, 'T-shirt', 'Patagonia', 35.0, 1),
  (4626377, 'Hoody', 'Animal', 44.0, 1),
  (4626377, 'Cargo Shorts', 'Animal', 38.0, 1),
  (4626412, 'Shirt', 'Volcom', 78.0, 1),
  (9423783, 'Boxer Shorts', 'Superdry', 30.0, 2),
  (9423783, 'Shorts', 'Globe', 26.0, 1),
  (4626490, 'Cargo Shorts', 'Billabong', 54.0, 1),
  (4626490, 'Sweater', 'Dickies', 56.0, 1)
]
# converting the list into a DataFrame
df_details = pd.DataFrame(details, columns =['OrderNo', 'Item', 'Brand', 'Price', 'Quantity'])
```

We'll store information about the company's employees in a third DataFrame. Create it from another list of tuples called emps with employee numbers, names, and locations:

```
emps = [
  (9001, 'Jeff Russell', 'LA'),
  (9002, 'Jane Boorman', 'San Francisco'),
  (9003, 'Tom Heints', 'NYC'),
  (9004, 'Maya Silver', 'Philadelphia')
]

df_emps = pd.DataFrame(emps, columns =['Empno', 'Empname', 'Location'])
```

Finally, we have the city and region of each warehouse in a list of tuples named locations, which you'll store in a fourth DataFrame:

```
locations = [
  ('LA', 'West'),
  ('San Francisco', 'West'),
  ('NYC', 'East'),
  ('Philadelphia', 'East')
]

df_locations = pd.DataFrame(locations, columns =['Location', 'Region'])
```

Now that you've loaded the data into DataFrames, you can aggregate it in many ways, allowing you to answer all sorts of questions about the state of the business. For example, you might want to look at the sales performance for different regions, generating subtotals by date. To do this, you'll first need to combine the relevant data into a single DataFrame. Then you can group the data and apply aggregate functions to the groups.

## Combining DataFrames

You'll often need to collect data from many different containers before you have everything you need to produce the desired aggregation. Our example is no exception. Even the data representing the orders is distributed between two different DataFrames: df_orders and df_details. Your goal is to generate the sums of sales by region and by date. What DataFrames do you need to combine, and what columns from each should you include?

Since you need to total up the sales numbers, you'll have to include the Price and Quantity columns from df_details. The Date column from df_orders and the Region column from df_locations have to be included as well. This means you'll have to join the following DataFrames: df_orders, df_details, and df_locations.

The df_orders and df_details DataFrames can be joined directly with a single call of the pandas merge() method, as follows:

```
df_sales = df_orders.merge(df_details)
```

**NOTE**  *To brush up on how merge() works, refer back to "One-to-Many Joins" in Chapter 3.*

You join the DataFrames based on the OrderNo column. You don't have to specify this explicitly, because OrderNo is present in both DataFrames and is therefore chosen by default. The newly merged DataFrame now contains one record for each order line, as in df_details, but with the information added from the corresponding records from df_orders. To see the records in the merged DataFrame, you can simply print the DataFrame:

```
print(df_sales)
```

The content of df_sales will look as follows:

|    | OrderNo | Date       | Empno | Item         | Brand          | Price | Quantity |
|----|---------|------------|-------|--------------|----------------|-------|----------|
| 0  | 9423517 | 2022-02-04 | 9001  | Jeans        | Rip Curl       | 87.0  | 1        |
| 1  | 9423517 | 2022-02-04 | 9001  | Jacket       | The North Face | 112.0 | 1        |
| 2  | 4626232 | 2022-02-04 | 9003  | Socks        | Vans           | 15.0  | 1        |
| 3  | 4626232 | 2022-02-04 | 9003  | Jeans        | Quiksilver     | 82.0  | 1        |
| 4  | 9423534 | 2022-02-04 | 9001  | Socks        | DC             | 10.0  | 2        |
| 5  | 9423534 | 2022-02-04 | 9001  | Socks        | Quiksilver     | 12.0  | 2        |
| 6  | 9423679 | 2022-02-05 | 9002  | T-shirt      | Patagonia      | 35.0  | 1        |
| 7  | 4626377 | 2022-02-05 | 9003  | Hoody        | Animal         | 44.0  | 1        |
| 8  | 4626377 | 2022-02-05 | 9003  | Cargo Shorts | Animal         | 38.0  | 1        |
| 9  | 4626412 | 2022-02-05 | 9004  | Shirt        | Volcom         | 78.0  | 1        |
| 10 | 9423783 | 2022-02-06 | 9002  | Boxer Shorts | Superdry       | 30.0  | 2        |
| 11 | 9423783 | 2022-02-06 | 9002  | Shorts       | Globe          | 26.0  | 1        |
| 12 | 4626490 | 2022-02-06 | 9004  | Cargo Shorts | Billabong      | 54.0  | 1        |
| 13 | 4626490 | 2022-02-06 | 9004  | Sweater      | Dickies        | 56.0  | 1        |

As you can see in the Quantity column, there may be more than one of an item in a single order line. You therefore need to multiply the values of the Price and Quantity fields to calculate the total of an order line. You can store the result of this multiplication in a new field of the DataFrame, as follows:

```
df_sales['Total'] = df_sales['Price'] * df_sales['Quantity']
```

This adds a Total column to the DataFrame, in addition to the existing seven columns. You now have the option to remove the columns that you don't need for generating the sums of sales by region and date. At this stage, you only need to retain the Date, Total, and Empno columns. The first two will obviously be essential to your calculations. We'll discuss the need for Empno momentarily.

To filter the DataFrame down to the necessary columns, pass a list of the column names in to the [] operator of the DataFrame, as shown here:

```
df_sales = df_sales[['Date','Empno','Total']]
```

You now need to join the df_sales DataFrame that you just created with the df_regions DataFrame. However, you can't join them directly, because they don't have any columns in common. Instead, you'll have to join them via the df_emps DataFrame, which shares one column with df_sales and one with df_regions. Specifically, df_sales and df_emps can be joined on the Empno column, which is why we kept the column in df_sales, while df_emps and df_locations can be joined on the Location column. Implement these joins with the merge() method:

```
df_sales_emps = df_sales.merge(df_emps)
df_result = df_sales_emps.merge(df_locations)
```

A printout of this df_result DataFrame will look like this:

|    | Date       | Empno | Total | Empname      | Location      | Region |
|----|------------|-------|-------|--------------|---------------|--------|
| 0  | 2022-02-04 | 9001  | 87.0  | Jeff Russell | LA            | West   |
| 1  | 2022-02-04 | 9001  | 112.0 | Jeff Russell | LA            | West   |
| 2  | 2022-02-04 | 9001  | 20.0  | Jeff Russell | LA            | West   |
| 3  | 2022-02-04 | 9001  | 24.0  | Jeff Russell | LA            | West   |
| 4  | 2022-02-04 | 9003  | 15.0  | Tom Heints   | NYC           | East   |
| 5  | 2022-02-04 | 9003  | 82.0  | Tom Heints   | NYC           | East   |
| 6  | 2022-02-05 | 9003  | 44.0  | Tom Heints   | NYC           | East   |
| 7  | 2022-02-05 | 9003  | 38.0  | Tom Heints   | NYC           | East   |
| 8  | 2022-02-05 | 9002  | 35.0  | Jane Boorman | San Francisco | West   |
| 9  | 2022-02-06 | 9002  | 60.0  | Jane Boorman | San Francisco | West   |
| 10 | 2022-02-06 | 9002  | 26.0  | Jane Boorman | San Francisco | West   |
| 11 | 2022-02-05 | 9004  | 78.0  | Maya Silver  | Philadelphia  | East   |
| 12 | 2022-02-06 | 9004  | 54.0  | Maya Silver  | Philadelphia  | East   |
| 13 | 2022-02-06 | 9004  | 56.0  | Maya Silver  | Philadelphia  | East   |

Once again, you might want to remove unnecessary columns and keep only those that you actually need. This time you can get rid of the Empno, Empname, and Location columns, leaving only Date, Region, and Total:

```
df_result = df_result[['Date','Region','Total']]
```

Now the content of `df_result` appears as follows:

```
     Date        Region   Total
0    2022-02-04  West     87.0
1    2022-02-04  West     112.0
2    2022-02-04  West     20.0
3    2022-02-04  West     24.0
4    2022-02-04  East     15.0
5    2022-02-04  East     82.0
6    2022-02-05  East     44.0
7    2022-02-05  East     38.0
8    2022-02-05  West     35.0
9    2022-02-06  West     60.0
10   2022-02-06  West     26.0
11   2022-02-05  East     78.0
12   2022-02-06  East     54.0
13   2022-02-06  East     56.0
```

Without including unnecessary columns, the `df_result` DataFrame is now ideally formatted for aggregating the sales data by region and by date.

## Grouping and Aggregating the Data

To perform aggregate calculations on your data, you must first sort it into relevant groups. The pandas `groupby()` function splits a DataFrame's data into subsets that have matching values for one or more columns. For our example, you can use `groupby()` to group the df_result DataFrame by date and region. Then you can apply the pandas `sum()` aggregation function to each group. You can perform both operations in a single line of code:

```
df_date_region = df_result.groupby(['Date','Region']).sum()
```

The first grouping is based on the `Date` column. Then, within each date, you group based on `Region`. The `groupby()` function returns an object to which you then apply the `sum()` aggregation function. This function sums up the values of numeric columns. In this particular example, `sum()` is applied only to the `Total` column because this is the only numeric column in the DataFrame. (If the DataFrame had other numeric columns, the aggregation function would be applied to those too.) You end up with the following DataFrame:

```
                         Total
Date        Region
2022-02-04  East         97.0
            West         243.0
2022-02-05  East         160.0
            West         35.0
2022-02-06  East         110.0
            West         86.0
```

Both `Date` and `Region` are index columns of the new DataFrame. Together they form a *hierarchical index*, also known as a *multilevel index*, or just a *MultiIndex*.

A MultiIndex makes it possible to work with data that has an arbitrary number of dimensions within the 2D structure of a DataFrame by using multiple columns to uniquely identify each row. In our case, the df_date_region DataFrame can be viewed as a 3D dataset, with three axes corresponding to dates, regions, and aggregate values (each axis represents the corresponding dimension), as described in Table 6-1.

**Table 6-1:** The Three Dimensions of the df_date_region DataFrame

| Axis | Coordinates |
| --- | --- |
| Date | 2022-02-04, 2022-02-05, 2022-02-06 |
| Region | West, East |
| Aggregation | Total |

**NOTE** *In this context,* coordinates *are possible values for a given axis.*

Our DataFrame's MultiIndex enables us to write queries that navigate the DataFrame's dimensions, accessing totals by date, region, or both. We'll be able to uniquely identify each row of the DataFrame and access selected aggregated values within different groups of data.

### Viewing Specific Aggregations by MultiIndex

Viewing specific categories of information in a DataFrame is a common requirement. For example, in the case of the df_date_region DataFrame you've just created, you might need to obtain the aggregated sales figures only for a certain date, or for a particular region and a certain date at the same time. You can use the DataFrame's index (or MultiIndex) to find the required aggregation.

To get a feel for working with a MultiIndex, it will help to see how each MultiIndex value is represented in Python. You can use the df_date_region DataFrame's index property for this:

```
print(df_date_region.index)
```

The index property returns all the index values, or row labels, of a DataFrame, whether that DataFrame has a simple index or a MultiIndex. Here are the MultiIndex values for df_date_region:

```
MultiIndex([('2022-02-04', 'East'),
            ('2022-02-04', 'West'),
            ('2022-02-05', 'East'),
            ('2022-02-05', 'West'),
            ('2022-02-06', 'East'),
            ('2022-02-06', 'West')],
           names=['Date', 'Region'])
```

As you can see, each MultiIndex value is a tuple that you can use to access a corresponding sales figure in the Total field. With this in mind, here's how to access the total figures for a certain date and region:

```
df_date_region❶ [df_date_region.index.isin(❷ [('2022-02-05', 'West')])]
```

You place the tuple representing the desired MultiIndex in the [] operator ❷ and pass it to the pandas index.isin() method. The method requires the passed parameter to be an iterable (list or tuple), Series, DataFrame, or dictionary, which is why you place the desired MultiIndex in square brackets. The method returns a Boolean array indicating whether the data at each of the DataFrame's index values corresponds to the index value(s) you specify: True for matches or False otherwise. In this particular example, the isin() method generates the array [False, False, False, True, False, False], meaning that the fourth index value is a match.

You then pass the Boolean array to the df_date_region DataFrame in the [] operator ❶, resulting in the corresponding sales figure being selected, as shown here:

```
                 Total
Date        Region
2022-02-05 West     35.0
```

You aren't limited to retrieving only a single row from the DataFrame. You can pass more than one index value to index.isin() to get a set of corresponding sales figures, as shown here:

```
df_date_region[df_date_region.index.isin([('2022-02-05', 'East'), ('2022-02-05', 'West')])]
```

This will retrieve the following two rows from df_date_region:

```
                 Total
Date        Region
2022-02-05 East     160.0
           West      35.0
```

Although this particular example uses two neighboring indices, you can in fact pass any indices into index.isin() in any order, like so:

```
df_date_region[df_date_region.index.isin([('2022-02-06', 'East'),
              ('2022-02-04', 'East'), ('2022-02-05', 'West')])]
```

The set of retrieved rows will appear as follows:

```
                 Total
Date        Region
2022-02-04 East      97.0
2022-02-05 West      35.0
2022-02-06 East     110.0
```

Notice that the order of the retrieved records matches the order of the records in the DataFrame rather than the order in which you specified the indices.

## Slicing a Range of Aggregated Values

Just as you can use slicing to obtain a range of values from a list, you can use it to extract a range of aggregated values from a DataFrame. You would do this in the df_date_region DataFrame by providing two tuples specifying the MultiIndex keys of the start and end positions of the slice range. The following example obtains the range of aggregated values for dates from 2022-02-04 through 2022-02-05 for all regions. You simply place the start and end MultiIndex keys in square brackets, separated by a colon:

```
df_date_region[('2022-02-04', 'East'):('2022-02-05', 'West')]
```

As a result, you get the following rows of the DataFrame:

```
                   Total
Date       Region
2022-02-04 East     97.0
           West    243.0
2022-02-05 East    160.0
           West     35.0
```

Since in this particular example you're obtaining the sales figures for all regions within a specified date range, you can leave off the region names and pass only the dates:

```
df_date_region['2022-02-04':'2022-02-05']
```

This should give you exactly the same result as the preceding example.

## Slicing Within Aggregation Levels

You might want to slice your aggregations within the different levels of a hierarchical index. In our example, the highest aggregation level is the Date level, within which we have the Region level. Say you need to obtain the sales figures for a specific slice of dates, selecting all the contents of the Region level. You can do this with Python's slice() function in conjunction with the DataFrame's loc property, as illustrated here:

```
df_date_region.loc[(slice('2022-02-05', '2022-02-06'), slice(None)), :]
```

You use slice() twice here. In the first instance, slice() defines the slicing range for Date, the highest aggregation level, generating the slice object that specifies the start and end dates. The second time you invoke slice(), you do so for the Region level (the next lowest level). By specifying None, you select all the contents of the Region level. In the [] operator of the loc property, you also include a comma followed by a colon (:). This syntax specifies that you're using row labels rather than column labels.

The result set is as follows:

```
                   Total
Date       Region
2022-02-05 East    160.0
```

```
         West     35.0
2022-02-06 East   110.0
         West     86.0
```

In the next example, you replace slice(None) with slice('East'), thus reducing the sales figures being retrieved to only rows containing East, taken from within the specified date range:

```
df_date_region.loc[(slice('2022-02-05', '2022-02-06'), slice('East')), :]
```

This will retrieve the following rows:

```
                  Total
Date       Region
2022-02-05 East   160.0
2022-02-06 East   110.0
```

You could specify a range for the Region level rather than a single value, just as you specify a range for the Date level. In this particular example, however, that range could only start with 'East' and end with 'West', implemented as slice('East','West'). Since this is the maximum possible range, a call of slice('East','West') will be equal to a call of slice(None).

### Adding a Grand Total

When it comes to aggregating sales data, you might ultimately want to calculate the grand total, or the sum of all the other sales value totals, and add it to the DataFrame. In our example, since all the totals are in a single DataFrame, df_date_region, you can use the pandas sum() method to find the total sales across all regions and all dates. The method calculates the sum of the values for a specified axis, as shown here:

```
ps = df_date_region.sum(axis = 0)
print(ps)
```

Here, sum() returns a pandas Series with the sum over the Total column in the df_date_region DataFrame. Remember that it isn't necessary to specify the Total column in your call to sum(), since it automatically applies to any numeric data. The content of the ps Series will be as follows:

```
Total    731.0
dtype: float64
```

To append the newly created Series to the df_date_region DataFrame, you have to first give it a name. This name will be used as the index for the grand total row in the DataFrame. Because index keys are tuples in the df_date_region DataFrame, you use a tuple for the Series name as well:

```
ps.name=('All','All')
```

The first 'All' in the tuple relates to the Date component of the index key, while the second relates to the Region index key component. Now you can append the Series to the DataFrame:

```
df_date_region_total = df_date_region.append(ps)
```

If you print out the newly created DataFrame, its content will look like this:

```
                   Total
Date       Region
2022-02-04 East     97.0
           West    243.0
2022-02-05 East    160.0
           West     35.0
2022-02-06 East    110.0
           West     86.0
All        All     731.0
```

You can access the grand total row by its index, as you would any other row in a DataFrame. Here, you pass the tuple representing the index of the row to the index.isin() method, as discussed earlier:

```
df_date_region_total[df_date_region_total.index.isin([('All', 'All')])]
```

This will give you the grand total row:

```
            Total
Date Region
All  All    731.0
```

## Adding Subtotals

Apart from adding up the grand total, you might also want to add subtotals for each date to the DataFrame so that the resulting DataFrame appears as follows:

```
                   Total
Date       Region
2022-02-04 East     97.0
           West    243.0
           All     340.0
2022-02-05 East    160.0
           West     35.0
           All     195.0
2022-02-06 East    110.0
           West     86.0
           All     196.0
All        All     731.0
```

Generating this DataFrame requires a few steps. First you group the DataFrame by the Date level of the index. Then you iterate over the resulting GroupBy object, accessing each date along with a set of rows (known as a *subframe*) containing the region and total information for that date. You then select and append each subframe to an empty DataFrame, along with a corresponding subtotal row. Here's how:

```
❶ df_totals = pd.DataFrame()
  for date, date_df in ❷ df_date_region.groupby(level=0):
❸ df_totals = df_totals.append(date_df)
❹ ps = date_df.sum(axis = 0)
❺ ps.name=(date,'All')
❻ df_totals = df_totals.append(ps)
```

You begin by creating an empty DataFrame, df_totals, to receive the final data ❶. You then create a GroupBy object ❷, grouping the df_date_region DataFrame by the top hierarchical level (level=0) of its index (that is, the Date column) and enter a for loop iterating over the GroupBy object. With each iteration, you get a date and its corresponding subframe. You append the subframe to the df_totals DataFrame ❸, then create the subtotal row in the form of a Series containing the sum of the subframe's rows ❹. Next, you name that Series with its associated date and 'All' to denote all regions ❺, then append the Series to the df_totals DataFrame ❻.

Finally, you append the grand total row to the DataFrame, as shown here:

```
df_totals = df_totals.append(df_date_region_total.loc[('All','All')])
```

As a result, you get a DataFrame that has both the sales sum for each date and the overall total for all the dates.

---

**EXERCISE #10: EXCLUDING TOTAL ROWS FROM THE DATAFRAME**

Having rows for totals in a DataFrame allows you to use it as a report without having to add further steps. However, if you're going to use the DataFrame in further aggregation operations, you may need to exclude rows for totals.

Try filtering the df_totals DataFrame created in the previous section, excluding the grand total and subtotal rows. Use the slicing techniques discussed in this chapter.

---

## Selecting All Rows in a Group

In addition to aiding with aggregation, the groupby() function also helps you to select all the rows belonging to a certain group. To accomplish this, objects returned by groupby() provide the get_group() method. Here's how it works:

```
group = df_result.groupby(['Date','Region'])
group.get_group(('2022-02-04','West'))
```

You group the df_result DataFrame by Date and Region, passing the column names in as a list to groupby(), just like you did previously. Then you invoke the get_group() method on the resulting GroupBy object, passing a tuple with the desired index. This returns the following DataFrame:

```
     Date Region  Total
0  2022-02-04   West   87.0
1  2022-02-04   West  112.0
2  2022-02-04   West   20.0
3  2022-02-04   West   24.0
```

As you can see, the result set isn't an aggregation. Rather, it includes all the order rows related to the specified date and region.

## Summary

You learned in this chapter that aggregation is the process of gathering data and expressing it in a summarized format. Typically, this process involves splitting data into groups and then computing summaries for each group. The examples in this chapter showed how to aggregate data contained in pandas DataFrames, employing DataFrame methods and properties such as merge(), groupby(), sum(), index, and loc. You learned to take advantage of a DataFrame's hierarchical index, or MultiIndex, to model multilevel relationships in the data being aggregated. You also learned to view and slice aggregated data selectively using a MultiIndex.

# 7

## COMBINING DATASETS

It's common for data to be split across multiple containers. Therefore, you'll often need to combine different datasets into one. You've done some combining in previous chapters, but in this chapter we'll look at techniques for combining datasets in more depth.

In some cases, combining datasets may simply be a matter of adding one dataset to the end of another. For example, a financial analyst may receive a new batch of stock data each week that needs to be added to an existing collection of stock data. Other times, you may need to more selectively combine datasets that share a common column, joining them into a summary dataset. For instance, a retailer may want to merge general data about online orders with specific details about the items ordered, as you saw in Chapter 6. In either case, once you've combined the data, you can use it for further analysis. For example, you can run a range of filtering, grouping, or aggregation operations on the combined dataset.

As you've learned in previous chapters, datasets in Python can take the form of built-in data structures such as lists, tuples, and dictionaries, or they can be organized using third-party data structures such as NumPy arrays or pandas DataFrames. In the latter case, you have a richer set of tools for combining data, and therefore you have more options when you need to satisfy certain join conditions. This doesn't mean, however, that you won't be able to effectively combine built-in Python data structures. This chapter will show you how to do so, as well as how to combine third-party data structures.

## Combining Built-in Data Structures

The syntax for combining Python's built-in data structures is quite straightforward. In this section, you'll see how to combine lists or tuples using the + operator. Then, you'll learn to combine dictionaries with the ** operator. You'll also explore how to perform joins, aggregations, and other operations on lists of tuples, essentially treating them as if they were database tables, with each tuple representing a row.

### Combining Lists and Tuples with +

The easiest way to combine two or more lists or two or more tuples is with the + operator. You simply write a statement adding the lists or tuples together, just as you would add multiple numbers. This method works well when you need to put the elements from the structures being combined into a single new structure without changing the elements themselves. This process is often referred to as *concatenation*.

To demonstrate, we'll return to the example of the online fashion retailer introduced in the previous chapter. Suppose the information about orders placed throughout a day is collected in a list, so you have one list for each day. You might have the following three lists:

```
orders_2022_02_04 = [
  (9423517, '2022-02-04', 9001),
  (4626232, '2022-02-04', 9003),
  (9423534, '2022-02-04', 9001)
]
orders_2022_02_05 = [
  (9423679, '2022-02-05', 9002),
  (4626377, '2022-02-05', 9003),
  (4626412, '2022-02-05', 9004)
]
orders_2022_02_06 = [
  (9423783, '2022-02-06', 9002),
  (4626490, '2022-02-06', 9004)
]
```

For the purpose of further analysis, you may need to combine these lists into a single one. The + operator makes this easy; you simply add the three lists together:

```
orders = orders_2022_02_04 + orders_2022_02_05 + orders_2022_02_06
```

The resulting orders list looks as follows:

```
[
    (9423517, '2022-02-04', 9001),
    (4626232, '2022-02-04', 9003),
    (9423534, '2022-02-04', 9001),
    (9423679, '2022-02-05', 9002),
    (4626377, '2022-02-05', 9003),
    (4626412, '2022-02-05', 9004),
    (9423783, '2022-02-06', 9002),
    (4626490, '2022-02-06', 9004)
]
```

As you can see, the elements from the three original lists now all appear in a single list, with their order determined by the order in which you wrote the concatenation statement. In this particular example, the elements of the lists that were combined were all tuples. However, the + operator works for concatenating lists whose elements are of any type. Thus, you could just as easily combine lists of integers, strings, dictionaries, or anything else.

You can use the same + syntax to combine multiple tuples. However, if you try to use + to combine dictionaries, you'll end up with an unsupported operand type(s) error. The following section explains the proper syntax for combining dictionaries.

## Combining Dictionaries with **

The ** operator breaks up, or unpacks, a dictionary into its individual key-value pairs. To combine two dictionaries into one, you unpack both dictionaries with ** and store the results in a new dictionary. This works even if one or both of the dictionaries has a hierarchical structure. In the context of our retailer example, consider the following dictionary that contains some additional fields pertaining to an order:

```
extra_fields_9423517 = {
    'ShippingInstructions' : { 'name'    : 'John Silver',
                               'Phone' : [{ 'type' : 'Office', 'number' : '809-123-9309' },
                                          { 'type' : 'Mobile', 'number' : '417-123-4567' }
                                         ]}
}
```

Thanks to the use of meaningful key names, the dictionary's nested structure is clear. Indeed, the ability to access data by keys rather than by positions makes dictionaries preferable to lists when you're working with hierarchical data structures.

Now suppose you have the other fields for this same order in another dictionary:

```
order_9423517 = {'OrderNo':9423517, 'Date':'2022-02-04', 'Empno':9001}
```

Your task is to concatenate these dictionaries into a single dictionary that includes all the key-value pairs from both the original ones. You use the ** operator as follows:

```
order_9423517 = {**order_9423517, **extra_fields_9423517}
```

You place the dictionaries you want to concatenate inside curly brackets, preceding each dictionary name with **. The ** operator unpacks the two dictionaries into their key-value pairs, and then the curly brackets package them back up into a single dictionary. Now order_9423517 looks like this:

```
{
 'OrderNo': 9423517,
 'Date': '2022-02-04',
 'Empno': 9001,
 'ShippingInstructions': {'name': 'John Silver',
                 'Phone': [{'type': 'Office', 'number': '809-123-9309'},
                          {'type': 'Mobile', 'number': '417-123-4567'}
                          ]}
}
```

As you can see, all the elements from the original dictionaries are present, and their hierarchical structure has been preserved.

### Combining Corresponding Rows from Two Structures

You already know how to combine several lists into a single list without changing the elements of those lists. In practice, you'll also often have to join two or more data structures that share a common column into a single structure, combining corresponding rows from these data structures into a single row. If your data structures are pandas DataFrames, you can use methods like join() and merge(), as you've seen in previous chapters. However, if your data structures are lists containing "rows" of tuples, these methods aren't available. Instead, you need to iterate over the lists and join each row individually.

To illustrate, we'll join the orders list you created in "Combining Lists and Tuples with +" earlier in this chapter with the details list introduced in "Data to Aggregate" in Chapter 6. As a reminder, here's what that list looks like:

```
details = [
 (9423517, 'Jeans', 'Rip Curl', 87.0, 1),
 (9423517, 'Jacket', 'The North Face', 112.0, 1),
 (4626232, 'Socks', 'Vans', 15.0, 1),
 (4626232, 'Jeans', 'Quiksilver', 82.0, 1),
 (9423534, 'Socks', 'DC', 10.0, 2),
 (9423534, 'Socks', 'Quiksilver', 12.0, 2),
 (9423679, 'T-shirt', 'Patagonia', 35.0, 1),
 (4626377, 'Hoody', 'Animal', 44.0, 1),
 (4626377, 'Cargo Shorts', 'Animal', 38.0, 1),
 (4626412, 'Shirt', 'Volcom', 78.0, 1),
 (9423783, 'Boxer Shorts', 'Superdry', 30.0, 2),
 (9423783, 'Shorts', 'Globe', 26.0, 1),
```

```
    (4626490, 'Cargo Shorts', 'Billabong', 54.0, 1),
    (4626490, 'Sweater', 'Dickies', 56.0, 1)
]
```

Both lists contain tuples whose first element is an order number. The goal is to find the tuples with matching order numbers, merge them into a single tuple, and store all the tuples in a list. Here's how this is done:

```
❶ orders_details = []
❷ for o in orders:
      for d in details:
❸       if d[0] == o[0]:
            orders_details.append(o + ❹ d[1:])
```

First you create an empty list to receive the merged tuples ❶. Then you use a nested pair of loops to iterate over the lists ❷ and an if statement ❸ to merge only tuples with matching order numbers. To avoid repeating the order number twice in the tuple being combined and appended to the orders_details list, you use slicing for each details tuple ❹, picking up all its fields except for the first one, which contains the redundant order number.

Looking at this code, you might wonder if it could be implemented more elegantly as a one-liner. Indeed, with the help of list comprehensions, you can achieve the same result as follows:

```
orders_details = [[o for o in orders if d[0] == o[0]][0] + d[1:] for d in details]
```

In the outer list comprehension, you iterate over the tuples in the details list. In the inner list comprehension, you find a tuple in the orders list whose order number matches the current tuple from details. Since an order line in details is supposed to have only one matching tuple in orders, the inner list comprehension should generate a list with a single element (a tuple representing an order). So, you take the first element of the inner list comprehension with the [0] operator, then you concatenate this order's tuple with the corresponding tuple from details using the + operator, excluding the redundant order number with [1:].

Whether you've created orders_details through list comprehensions or with the help of two for loops, as shown previously, the resulting list will look as follows:

```
[
    (9423517, '2022-02-04', 9001, 'Jeans', 'Rip Curl', 87.0, 1),
    (9423517, '2022-02-04', 9001, 'Jacket', 'The North Face', 112.0, 1),
    (4626232, '2022-02-04', 9003, 'Socks', 'Vans', 15.0, 1),
    (4626232, '2022-02-04', 9003, 'Jeans', 'Quiksilver', 82.0, 1),
    (9423534, '2022-02-04', 9001, 'Socks', 'DC', 10.0, 2),
    (9423534, '2022-02-04', 9001, 'Socks', 'Quiksilver', 12.0, 2),
    (9423679, '2022-02-05', 9002, 'T-shirt', 'Patagonia', 35.0, 1),
    (4626377, '2022-02-05', 9003, 'Hoody', 'Animal', 44.0, 1),
    (4626377, '2022-02-05', 9003, 'Cargo Shorts', 'Animal', 38.0, 1),
    (4626412, '2022-02-05', 9004, 'Shirt', 'Volcom', 78.0, 1),
    (9423783, '2022-02-06', 9002, 'Boxer Shorts', 'Superdry', 30.0, 2),
```

```
(9423783, '2022-02-06', 9002, 'Shorts', 'Globe', 26.0, 1),
(4626490, '2022-02-06', 9004, 'Cargo Shorts', 'Billabong', 54.0, 1),
(4626490, '2022-02-06', 9004, 'Sweater', 'Dickies', 56.0, 1)
]
```

The list contains all the tuples from the details list, and each tuple also contains additional information from the corresponding tuple of the orders list.

### Implementing Different Types of Joins for Lists

The operation you performed in the previous section is a standard one-to-many join: each order line in details has a matching order in orders, and each order in orders has one or more order lines in details. In practice, however, either or both of the datasets being joined might have rows with no matches in the other dataset. To account for these situations, you must be able to perform operations equivalent to the various database-style joins we discussed in Chapter 3: left joins, right joins, inner joins, and outer joins.

As an example, the details list might have order lines for orders not found in the orders list. One way this could happen is if you filter orders for a certain date range; since details doesn't include a date field, you can't filter the details list accordingly. To simulate this situation, add a new row to the details list that refers to an order that isn't in orders:

```
details.append((4626592, 'Shorts', 'Protest', 48.0, 1))
```

If you now try to generate the orders_details list as you did before:

```
orders_details = [[o for o in orders if d[0] == o][0] + d[1:] for d in details]
```

you'll get the following error:

```
IndexError: list index out of range
```

The problem occurs when you get to the unmatched order number in the details list and you try to retrieve the first element of the corresponding inner list comprehension. No such element exists, since the order number isn't in the orders list. One way to solve this is to add an if clause to the for d in details loop within the outer list comprehension, checking whether the order number in a details row can be found in any row of orders, as shown here:

```
orders_details = [[o for o in orders if d[0] in o][0] + d[1:] for d in details
❶ if d[0] in [o[0] for o in orders]]
```

You eliminate the problem by excluding any details rows that don't have a matching row in the orders list, implementing the check in the if clause that follows the for d in details loop ❶. Thus, the list comprehension shown here results in an inner join.

But what if you want to include all the details rows in the resulting orders_details list? You may want to do this, for example, so you can summarize the totals for all the orders, not only for those orders in the current orders list (which has hypothetically been filtered by date). You might then summarize totals for the orders that *are* in the current orders list and compare these sums.

What you want to implement in this case is a right join, assuming the orders list is on the left side of the relationship and the details list is on the right. Recall that a right join returns all rows from the right dataset and only the matched rows from the left dataset. Update the previous list comprehension as follows:

```
orders_details_right = [[o for o in orders if d[0] in o][0] + d[1:] if d[0] in [o[0] for o
                        in orders] ❶ else (d[0], None, None) + d[1:] for d in details]
```

Here, you add an else clause ❶ to the if clause assigned to the for d in details loop. This else clause works for any details row that doesn't have a matching row in orders. It creates a new tuple containing the order number plus two None entries to take the place of the missing orders fields, and it concatenates that tuple with the row from details, yielding a row with the same structure as all the others. So, the generated dataset will include the details row that doesn't have a matched row in orders in addition to all the matching rows:

```
[
--snip--
(4626490, '2022-02-06', 9004, 'Sweater', 'Dickies', 56.0, 1),
(4626592, None, None, 'Shorts', 'Protest', 48.0, 1)
]
```

Now that you have the orders_details_right list (the right join of the orders and details lists), you can total up all the orders and compare the result with the total of just those orders included in the orders list. You add up the total of all the orders with Python's built-in sum() function:

```
sum(pr*qt for _, _, _, _, _, pr, qt in orders_details_right)
```

The for loop passed as a parameter to sum() is somewhat similar to the loop used in a list comprehension in that it allows you to take only the necessary elements with each iteration of the loop. In this particular example, all you need to find with each iteration is pr*qt, the multiplication of the Price and Quantity values from the tuple at hand. Since you're not actually interested in the other values of each tuple, you use _ placeholders for them in the clause after the for keyword.

If you've followed the steps presented in this chapter so far, the preceding call will return:

```
779.0
```

You can calculate the totals of only those orders that are in the orders list with a modified version of the sum() call:

```
sum(pr*qt for _, dt, _, _, _, pr, qt in orders_details_right ❶ if dt != None)
```

Here you add an `if` clause to the loop to filter out orders that weren't in the orders list ❶. You ignore rows where the Date (`dt`) field contains `None`, indicating that the row's order information wasn't retrieved from `orders`. The generated sum will be:

```
731.0
```

## Concatenating NumPy Arrays

Unlike with lists, you can't use the + operator to concatenate NumPy arrays. This is because, as discussed in Chapter 3, NumPy reserves the + operator for performing element-wise addition operations on multiple arrays. To concatenate two NumPy arrays, you instead use the `numpy.concatenate()` function.

To demonstrate, we'll use the `base_salary` array from "Creating a NumPy Array" in Chapter 3, which was created as follows (here, we'll call it base_salary1):

```
import numpy as np
jeff_salary = [2700,3000,3000]
nick_salary = [2600,2800,2800]
tom_salary = [2300,2500,2500]
base_salary1 = np.array([jeff_salary, nick_salary, tom_salary])
```

Recall that each row in the array contains three months' worth of base salary data for a particular employee. Now suppose you have salary information for two more employees in another array, base_salary2:

```
maya_salary = [2200,2400,2400]
john_salary = [2500,2700,2700]
base_salary2 = np.array([maya_salary, john_salary])
```

You want to store the salary information for all five employees in the same array. To do so, you concatenate base_salary1 and base_salary2 using `numpy.concatenate()`, as follows:

```
base_salary = np.concatenate((base_salary1, base_salary2), axis=0)
```

The first parameter is a tuple containing the arrays to be concatenated. The second parameter, axis, is critical: it specifies whether the arrays should be concatenated horizontally or vertically, or in other words whether the second array will be added as new rows or new columns. The first axis (axis 0) runs vertically. Thus, axis=0 instructs the `concatenate()` function to append the rows of base_salary2 beneath those of base_salary1. The resulting array will look as follows:

```
[[2700 3000 3000]
 [2600 2800 2800]
 [2300 2500 2500],
```

```
 [2200 2400 2400],
 [2500 2700 2700]]
```

Now imagine that the salary information for the next month has come in. You might put these new figures in another NumPy array, as follows:

```
new_month_salary = np.array([[3000],[2900],[2500],[2500],[2700]])
```

If you print the array, you'll see the following output:

```
[[3000]
 [2900]
 [2500]
 [2500]
 [2700]]
```

You need to add this new_month_salary array to the base_salary array as an extra column. Assuming the order of employees is the same in both arrays, you can use concatenate() for this as follows:

```
base_salary = np.concatenate((base_salary, new_month_salary), axis=1)
```

Since axis 1 runs horizontally across the columns, axis=1 instructs the concatenate() function to append the new_month_salary array as a column to the right of the base_salary array's columns. Now base_salary will look like this:

```
[[2700 3000 3000 3000]
 [2600 2800 2800 2900]
 [2300 2500 2500 2500]
 [2200 2400 2400 2500]
 [2500 2700 2700 2700]]
```

---

**EXERCISE #11: ADDING NEW ROWS/COLUMNS TO A NUMPY ARRAY**

Continuing with the preceding example, create a new two-column NumPy array with salary information for two more months for each employee. Then, concatenate the existing base_salary array with the newly created array. Similarly, append a new row to the base_salary array, thus adding salary information for another employee. Note that when adding a single row or column to a NumPy array, you can use the numpy.append() function rather than numpy.concatenate().

---

# Combining pandas Data Structures

In Chapter 3, we covered some basic techniques for combining pandas data structures. You saw examples of how Series objects can be combined into a DataFrame and how two DataFrames can be joined on their indexes. You also learned about the different types of joins you can create when merging two DataFrames into a single one, by passing the `how` parameter in to the pandas `join()` or `merge()` method. In this section, you'll see more examples of how to use this parameter to create nondefault DataFrame joins, such as a right join. Before that, however, you'll learn to concatenate two DataFrames along a particular axis.

### Concatenating DataFrames

Like with NumPy arrays, you might need to concatenate two DataFrames along a particular axis, appending either the rows or the columns of one DataFrame to the other. The examples in this section show how to do this with the pandas `concat()` function. Before proceeding to the examples, you'll need to create two DataFrames to be concatenated.

Using the `jeff_salary`, `nick_salary`, and `tom_salary` lists from earlier in this chapter, you can create a DataFrame using a dictionary, like so:

```
import pandas as pd
salary_df1 = pd.DataFrame(
    {'jeff': jeff_salary,
     'nick': nick_salary,
     'tom': tom_salary
    })
```

Each list becomes a value in the dictionary, which in turn becomes a column in the new DataFrame. The dictionary's keys, which are the corresponding employee names, become the column labels. Each row of the DataFrame contains all the salary data for a single month. By default the rows are indexed numerically, but it would be more meaningful to index them by month. You can update the indices as follows:

```
salary_df1.index = ['June', 'July', 'August']
```

The salary_df1 DataFrame will now look like this:

```
        jeff  nick  tom
June    2700  2600  2300
July    3000  2800  2500
August  3000  2800  2500
```

You may find it more convenient to view the salary data of an employee as a row rather than a column. You make this change with the DataFrame's `T` property, which is a shorthand for the `DataFrame.transpose()` method:

```
salary_df1 = salary_df1.T
```

This statement *transposes* the DataFrame, turning its columns into rows and vice versa. The DataFrame is now indexed by employee name and looks as follows:

```
      June  July  August
jeff  2700  3000    3000
```

| | | | |
|------|------|------|------|
| nick | 2600 | 2800 | 2800 |
| tom  | 2300 | 2500 | 2500 |

Now you need to create another DataFrame with the same columns to be concatenated with salary_df1. Following in line with the example of concatenating NumPy arrays, here you create a DataFrame that holds salary data for two more employees:

```
salary_df2 = pd.DataFrame(
    {'maya': maya_salary,
     'john': john_salary
    },
    index = ['June', 'July', 'August']
).T
```

You create the DataFrame, set the index, and transpose the rows and columns all in a single statement. The newly created DataFrame will look as follows:

| | June | July | August |
|------|------|------|--------|
| maya | 2200 | 2400 | 2400 |
| john | 2500 | 2700 | 2700 |

Now that you've created both DataFrames, you're ready to concatenate them.

### Concatenation Along Axis 0

The pandas concat() function concatenates pandas objects along a certain axis. By default, this function uses axis 0, meaning the rows of the DataFrame that appears second in the argument list will be appended below the rows of the DataFrame that appears first. Thus, to concatenate the salary_df1 and salary_df2 DataFrames in this manner, you can call concat() without passing the axis argument explicitly. All you have to do is specify the names of the DataFrames within square brackets:

```
salary_df = pd.concat([salary_df1, salary_df2])
```

This will generate the following DataFrame:

| | June | July | August |
|------|------|------|--------|
| jeff | 2700 | 3000 | 3000 |
| nick | 2600 | 2800 | 2800 |
| tom  | 2300 | 2500 | 2500 |
| maya | 2200 | 2400 | 2400 |
| john | 2500 | 2700 | 2700 |

As you can see, the maya and john rows from the second DataFrame have been added beneath the rows from the first DataFrame.

## Concatenation Along Axis 1

When concatenating along axis 1, the concat() function will append the columns of the second DataFrame to the right of the columns of the first one. To illustrate this, you can use salary_df from the preceding section as the first DataFrame. For the second DataFrame, create the following structure, which holds two more months' worth of salary data:

```
salary_df3 = pd.DataFrame(
    {'September': [3000,2800,2500,2400,2700],
     'October': [3200,3000,2700,2500,2900]
    },
    index = ['jeff', 'nick', 'tom', 'maya', 'john']
)
```

Now call concat(), passing in the two DataFrames and specifying axis=1 to ensure the concatenation is horizontal:

```
salary_df = pd.concat([salary_df, salary_df3], axis=1)
```

The resulting DataFrame will look as follows:

```
      June  July  August  September  October
jeff  2700  3000  3000    3000       3200
nick  2600  2800  2800    2800       3000
tom   2300  2500  2500    2500       2700
maya  2200  2400  2400    2400       2500
john  2500  2700  2700    2700       2900
```

The salary data from the second DataFrame appears as new columns to the right of the salary data from the first DataFrame.

## Removing Columns/Rows from a DataFrame

After combining DataFrames, you may need to remove some unnecessary rows or columns. Let's say, for example, you want to remove the September and October columns from the salary_df DataFrame. You can do this with the DataFrame.drop() method, as follows:

```
salary_df = salary_df.drop(['September', 'October'], axis=1)
```

The first argument takes the names of the columns or rows to be deleted from the DataFrame. Then you use the axis argument to specify whether they're rows or columns. In this example you're deleting columns, because axis is set to 1.

With drop(), you aren't limited to only deleting the last columns/rows of a DataFrame. You can pass in an arbitrary list of columns or rows to be deleted, as shown here:

```
salary_df = salary_df.drop(['nick', 'maya'], axis=0)
```

After performing the two previous operations, `salary_df` will appear as follows:

|      | June | July | August |
|------|------|------|--------|
| jeff | 2700 | 3000 | 3000   |
| tom  | 2300 | 2500 | 2500   |
| john | 2500 | 2700 | 2700   |

You've removed the columns for September and October and the rows for Nick and Maya.

### Concatenating DataFrames with a Hierarchical Index

So far you've seen examples of concatenating DataFrames with simple indexes. Now let's consider how to concatenate DataFrames with a MultiIndex. The following example uses the `df_date_region` DataFrame introduced in "Grouping and Aggregating the Data" in Chapter 6. The DataFrame was created as a result of several successive operations and looked as follows:

|            |        | Total |
|------------|--------|-------|
| Date       | Region |       |
| 2022-02-04 | East   | 97.0  |
|            | West   | 243.0 |
| 2022-02-05 | East   | 160.0 |
|            | West   | 35.0  |
| 2022-02-06 | East   | 110.0 |
|            | West   | 86.0  |

To re-create this DataFrame, you don't have to follow the steps from Chapter 6. Instead, execute the following statement:

```
df_date_region1 = pd.DataFrame(
 [
  ('2022-02-04', 'East', 97.0),
  ('2022-02-04', 'West', 243.0),
  ('2022-02-05', 'East', 160.0),
  ('2022-02-05', 'West', 35.0),
  ('2022-02-06', 'East', 110.0),
  ('2022-02-06', 'West', 86.0)
 ],
 columns =['Date', 'Region', 'Total']).set_index(['Date','Region'])
```

Now you'll need another DataFrame that's also indexed by `Date` and `Region`. Create it like this:

```
df_date_region2 = pd.DataFrame(
 [
  ('2022-02-04', 'South', 114.0),
  ('2022-02-05', 'South', 325.0),
  ('2022-02-06', 'South', 212.0)
 ],
 columns =['Date', 'Region', 'Total']).set_index(['Date','Region'])
```

The second DataFrame features the same three dates as the first but has data for a new region, South. The challenge when concatenating these two DataFrames is to keep the result sorted by date rather than simply appending the second DataFrame beneath the first one. Here's how you can do this:

```
df_date_region = pd.concat([df_date_region1,
           df_date_region2]).sort_index(level=['Date','Region'])
```

You start with a concat() call that looks the same as it would if it were concatenating DataFrames with single-column indexes. You identify the DataFrames to be combined, and since you omit the axis parameter, they'll be concatenated vertically by default. To sort the rows in the resulting DataFrame by date and region, you then have to call the sort_index() method. As a result, you'll get the following DataFrame:

```
                    Total
Date       Region
2022-02-04 East      97.0
           South    114.0
           West     243.0
2022-02-05 East     160.0
           South    325.0
           West      35.0
2022-02-06 East     110.0
           South    212.0
           West      86.0
```

As you can see, the rows from the second DataFrame have been integrated among the rows from the first DataFrame, maintaining the top-level grouping by date.

## Joining Two DataFrames

When you join two DataFrames, you combine each row from one dataset with the matching row(s) from the other, rather than simply appending one DataFrame's rows or columns beneath or beside the other's. To review the basics of joining DataFrames, refer back to "Combining DataFrames" in Chapter 3, which covers the different types of joins you can implement. In this section, you'll go beyond what you learned in Chapter 3 by implementing a right join and a join based on a many-to-many relationship.

### Implementing a Right Join

A right join takes all the rows from a second DataFrame and combines them with any matching rows from a first DataFrame. As you'll see, this type of join comes with the possibility that some rows in the resulting DataFrame will have undefined fields, which can lead to unexpected challenges.

To demonstrate, you'll perform a right join of the df_orders and df_details DataFrames created from the orders and details lists introduced in Chapter 6, which you used in the examples in the opening section of this chapter. Create the DataFrames from these lists as follows:

```
import pandas as pd
df_orders = pd.DataFrame(orders, columns =['OrderNo', 'Date', 'Empno'])
df_details = pd.DataFrame(details, columns =['OrderNo', 'Item', 'Brand',
                                             'Price', 'Quantity'])
```

Recall that each row in the original details list has a matching row in the orders list. Therefore, the same is true for the df_details and df_orders DataFrames. To properly illustrate a right join, you need to add one or more new rows to df_details that don't have matches in df_orders. You can add a row using the DataFrame.append() method, which takes the row being appended either as a dictionary or a Series.

If you followed along with the example in "Implementing Different Types of Joins for Lists" earlier in this chapter, you've already added the following row to the details list, and therefore it should already appear in the df_details DataFrame. In that case, you can ignore the following append operation. Otherwise, append this row to df_details as a dictionary. Note that the value of the new row's OrderNo field can't be found among the values of the OrderNo column in the df_orders DataFrame:

```
df_details = df_details.append(
  {'OrderNo': 4626592,
   'Item': 'Shorts',
   'Brand': 'Protest',
   'Price': 48.0,
   'Quantity': 1
  },
❶ ignore_index = True
)
```

You must set the ignore_index parameter to True ❶, or you won't be able to append a dictionary to a DataFrame. Setting this parameter to True also resets the DataFrame's index, maintaining continuous index values (0, 1, ...) for the rows.

Next, you join the df_orders and df_details DataFrames using the merge() method. As discussed in Chapter 3, merge() provides a convenient way of joining two DataFrames with a common column:

```
df_orders_details_right = df_orders.merge(df_details, ❶ how='right',
                   ❷ left_on='OrderNo', right_on='OrderNo')
```

You use the how parameter to specify the type of join—in this example, a right join ❶. With the left_on and right_on parameters, you specify the columns to join on from the df_orders and df_details DataFrames, respectively ❷. The resulting DataFrame will look as follows:

|   | OrderNo | Date | Empno | Item | Brand | Price | Quantity |
|---|---------|------|-------|------|-------|-------|----------|
| 0 | 9423517 | 2022-02-04 | 9001.0 | Jeans | Rip Curl | 87.0 | 1 |
| 1 | 9423517 | 2022-02-04 | 9001.0 | Jacket | The North Face | 112.0 | 1 |

| | | | | | | | |
|---|---|---|---|---|---|---|---|
| 2 | 4626232 | 2022-02-04 | 9003.0 | Socks | Vans | 15.0 | 1 |
| 3 | 4626232 | 2022-02-04 | 9003.0 | Jeans | Quiksilver | 82.0 | 1 |
| 4 | 9423534 | 2022-02-04 | 9001.0 | Socks | DC | 10.0 | 2 |
| 5 | 9423534 | 2022-02-04 | 9001.0 | Socks | Quiksilver | 12.0 | 2 |
| 6 | 9423679 | 2022-02-05 | 9002.0 | T-shirt | Patagonia | 35.0 | 1 |
| 7 | 4626377 | 2022-02-05 | 9003.0 | Hoody | Animal | 44.0 | 1 |
| 8 | 4626377 | 2022-02-05 | 9003.0 | Cargo Shorts | Animal | 38.0 | 1 |
| 9 | 4626412 | 2022-02-05 | 9004.0 | Shirt | Volcom | 78.0 | 1 |
| 10 | 9423783 | 2022-02-06 | 9002.0 | Boxer Shorts | Superdry | 30.0 | 2 |
| 11 | 9423783 | 2022-02-06 | 9002.0 | Shorts | Globe | 26.0 | 1 |
| 12 | 4626490 | 2022-02-06 | 9004.0 | Cargo Shorts | Billabong | 54.0 | 1 |
| 13 | 4626490 | 2022-02-06 | 9004.0 | Sweater | Dickies | 56.0 | 1 |
| 14 | 4626592 | NaN | NaN | Shorts | Protest | 48.0 | 1 |

Since the row newly appended to df_details has no matching row in df_orders, the corresponding row in the resulting DataFrame contains NaN (the default missing value marker) in the Date and Empno fields. However, this causes a problem: NaNs can't be stored in integer columns, so pandas automatically converts an integer column into a float column when a NaN is being inserted. For this reason, the values in the Empno column have been converted into floats. You can confirm this using the df_orders_details_right DataFrame's dtypes property, which shows the type of each column:

```
print(df_orders_details_right.dtypes)
```

This will give you the following output:

```
OrderNo      int64
Date        object
Empno      float64
Item        object
Brand       object
Price      float64
Quantity     int64
dtype: object
```

As you can see, the Empno column is of type float64. If you similarly check the dtypes property of df_orders, you'll see that the Empno column was originally of type int64.

Obviously this conversion from integers to floats isn't desirable behavior: the employee numbers shouldn't have decimal points! Is there a way to convert the Empno column back to integers? One workaround is to replace NaNs in this columns with some integer value, say 0. As long as 0 isn't someone's employee ID, this replacement can be perfectly acceptable. Here's how to implement the change:

```
df_orders_details_right = df_orders_details_right.fillna({'Empno':0}).astype({'Empno':'int64'})
```

You use the DataFrame's fillna() method, which replaces NaNs in the specified column(s) with a specified value. The column and replacement value are defined as a dictionary. In this particular example, you replace

NaNs in the `Empno` column with `0`s. Then, you convert the type of the column to `int64` using the `astype()` method. Once again, the column and new type are specified as a key-value pair in a dictionary.

You end up with the following DataFrame:

| | OrderNo | Date | Empno | Item | Brand | Price | Quantity |
|---|---|---|---|---|---|---|---|
| 0 | 9423517 | 2022-02-04 | 9001 | Jeans | Rip Curl | 87.0 | 1 |
| 1 | 9423517 | 2022-02-04 | 9001 | Jacket | The North Face | 112.0 | 1 |
| --snip-- | | | | | | | |
| 14 | 4626592 | NaN | 0 | Shorts | Protest | 48.0 | 1 |

The `NaN` in the `Empno` column has become a `0`, and the employee numbers once again appear as integers. No more pesky decimal points!

### Implementing a Many-to-Many Join

A many-to-many join can be established between datasets where a row in each dataset may relate to multiple rows in the other. For example, suppose you have two datasets containing books and authors, respectively. Every record in the authors dataset can be linked to one or more records in the books dataset, and every record in the books dataset can be linked to one or more records in the authors dataset.

Typically, you join datasets that have a many-to-many relationship using an *associative table*, also known as a *matching table*. This table maps two (or more) datasets together by referencing the primary keys of each dataset. The associative table has a one-to-many relationship with each of the datasets and functions as an intermediary between them, allowing them to be merged.

To see how a many-to-many join can be implemented through a matching table, create a `books` DataFrame and an `authors` DataFrame as follows:

```
import pandas as pd
books = pd.DataFrame({'book_id': ['b1', 'b2', 'b3'],
                      'title': ['Beautiful Coding', 'Python for Web
                                Development', 'Pythonic Thinking'],
                      'topic': ['programming', 'Python, Web', 'Python']})
authors = pd.DataFrame({'author_id': ['jsn', 'tri', 'wsn'],
                        'author': ['Johnson', 'Treloni', 'Willson']})
```

The `books` DataFrame includes three books, each with a unique `book_id`, while the `authors` DataFrame includes three authors, each with a unique `author_id`. Now create a third DataFrame, `matching`, that will serve as the associative table, connecting each book with its respective author(s) and vice versa:

```
matching = pd.DataFrame({'author_id': ['jsn', 'jsn','tri', 'wsn'],
                         'book_id': ['b1', 'b2', 'b2', 'b3']})
```

The `matching` DataFrame has two columns: one corresponding to author IDs and one corresponding to book IDs. Unlike in the other two DataFrames, each row in `matching` doesn't just represent a single author or a single book. Instead, it contains information about the *relationship between* one particular author and one particular book. The DataFrame looks as follows:

```
   author_id book_id
0        jsn      b1
1        jsn      b2
2        tri      b2
3        wsn      b3
```

The first and second rows both reference the author_id of jsn, establishing that Johnson is the author of two different books. Likewise, the second and third rows both reference the book_id of b2, establishing that *Python for Web Development* has two authors.

Now you can create a many-to-many join between the authors and books datasets via matching, as shown here:

```
authorship = books.merge(matching).merge(authors)[['title','topic','author']]
```

The operation actually consists of two separate joins using the merge() method. First you join the books and matching DataFrames on their respective book_id columns. Then you join the result of the first join with the authors DataFrame via their author_id columns. Both of these are straightforward one-to-many joins, but together they result in a new DataFrame illustrating the many-to-many relationship between the books and authors datasets. You filter the DataFrame to include just the title, topic, and author columns, so that result looks as follows:

```
                       title         topic   author
0             Beautiful Coding   programming  Johnson
1  Python for Web Development   Python, Web  Johnson
2  Python for Web Development   Python, Web  Treloni
3            Pythonic Thinking        Python  Willson
```

As you can see, Johnson is listed twice as the author of both *Beautiful Coding* and *Python for Web Development*, while *Python for Web Development* is listed twice, once for each of its authors.

## Summary

In this chapter, you looked at different ways of combining datasets presented in the form of built-in data structures such as lists, or third-party data structures such as NumPy arrays and pandas DataFrames. You learned to concatenate datasets, appending the columns or rows of one dataset to another. You also learned to join datasets, combining their matching rows.

# 8

## CREATING VISUALIZATIONS

Data can be viewed more clearly in a visual form than it can be as raw numbers. For example, you might want to create a line chart graphing the changes in a stock price over time. Or you could track the interest in the articles on your website using a histogram showing daily views of each. Visualizations such as these help you immediately recognize trends in your data.

This chapter provides an overview of the most common types of data visualizations and covers how to create them using Matplotlib, a popular Python plotting library. You'll also learn how to integrate Matplotlib with pandas and how to create maps with Matplotlib and the Cartopy library.

# Common Visualizations

Several chart types are available for visualizing data, including line graphs, bar graphs, pie charts, and histograms. In this section, we'll discuss these common visualizations and explore typical use cases for each.

## Line Graphs

*Line graphs*, also known as *line charts*, are useful when you need to illustrate trends in data over a period of time. In a line graph, you place the timestamp column of a dataset along the x-axis and one or more numeric columns on the y-axis.

Consider a website where users can view different articles. You can create a chart for an article in which the x-axis plots a series of days and the y-axis displays how many times the article has been viewed each day. This is shown in Figure 8-1.

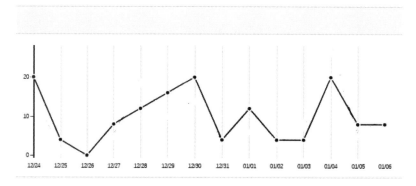

*Figure 8-1: A line graph showing article views over time*

You can overlay data from multiple parameters in one line chart to illustrate the correlation between them, plotting each parameter's data with a line of a different color. For example, Figure 8-2 shows the website's daily number of unique users on top of the number of article views.

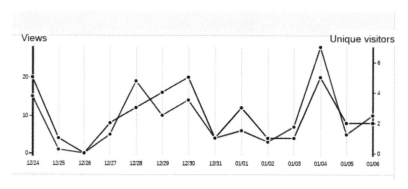

*Figure 8-2: A line graph showing the relationship between various parameters*

The left-hand y-axis in this line graph shows article views, while the right-hand y-axis shows unique visitors. Overlaying the data for both parameters, it's visually clear that there's a general correlation between the numbers of article views and unique visitors.

**NOTE**   *Article views might be plotted as a histogram instead of a line graph. We'll discuss histograms later in this section.*

## Bar Graphs

*Bar graphs*, also referred to as *bar charts* or *column charts*, show categorical data using rectangular bars with heights proportional to the values they represent, allowing for comparisons between categories. For example, consider the following figures, which represent a company's annual sales aggregated on a regional basis:

| | |
|---|---|
| New England | $882,703 |
| Mid-Atlantic | $532,648 |
| Midwest | $714,406 |

Figure 8-3 illustrates what this sales data looks like when plotted on a bar graph.

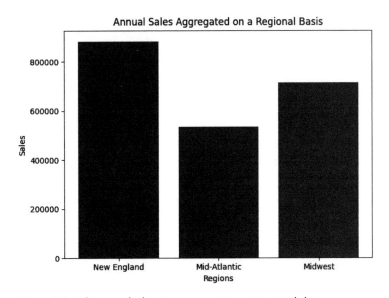

*Figure 8-3: A bar graph showing comparative categorical data*

In this chart, the y-axis displays comparative sales figures for the regions shown on the x-axis.

## Pie Charts

*Pie charts* illustrate the proportion of each category in the full dataset, expressed as a percentage. Figure 8-4 illustrates the sales figures from the previous example when plotted on a pie chart.

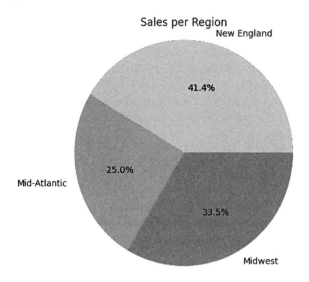

*Figure 8-4: Pie charts represent the percentage of each category as a slice of a circle.*

Here, the size of each slice provides a visual representation of the proportion that each category contributes to the whole. You can easily see how the sales for each region compare to each other. This works well when each slice represents a substantial portion of the pie, but as you might guess, a pie chart isn't the best choice when you have to represent very small portions. For example, a slice representing 0.01 percent of the whole may not even be visible in the chart.

## Histograms

*Histograms* show frequency distributions, or how many times a particular value or range of values appears in a dataset. Each value, or outcome, is represented by a vertical bar whose height corresponds to that value's frequency. For example, the histogram in Figure 8-5 immediately makes apparent the frequency of different salary groups in a sales department.

In this histogram, salaries are grouped into $50 ranges, with each vertical bar representing the number of people who have salaries within a certain range. The visualization lets you quickly see how many employees earn between $1,200 and $1,250, for example, as compared to other ranges, like $1,250 to $1,300.

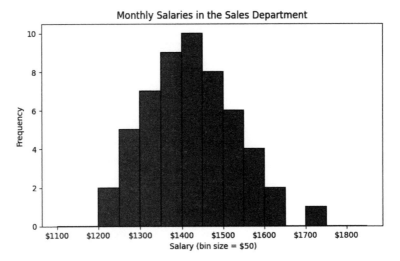

Figure 8-5: A histogram showing a salary distribution

## Plotting with Matplotlib

Now that you've seen the most common types of charts, we'll consider how to create them using Matplotlib, one of the most popular Python libraries for data visualization. You'll learn how to make line graphs, pie charts, bar graphs, and histograms.

Each Matplotlib visualization, or *figure*, is built from a hierarchy of nested objects. You can work with those objects directly to create highly customizable visualizations, or you can manipulate the objects indirectly through the functions provided in the matplotlib.pyplot module. The latter approach is simpler and is often sufficient for creating basic charts and graphs.

### Installing Matplotlib

Check if Matplotlib is already installed by trying to import it in a Python interpreter session:

```
> import matplotlib
```

If you get a ModuleNotFoundError, install Matplotlib with pip as follows:

```
$ python -m pip install -U matplotlib
```

### Using matplotlib.pyplot

The matplotlib.pyplot module, typically referred to in code as plt, provides a collection of functions for building good-looking figures. The module lets you easily define various aspects of a figure, such as its title, its axis labels, and so on. For example, here's how to construct a line graph plotting Tesla's closing stock price over five consecutive days:

```
from matplotlib import pyplot as plt

days = ['2021-01-04', '2021-01-05', '2021-01-06', '2021-01-07', '2021-01-08']
prices = [729.77, 735.11, 755.98, 816.04, 880.02]

plt.plot(days,prices)
plt.title('NASDAQ: TSLA')
plt.xlabel('Date')
plt.ylabel('USD')
plt.show()
```

First, you define your dataset as two lists: days, which contains the dates that will be plotted along the x-axis, and prices, which contains the prices that will be plotted along the y-axis. Then you create a *plot*, the part of the figure that actually shows the data, with the plt.plot() function, passing it the data for the x- and y-axes. In the next three lines of code, you customize the figure: you add a title with plt.title() and labels for the x- and y-axes with plt.xlabel() and plt.ylabel(). Finally, you display the figure with plt.show(). Figure 8-6 shows the result.

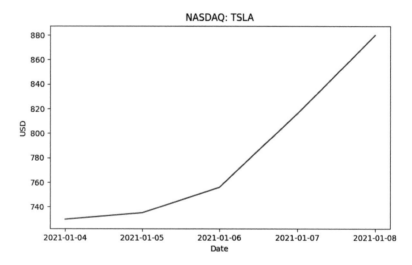

Figure 8-6: A simple line graph generated with the matplotlib.pyplot module

By default, plt.plot() yields a visualization rendered as a series of lines connecting the data points, which are plotted on the x- and y-axes. Matplotlib has automatically chosen a range of 720 to 880 for the y-axis, demarcated in intervals of 20, making it easy to see each day's stock price.

Building a basic pie chart is just as simple as making a line graph. For example, the following code generates the pie chart shown earlier in Figure 8-4:

```
import matplotlib.pyplot as plt

regions = ['New England', 'Mid-Atlantic', 'Midwest']
sales = [882703, 532648, 714406]

plt.pie(sales, labels=regions, autopct='%1.1f%%')
plt.title('Sales per Region')
plt.show()
```

The script follows the same basic pattern you used to make the line graph: you define the data to be plotted, create a plot, customize some of its features, and display it. This time, the data consists of a list of regions, which will serve as labels for each slice of the pie chart, and a list of the sales totals for each region, which will define the size of each slice. To make the plot a pie chart rather than a line graph, you call the plt.pie() function, passing in sales as the data to be plotted and regions as the labels for the data. You also use the autopct parameter to display percent values in the pie slices, using Python string formatting to show the values to the nearest tenth of a percent.

Here you visualize the same input data as a bar graph, like the one in Figure 8-3:

```
import matplotlib.pyplot as plt
regions = ['New England', 'Mid-Atlantic', 'Midwest']
sales = [882703, 532648, 714406]

plt.bar(regions, sales)
plt.xlabel("Regions")
plt.ylabel("Sales")
plt.title("Annual Sales Aggregated on a Regional Basis")

plt.show()
```

You pass the regions list to the plt.bar() function as the x-axis labels for the bars. The second argument you pass to plt.bar() is the list with the sales figures corresponding to the items in regions. Both here and in the pie chart example, you're able to use separate lists for labels and sales figures because the order of elements in a Python list is persistent.

## Working with Figure and Axes Objects

At heart, a Matplotlib visualization is built from two main types of objects: a Figure object and one or more Axes objects. In the previous examples, matplotlib.pyplot served as an interface for working indirectly with these objects, allowing you to customize some elements of a visualization. However, you can exert more control over your visualizations by working directly with the Figure and Axes objects themselves.

The Figure object is the top-level, outermost container for a Matplotlib visualization. It can include one or more plots. You work with a Figure object when you need to do something with the overall visualization, such as resize it or save it to a file. Meanwhile, each Axes object represents one plot in the figure. You use an Axes object to customize a plot and define its layout. For example, you can set the coordinate system of the plot and mark positions on an axis.

You access the Figure and Axes objects through the matplotlib.pyplot.subplots() function. When invoked without arguments, this function returns a Figure instance and a single Axes instance associated with the Figure. By adding arguments to the subplots() function, you can create a Figure instance and multiple associated Axes instances. In other words, you'll create a figure with multiple plots. For example, a call of subplots(2,2) creates a figure with four plots, arranged in two rows of two. Each plot is represented by one Axes object.

**NOTE** *For further details on the use of subplots(), refer to the Matplotlib documentation at* https://matplotlib.org/3.3.3/api/_as_gen/matplotlib.pyplot.subplots.html.

### Creating a Histogram with subplots()

In the following script, you use subplots() to create a Figure object and a single Axes object. You then manipulate the objects to produce the histogram shown earlier in Figure 8-5, displaying the salary distribution of a collection of employees. In addition to working with the Figure and Axes objects, you also work with a Matplotlib module called matplotlib.ticker to format the ticks along the x-axis of the plot as well as with NumPy to define a sequence of bins for the histogram in $50 increments:

```
# importing modules
import numpy as np
from matplotlib import pyplot as plt
import matplotlib.ticker as ticker

# data to plot
❶ salaries = [1215, 1221, 1263, 1267, 1271, 1274, 1275, 1318, 1320, 1324, 1324,
             1326, 1337, 1346, 1354, 1355, 1364, 1367, 1372, 1375, 1376, 1378,
             1378, 1410, 1415, 1415, 1418, 1420, 1422, 1426, 1430, 1434, 1437,
             1451, 1454, 1467, 1470, 1473, 1477, 1479, 1480, 1514, 1516, 1522,
             1529, 1544, 1547, 1554, 1562, 1584, 1595, 1616, 1626, 1717]

# preparing a histogram
❷ fig, ax = plt.subplots()
❸ fig.set_size_inches(5.6, 4.2)
❹ ax.hist(salaries, bins=np.arange(1100, 1900, 50), edgecolor='black',
          linewidth=1.2)
❺ formatter = ticker.FormatStrFormatter('$%1.0f')
❻ ax.xaxis.set_major_formatter(formatter)
❼ plt.title('Monthly Salaries in the Sales Department')
  plt.xlabel('Salary (bin size = $50)')
  plt.ylabel('Frequency')
  # showing the histogram
  plt.show()
```

You start by defining a `salaries` list with the salary data you want to visualize ❶. You then invoke the `subplots()` function without parameters ❷, thus instructing it to create a figure containing a single plot. The function returns a tuple containing two objects, `fig` and `ax`, representing the figure and the plot, respectively.

Now that you have these `Figure` and `Axes` instances, you can begin to customize them. To start, you invoke the `set_size_inches()` method of the `Figure` object to resize the overall figure ❸. Then you invoke the `hist()` method of the `Axes` object to plot a histogram ❹. You pass the method the `salaries` list as the input data for the histogram, as well as a NumPy array defining the x-axis points for the histogram bins. You generate the array with NumPy's `arange()` function, which produces an array of evenly spaced values within a given interval (in this case, increments of 50 between 1100 and 1900). You use the `hist()` method's `edgecolor` parameter to draw black line boundaries for the bins and the `linewidth` parameter to define the width of those boundaries.

Next, you use the `FormatStrFormatter()` function from the `matplotlib.ticker` module to create a formatter that will prepend a dollar sign to each x-axis label ❺. You apply the formatter to the x-axis labels using the `set_major_formatter()` method of the `ax.xaxis` object ❻. Finally, you set the general aspects of the plot, such as its title and main axis labels, via the `matplotlib.pyplot` interface ❼ and display the plot.

### Showing Frequency Distributions on a Pie Chart

While histograms are well suited for visualizing frequency distributions, you can also use a pie chart to convey frequency distributions as percentages. As an example, this section shows how to transform the salary distribution histogram you just created into a pie chart displaying how the salaries are distributed as parts of a whole.

Before you can create such a pie chart, you need to extract and organize some key information from the histogram. In particular, you need to learn the number of salaries in each $50 range. You can use NumPy's `histogram()` function for this; it computes a histogram without displaying it:

```
import numpy as np
count, labels = np.histogram(salaries, bins=np.arange(1100, 1900, 50))
```

Here, you call the `histogram()` function, passing it the same `salaries` list you created earlier and again using NumPy's `arange()` function to generate evenly spaced bins. Calling `histogram()` returns two NumPy arrays: `count` and `labels`. The `count` array represents the number of employees with salaries in each interval and looks as follows:

```
[0,  0,  2,  5,  7,  9, 10,  8,  6,  4,  2,  0,  1,  0,  0]
```

Meanwhile, the `labels` array contains the edges of the bin intervals:

```
[1100, 1150, 1200, 1250, 1300, 1350, 1400, 1450, 1500, 1550, 1600, 1650,
 1700, 1750, 1800, 1850]
```

Next you need to combine neighboring elements of the `labels` array, turning them into the labels for the slices of the pie chart. For example, neighboring elements 1100 and 1150 should become a single label formatted as '$1100-1150'. Use the following list comprehension:

```
labels = ['$'+str(labels[i])+'-'+str(labels[i+1]) for i, _ in enumerate(labels[1:])]
```

As a result, the `labels` list will look as follows:

```
['$1100-1150', '$1150-1200', '$1200-1250', '$1250-1300', '$1300-1350',
 '$1350-1400', '$1400-1450', '$1450-1500', '$1500-1550', '$1550-1600',
 '$1600-1650', '$1650-1700', '$1700-1750', '$1750-1800', '$1800-1850']
```

Each element in `labels` corresponds to the element in the `count` array with the same index. Looking back at the `count` array, however, you may notice a problem: the count for some intervals is 0, and you wouldn't want to include these empty intervals to the pie chart. To exclude them, you need to generate a list of the indices corresponding to nonempty intervals in the `count` array:

```
non_zero_pos = [i for i, x in enumerate(count) if x != 0]
```

Now you can use `non_zero_pos` to filter `count` and `labels`, excluding those elements that represent empty intervals:

```
labels = [e for i, e in enumerate(labels) if i in non_zero_pos]
count = [e for i, e in enumerate(count) if i in non_zero_pos]
```

Now all that remains is to create and display the pie chart using the `matplotlib.pyplot` interface and `plt.pie()`:

```
from matplotlib import pyplot as plt
plt.pie(count, labels=labels, autopct='%1.1f%%')
plt.title('Monthly Salaries in the Sales Department')
plt.show()
```

Figure 8-7 shows the result.

The pie chart visualizes the same data as the histogram in Figure 8-5, but it shows each bin as a percentage of the whole instead of indicating exactly how many employees have salaries that fall within that bin.

---

### EXERCISE #12: COMBINING BINS INTO AN "OTHER" SLICE

Looking at the chart in Figure 8-7, you may notice that some intervals are represented by a very thin slice in the pie. These are the bins with a count of one or two employees. Modify the chart so that these intervals are merged into a single slice labeled Other. To accomplish this, you'll need to alter the count array and the labels list. Then, you'll need to re-create the chart.

---

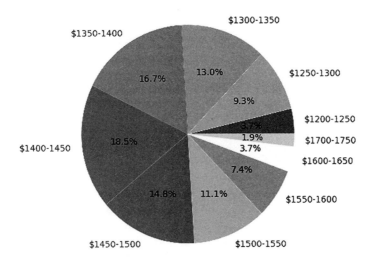

Monthly Salaries in the Sales Department

Figure 8-7: A pie chart visualizing a frequency distribution

# Using Other Libraries with Matplotlib

Matplotlib can easily interface with other Python libraries to plot data from different sources or create other kinds of visualizations. For example, you can use Matplotlib in conjunction with pandas to plot the data from a DataFrame, or you can create maps by combining Matplotlib with Cartopy, a library that specializes in handling geospatial data.

## Plotting pandas Data

The pandas library is closely integrated with Matplotlib. In fact, every pandas Series or DataFrame has a plot() method, which is actually a wrapper around the matplotlib.pyplot.plot() method. It allows you to directly convert a pandas data structure into a Matplotlib plot. To demonstrate, you'll create a bar chart from a DataFrame with population data for US cities. You'll use raw data from the *us-cities-top-1k.csv* file available at *https://github.com/plotly/datasets*. The bar chart will show the number of megacities (those with a population of 1,000,000 or greater) in each US state. Here's how to do it:

```
import pandas as pd
import matplotlib.pyplot as plt

# preparing the DataFrame
❶ us_cities = pd.read_csv("https://raw.githubusercontent.com/plotly/datasets/
                           master/us-cities-top-1k.csv")
❷ top_us_cities = us_cities[us_cities.Population.ge(1000000)]
❸ top_cities_count = top_us_cities.groupby(['State'], as_index = False)
                    .count().rename(columns={'City': 'cities_count'})
                    [['State','cities_count']]
```

```
# drawing the chart
❹ top_cities_count.plot.bar('State', 'cities_count', rot=0)
❺ plt.xlabel("States")
  plt.ylabel("Top cities count")
  plt.title("Number of Megacities per US State")
❻ plt.yticks(range(min(top_cities_count['cities_count']),
                    max(top_cities_count['cities_count'])+1 ))
  plt.show()
```

You first load the dataset into a DataFrame using the pandas read_csv() method ❶. The dataset contains the population, latitude, and longitude of the 1,000 largest US cities. To filter the dataset to just megacities, you use the DataFrame's ge() method, short for *greater than or equal to*, asking only for rows whose Population field is greater than or equal to 1000000 ❷. Then you group the data by the State column and apply the count() aggregate function to find the total number of megacities per state ❸. During the groupby operation, you set as_index to False to avoid converting the State column into the index of the resulting DataFrame. This is because you'll need to refer to the State column later in the script. You rename the City column to cities_count to reflect that it now holds aggregate information and include only the State and cities_count columns in the resulting top_cities_count DataFrame.

Next, you draw a bar chart with the DataFrame's plot.bar() method ❹. Remember, plot() is actually a wrapper for Matplotlib's pyplot.plot() method. In this call, you specify the DataFrame column names that will be used as the x- and y-axes of the plot, and you rotate the x-axis tick labels to 0 degrees. Having created the figure, you're then able to customize it with the matplotlib.pyplot interface, as you've done in earlier examples. You set the axis labels and the figure title ❺, and you use plt.yticks() to set number labels for the y-axis to reflect the top cities count ❻. Finally, you display the figure with plt.show(). Figure 8-8 shows the result.

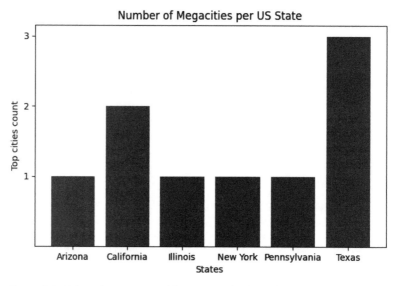

*Figure 8-8: A bar chart generated from a pandas DataFrame*

As you can see, the figure has the same general appearance as the others you've created in this chapter, particularly the bar chart in Figure 8-3. This is not surprising, since it was generated by the same Matplotlib library, which pandas uses behind the scenes.

## Plotting Geospatial Data with Cartopy

Cartopy is a Python library for creating geospatial visualizations, or maps. It includes the `matplotlib.pyplot` programmatic interface, which makes drawing maps easy. Essentially, drawing a map with Cartopy becomes a matter of creating a Matplotlib figure with longitude coordinates plotted along the x-axis and latitude coordinates plotted along the y-axis. Cartopy handles the complexity of translating Earth's spherical shape into the 2D plane of the plot. To demonstrate, you'll use the *us-cities-top-1k.csv* dataset introduced in the previous section to draw outline maps of Southern California showing the locations of various cities. But first you need to set up Cartopy.

### Using Cartopy in Google Colab

Installing Cartopy can be tricky, and the process varies depending on your system. Therefore, this section shows how to use Cartopy through the Google Colab web IDE, which allows you to write and execute Python code through your browser.

To load Colab, go to *https://colab.research.google.com*. Then click **New Notebook** to start a new Colab notebook, where you can create, populate, and run an arbitrary number of code cells. In each code cell, you can group one or more lines of Python code together and execute them with a click of the run button in the top-left corner of the cell. Colab remembers the execution state built by any previously executed cells, similar to a Python interpreter session. You create new code cells with the +Code button in the upper-left corner of the Colab window.

In the first code cell, enter and run the following command to install Cartopy within your Colab notebook:

```
!pip install cartopy
```

Once Cartopy installs, you can proceed to the examples in the next section, running each separate listing as its own code cell.

 *If you'd prefer to install Cartopy directly on your system, refer to the documentation at* https://scitools.org.uk/cartopy/docs/latest/installing.html.

### Creating Maps

In this section, you'll use Cartopy to create two maps of Southern California. First you'll draw a map showing all the Southern California cities included in the *us-cities-top-1k.csv* dataset. You start by importing all the required modules:

```
import pandas as pd
%matplotlib inline
import matplotlib.pyplot as plt
```

```
import cartopy.crs as ccrs
from cartopy.mpl.ticker import LongitudeFormatter, LatitudeFormatter
```

You'll need pandas, the `matplotlib.pyplot` interface, and a few different Cartopy modules: `cartopy.crs` to generate maps and `LongitudeFormatter` and `LatitudeFormatter` to format the tick labels properly. The `%matplotlib inline` command is required to include Matplotlib figures in a Google Colab notebook, next to the code.

Next, you load the required data and draw the map:

```
❶ us_cities = pd.read_csv("https://raw.githubusercontent.com/plotly/datasets/
                          master/us-cities-top-1k.csv")
❷ calif_cities = us_cities[us_cities.State.eq('California')]
❸ fig, ax = plt.subplots(figsize=(15,8))
❹ ax = plt.axes(projection=ccrs.Mercator())
❺ ax.coastlines('10m')
❻ ax.set_yticks([32,33,34,35,36], crs=ccrs.PlateCarree())
  ax.set_xticks([-121, -120, -119, -118, -117, -116, -115],
                crs=ccrs.PlateCarree())
❼ lon_formatter = LongitudeFormatter()
  lat_formatter = LatitudeFormatter()
  ax.xaxis.set_major_formatter(lon_formatter)
  ax.yaxis.set_major_formatter(lat_formatter)
❽ ax.set_extent([-121, -115, 32, 36])
  X = calif_cities['lon']
  Y = calif_cities['lat']
❾ ax.scatter(X, Y, color='red', marker='o', transform=ccrs.PlateCarree())
  plt.show()
```

You load the *us-cities-top-1k.csv* dataset into a DataFrame ❶, as you did in the previous section. Remember, it contains geospatial data in the form of latitude and longitude coordinates, as well as population data. You then filter the data to include only California cities using the DataFrame's `eq()` method ❷, short for *equal to*.

Since drawing a map requires more customization than the `matplotlib.pyplot` interface will allow, you need to work directly with the visualization's underlying Matplotlib objects. You therefore call the `plt.subplots()` function to obtain a `Figure` object and a single `Axes` object, setting the figure size in the process ❸. You then call `plt.axes()` to overwrite the `Axes` object, turning it into a Cartopy map ❹. You do this by telling Matplotlib to use Cartopy's Mercator projection when plotting coordinates on the flat surface of the figure. The Mercator projection is a standard mapmaking technique that converts Earth from a sphere to a cylinder, then unrolls that cylinder into a rectangle.

Next you call `ax.coastlines()` to show the outlines of landmasses on the map ❺. The coastal outlines are added to the current `Axes` object from the Natural Earth *coastline* shapefile collection. By specifying `10m`, you draw the coastlines at a scale of 1 to 10 million; that is, 1 centimeter on the map is equivalent to 100 kilometers in real life.

**NOTE** *Visit* https://www.naturalearthdata.com *for more information about Natural Earth datasets.*

To define what the ticks along the y- and x-axes will be, you use the set _yticks() and set_xticks() methods, passing a list of latitudes and longitudes, respectively ❻. Specifically, you pass 32 through 36 as the y ticks and -121 to -115 as the x ticks (that is, 32°N to 36°N and 121°W to 115°W), since these latitudes and longitudes cover the area of Southern California. In both cases, you add crs=ccrs.PlateCarree() to specify how the latitude and longitude information should be projected onto a flat plane. Like the Mercator projection, Plate Carrée treats Earth as a cylinder that's been flattened into a rectangle.

Next, you create formatters using Cartopy's LongitudeFormatter() and LatitudeFormatter() objects and apply them to the x- and y-axes ❼. Using these formatters ensures the longitude and latitude values will be shown with degree signs and a *W* or *N* for *west* or *north*, respectively. You also set the extent for the plot, specifying appropriate longitudes and latitudes to limit the map to showing only Southern California ❽. Then you extract two pandas Series objects from your DataFrame, X and Y, for the longitude and latitude values, respectively. Finally, you draw the map with Matplotlib's scatter() method ❾, passing the data to plot on the x- and y-axes along with instructions to display the cities as red dots. Figure 8-9 shows the result.

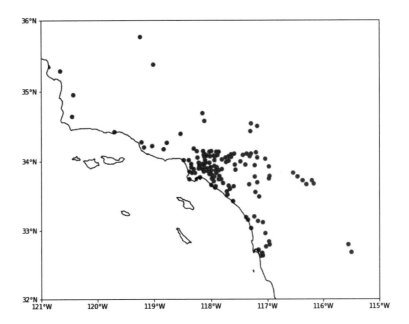

*Figure 8-9: An outline map of Southern California with cities*

The map provides a clear illustration of areas with a high population density. But what if you want to see only the largest cities marked with their names? Here's how you can do this:

```
❶ top_calif_cities = calif_cities[calif_cities.Population.ge(400000)]
fig, ax = plt.subplots(figsize=(15,8))
ax = plt.axes(projection=ccrs.Mercator())
```

```
ax.coastlines('10m')
ax.set_yticks([32,33,34,35,36], crs=ccrs.PlateCarree())
ax.set_xticks([-121, -120, -119, -118, -117, -116, -115],
              crs=ccrs.PlateCarree())
lon_formatter = LongitudeFormatter()
lat_formatter = LatitudeFormatter()
ax.xaxis.set_major_formatter(lon_formatter)
ax.yaxis.set_major_formatter(lat_formatter)
ax.set_extent([-121, -115, 32, 36])
X = top_calif_cities['lon']
Y = top_calif_cities['lat']
❷ cities = top_calif_cities['City']
ax.scatter(X, Y, color='red', marker='o', transform=ccrs.PlateCarree())
❸ for i in X.index:
    label = cities[i]
    plt.text(X[i], Y[i]+0.05, label, clip_on = True, fontsize = 20,
             horizontalalignment='center', transform=ccrs.Geodetic())
plt.show()
```

You filter the calif_cities DataFrame generated in the previous listing to only include those cities with populations of 400,000 or more ❶.
Then you generate the plot by following the same process as before, with
some extra steps for adding city labels. You store the city names in a pandas
Series called cities ❷, then you iterate over the city names, assigning them
as centered labels over the points on the map with Matplotlib's plt.text()
method ❸. You specify transform=ccrs.Geodetic() to make Matplotlib use
Cartopy's Geodetic coordinate system when adding the labels. This system
treats Earth as a sphere and specifies coordinates as latitude and longitude
values. Figure 8-10 shows the result.

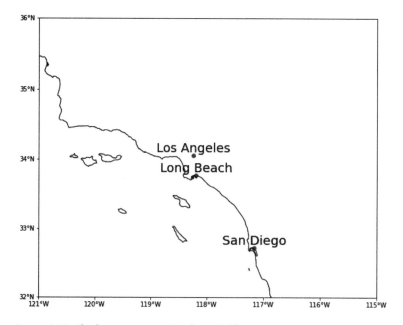

Figure 8-10: The largest cities in Southern California

The map now shows the locations and names of the three cities in Southern California with populations over 400,000.

**EXERCISE #13: DRAWING A MAP WITH CARTOPY AND MATPLOTLIB**

Now that you know how to create a map with Cartopy and Matplotlib, create a map showing the cities in another location in the US. For example, you might create a map for Northern California. You'll need to specify different latitude and longitude values for the y- and x-axes.

## Summary

As you've seen, data visualizations are a powerful tool for discovering trends and gaining insights from your data. For example, a line graph immediately reveals trends in a stock price, while a map can clearly illustrate areas of high population density. In this chapter, you learned how to create common visualizations like line graphs, bar graphs, pie charts, and histograms using the Matplotlib library. You saw how to build simple yet powerful visualizations with the `matplotlib.pyplot` interface and how to exert more control over the result by directly manipulating a visualization's underlying `Figure` and `Axes` objects. You also learned how to use Matplotlib alongside pandas to visualize DataFrame data, and you practiced creating maps with Matplotlib and the Cartopy geospatial data processing library.

# 9

# ANALYZING LOCATION DATA

Everything happens somewhere. That's why the location of an object can be just as important as its nonspatial attributes for the purposes of data analysis. In fact, spatial and nonspatial data often go hand in hand.

As an example, consider a ride-sharing app. Once you've ordered a ride, you might want to track the location of the car on a map in real time while it's heading to you. You might also want know some basic nonspatial information about the car and driver assigned to your order: the make and model of the car, the driver's rating, and so on.

In the last chapter, you saw how to work with location data to generate maps. In this chapter, you'll learn more about how to use Python to collect and analyze location data, and you'll see how to integrate both spatial and nonspatial data in your analysis. Throughout, we'll consider the example of a taxi management service, and we'll try to answer the central question of which cab should be assigned to a particular job.

# Obtaining Location Data

The first step in performing a spatial analysis is to obtain location data for the objects of interest. In particular, this location data should take the form of *geographical coordinates* (*geo coordinates* for short), or latitude and longitude values. This coordinate system enables every location on the planet to be specified as a set of numbers, meaning the locations can be analyzed programatically. In this section, we'll consider ways to obtain the geo coordinates of both stationary and moving objects. This will demonstrate how our example taxi service might determine a customer's pick-up location as well as the real-time locations of its various cabs.

## Turning a Human-Readable Address into Geo Coordinates

Most humans think in terms of street names and building numbers rather than geo coordinates. That's why it's common for taxi services, food delivery apps, and the like to let users specify pick-up and drop-off locations as street addresses. Behind the scenes, however, many of these services convert human-readable addresses into the corresponding geo coordinates. That way the app can perform calculations with the location data, such as determining the nearest available cab to the specified pick-up location.

How do you convert from street addresses to geo coordinates? One way is to use Geocoding, an API provided by Google for this purpose. To interact with the Geocoding API from a Python script, you'll need to use the googlemaps library. Install it using the pip command, as follows:

```
$ pip install -U googlemaps
```

You'll also need to get an API key for the Geocoding API using a Google Cloud account. For information about acquiring an API key, see *https://developers.google.com/maps/documentation/geocoding/get-api-key*. Details on the API's cost structure are available at *https://cloud.google.com/maps-platform/pricing*. As of this writing, Google provides a $200 monthly credit to API users, which is enough for you to experiment with the code in this book.

The following script illustrates a sample call to the Geocoding API using googlemaps. This call obtains the latitude and longitude coordinates corresponding to the address 1600 Amphitheatre Parkway, Mountain View, CA:

```
import googlemaps

gmaps = googlemaps.Client(key='YOUR_API_KEY_HERE')
address = '1600 Amphitheatre Parkway, Mountain View, CA'
geocode_result = gmaps.geocode(address)

print(geocode_result[0]['geometry']['location'].values())
```

In this script, you establish a connection to the API and send the address you want to convert. The API returns a JSON document with a nested structure. The geo coordinates are stored under the key location, which is a subfield of geometry. In the last line, you access and print the coordinates, yielding the following output:

```
dict_values([37.422388, -122.0841883])
```

## Getting the Geo Coordinates of a Moving Object

You now know how to obtain the geo coordinates of a fixed location via its street address, but how can you get the real-time geo coordinates of a moving object, such as a taxi? Some taxi services might use specialized GPS devices for this purpose, but we'll focus instead on a low-cost, easy-to-implement solution. All that's required is a smartphone.

Smartphones detect their location with built-in GPS sensors and can be tuned to share that information. Here, we'll look at how to collect smartphone GPS coordinates via the popular messaging app Telegram. Using the Telegram Bot API, you'll create a *bot*, an application that runs within Telegram. Bots are commonly used for natural language processing, but this one will collect and log the geolocation data of Telegram users who choose to share their data with the bot.

### Setting Up a Telegram Bot

To create a Telegram bot, you'll need to download the Telegram app and create an account. Then follow these steps using either a smartphone or a PC:

1. In the Telegram app, search for @BotFather. BotFather is a Telegram bot that manages all the other bots in your account.
2. On the BotFather page, click **Start** to see the list of commands that you can use to set up your Telegram bots.
3. Enter **/newbot** in the message box. You'll be prompted for a name and a username for your bot. Then you'll be given an authorization token for the new bot. Take note of this token; you'll need it when you program the bot.

After completing these steps, you can implement the bot with Python using the python-telegram-bot library. Install the library like so:

```
$ pip install python-telegram-bot -upgrade
```

The tools you'll need to program the bot are in the library's telegram.ext module. It's built on top of the Telegram Bot API.

## Programming the Bot

Here, you use the `telegram.ext` module of the python-telegram-bot library to program the bot to listen for and log GPS coordinates:

```
from telegram.ext import Updater, MessageHandler, Filters
from datetime import datetime
import csv

❶ def get_location(update, context):
    msg = None
    if update.edited_message:
      msg = update.edited_message
    else:
      msg = update.message
❷ gps = msg.location
    sender = msg.from_user.username
    tm = datetime.now().strftime("%H:%M:%S")
    with open(r'/HOME/PI/LOCATION_BOT/LOG.CSV', 'a') as f:
      writer = csv.writer(f)
❸    writer.writerow([sender, gps.latitude, gps.longitude, tm])
❹    context.bot.send_message(chat_id=msg.chat_id, text=str(gps))

def main():
❺ updater = Updater('TOKEN', use_context=True)
❻ updater.dispatcher.add_handler(MessageHandler(Filters.location,
                                    get_location))
❼ updater.start_polling()
❽ updater.idle()

if __name__ == '__main__':
    main()
```

The `main()` function contains the common invocations found in a script implementing a Telegram bot. You start by creating an `Updater` object ❺, passing it your bot's authorization token (generated by BotFather). This object orchestrates the bot execution process throughout the script. You then use the `Dispatcher` object associated with the `Updater` to add a handler function called `get_location()` for incoming messages ❻. By specifying `Filters.location`, you add a filter to the handler so it will only be called when the bot receives messages that include the sender's location data. You start the bot by invoking the `start_polling()` method of the `Updater` object ❼. Because `start_polling()` is a non-blocking method, you also have to call the `Updater` object's `idle()` method ❽ in order to block the script until a message is received.

At the beginning of the script, you define the `get_location()` handler ❶. Within the handler, you store the incoming message as `msg`, then you extract the sender's location data using the message's `location` property ❷. You also log the sender's username and generate a string containing the current time. Then, using Python's `csv` module, you store all this information as a row in a CSV file ❸ at a location of your choice. You also transmit the location data back to the sender so they know that their location has been received ❹.

### Getting Data from the Bot

Run the script on an internet-connected machine. Once it's running, users can follow a few simple steps to start sharing their real-time location data with the bot:

1. Create a Telegram account.
2. In Telegram, tap the name of the bot.
3. Tap the Paperclip icon and select **Location** from the menu.
4. Choose **Share My Location For** and set how long Telegram will share live location data with the bot. Options include 15 minutes, 1 hour, or 8 hours.

The screenshot in Figure 9-1 shows how easy it is to share your real-time location in Telegram.

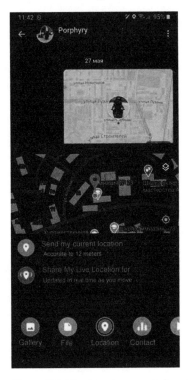

*Figure 9-1: Sharing your smartphone's live location in Telegram*

Once users start sharing their location data, the bot will start sending that data to a CSV file in the form of rows that might look as follows:

```
cab_26,43.602508,39.715685,14:47:44
cab_112,43.582243,39.752077,14:47:55
cab_26,43.607480,39.721521,14:49:11
cab_112,43.579258,39.758944,14:49:51
cab_112,43.574906,39.766325,14:51:53
cab_26,43.612203,39.720491,14:52:48
```

The first field in each row contains a username, the second and third fields contain the latitude and longitude of the user's location, and the fourth field contains a timestamp. For some tasks, such as finding the closest car to a certain pick-up location, you'd only need the latest row for each car. Other tasks, however, such as calculating the overall distance of a ride, would benefit from multiple rows of data for the given car, sorted by time.

# Spatial Data Analysis with geopy and Shapely

Spatial data analysis boils down to answering questions about relationships: Which object is closest to a certain location? Are two objects in the same area? In this section, you'll answer these common spatial analysis questions using two Python libraries, geopy and Shapely, all within the context of our example taxi service.

Since geopy is designed for performing calculations based on geo coordinates, it's particularly suited for answering questions about distance. Meanwhile, Shapely specializes in defining and analyzing geometric planes, so it's ideal for determining whether an object falls within a certain area. As you'll see, both libraries can play a role in identifying the best cab for a given job.

Before you proceed, install the libraries as follows:

```
$ pip install geopy
$ pip install shapely
```

## Finding the Closest Object

Continuing with our taxi service example, we'll look at how to use location data to identify the closest cab to a pick-up place. To start, you'll need some sample location data. If you deployed the Telegram bot discussed in the previous section, you may already have some data in the form of a CSV file. Here, you load the data into a pandas DataFrame so you can easily sort and filter it:

```
import pandas as pd
df = pd.read_csv("HOME/PI/LOCATION_BOT/LOG.CSV", names=['cab', 'lat',
                                                        'long', 'tm'])
```

If you didn't deploy a Telegram bot, you can instead create a list of tuples with some sample location data and load it into a DataFrame as follows:

```
import pandas as pd
locations = [
  ('cab_26',43.602508,39.715685,'14:47:44'),
  ('cab_112',43.582243,39.752077,'14:47:55'),
  ('cab_26',43.607480,39.721521,'14:49:11'),
  ('cab_112',43.579258,39.758944,'14:49:51'),
  ('cab_112',43.574906,39.766325,'14:51:53'),
```

```
('cab_26',43.612203,39.720491,'14:52:48')
]

df = pd.DataFrame(locations, columns =['cab', 'lat', 'long', 'tm'])
```

Either way, you'll get a DataFrame called df with columns for the cab ID, latitude, longitude, and timestamp.

**NOTE**    *If you'd like to build your own set of sample location data to manipulate, a simple method is to look up latitude and longitude coordinates using Google Maps. When you right-click a location on a map, the location's latitude and longitude coordinates will be the first thing to show up in the menu.*

The DataFrame has multiple rows for each cab, but to identify the cab closest to a pick-up place, you only need each cab's most recent location. You can filter out the unnecessary rows as follows:

```
latestrows = df.sort_values(['cab','tm'],ascending=False).drop_duplicates('cab')
```

Here, you sort the rows by the cab and tm fields in descending order. This operation groups the dataset by the cab column and puts the latest row for each cab first within its group. Then you apply the drop_duplicates() method to eliminate all but the first row for each cab. The resulting latestrows DataFrame looks as follows:

```
      cab        lat       long        tm
5   cab_26   43.612203   39.720491   14:52:48
3   cab_112  43.574906   39.766325   14:51:53
```

You now have a DataFrame with just the most recent location data for each cab. For the convenience of future computing, you next convert the DataFrame into a simpler Python structure, a list of lists. This way you'll be able to more easily append new fields to each row, such as a field for the distance between the cab and the pick-up place:

```
latestrows = latestrows.values.tolist()
```

The values property of latestrows returns a NumPy representation of the DataFrame, which you then convert to a list of lists using tolist().

You're now ready to calculate the distance between each cab and a pick-up place. You'll use the geopy library, which can accomplish this task with just a few lines of code. Here you use the distance() function from geopy's distance module to make the necessary calculations:

```
from geopy.distance import distance
pick_up = 43.578854, 39.754995

for i,row in enumerate(latestrows):
❶ dist = distance(pick_up, (row[1],row[2])).m
  print(row[0] + ':', round(dist))
  latestrows[i].append(round(dist))
```

For simplicity, you set the pick-up place by manually defining the latitude and longitude coordinates. In practice, however, you might use Google's Geocoding API to generate the coordinates automatically from a street address, as discussed earlier in the chapter. Next, you iterate over each row in your dataset and calculate the distance between each cab and the pick-up place by calling distance() ❶. This function takes two tuples containing latitude/longitude coordinates as arguments. By adding .m, you retrieve the distance in meters. For demonstration purposes, you'll print the result of each distance calculation; then you append it to the end of the row as a new field. The script produces the following output:

```
cab_112: 1015
cab_26: 4636
```

Clearly cab_112 is closer, but how can you determine that programmatically? Use Python's built-in min() function, as follows:

```
closest = min(latestrows, key=lambda x: x[4])
print('The closest cab is: ', closest[0], ' - the distance in meters: ', closest[4])
```

You feed the data to min() and use a lambda function to evaluate its sorting order based on the item at index 4 of each row. This is the newly appended distance calculation. You then print the result in a human-readable format, yielding the following:

```
The closest cab is:  cab_112  - the distance in meters:  1015
```

In this example, you calculated the straight-line distance between each cab and the pick-up location. While this information can certainly be useful, real-world cars almost never drive in a perfectly straight line from one place to another. The layout of streets means that the actual distance a cab must drive to reach a pick-up location will be greater than the straight-line distance. With this in mind, next we'll look at a more reliable way to match pick-up locations to cabs.

## Finding Objects in a Certain Area

Often, the right question to ask to determine the best cab for a job isn't "Which cab is the closest?" but rather "Which cab is in a certain area that includes the pick-up location?" This isn't just because the driving distance between two points is almost always greater than the straight-line distance between them. In practice, barriers such as rivers or railroad tracks often divide geographical areas into separate zones that are only connected at a limited number of points by bridges, tunnels, and the like. This can make straight-line distances highly misleading. Consider the example in Figure 9-2.

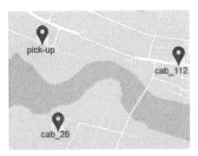

*Figure 9-2: Obstacles like rivers can make distance measurements misleading.*

As you can see, `cab_26` is spatially closest to the pick-up place in this scenario, but because of the river, `cab_112` will likely be able to get there faster. You can easily figure this out looking at the map, but how can you reach the same conclusion with a Python script? One way is to divide the area into a number of smaller *polygons*, or areas enclosed by a set of connected straight lines, and then check which cabs are within the same polygon as the pick-up location.

In this particular example, you should define a polygon that encompasses the pick-up location and has a boundary along the river. You can identify the polygon's boundaries manually through Google Maps: right-click several points that connect to form a closed polygon, and note each point's geo coordinates. Once you have the coordinates, you can define the polygon in Python using the Shapely library.

Here's how to create a polygon with Shapely and check whether a given point is inside that polygon:

```
❶ from shapely.geometry import Point, Polygon

  coords = [(46.082991, 38.987384), (46.075489, 38.987599), (46.079395,
            38.997684), (46.073822, 39.007297), (46.081741, 39.008842)]
❷ poly = Polygon(coords)
❸ cab_26 = Point(46.073852, 38.991890)
  cab_112 = Point(46.078228, 39.003949)
  pick_up = Point(46.080074, 38.991289)

❹ print('cab_26 within the polygon:', cab_26.within(poly))
  print('cab_112 within the polygon:', cab_112.within(poly))
  print('pick_up within the polygon:', pick_up.within(poly))
```

You first import two Shapely classes, `Point` and `Polygon` ❶, then you create a `Polygon` object using a list of latitude/longitude tuples ❷. This object represents the area north of the river, including the pick-up location. Next, you create several `Point` objects representing the locations of `cab_26`, `cab_112`, and the pick-up place, respectively ❸. Finally, you perform a series of spatial queries to detect if a certain point is inside the polygon using Shapely's within() method ❹. As a result, the script should produce the following output:

```
cab_26 within the polygon: False
cab_112 within the polygon: True
pick_up within the polygon: True
```

---

**EXERCISE #14: DEFINING TWO OR MORE POLYGONS**

In the preceding section, you used a single polygon covering an area on the map. Now try defining two or more polygons covering adjacent urban areas divided by an obstacle such as a river. Obtain coordinates for these polygons using the Google map of your own city or town, or of any other urban area on the planet. You'll also need the coordinates of several points within those polygons to simulate the locations of some cabs and a pick-up place.

In your script, define the polygons with Shapely and group them into a dictionary, then group the points representing the cabs into another dictionary. Next, divide the cabs into groups based on which polygon they're located in. This can be accomplished using two loops: the outer one to iterate over the polygons and the inner one to iterate over the points representing the cabs, checking whether a point is within a polygon on each iteration of the inner loop. The following code fragment illustrates how this might be implemented:

```
--snip--
cabs_dict ={}
polygons = {'poly1': poly1, 'poly2': poly2}
cabs = {'cab_26': cab_26, 'cab_112': cab_112}
for poly_name, poly in polygons.items():
  cabs_dict[poly_name] = []
  for cab_name, cab in cabs.items():
    if cab.within(poly):
      cabs_dict[poly_name].append(cab_name)
--snip--
```

Next, you'll need to determine which polygon contains the pick-up place. Once you know it, you can select the corresponding list of cabs from the cabs_dict dictionary, using the name of the polygon as the key. Finally, use geopy to determine which cab within the chosen polygon is closest to the pick-up location.

---

## Combining Both Approaches

So far, we've chosen the best cab for a pick-up by calculating linear distances and by finding the closest cab within a certain area. In fact, the most accurate way to find the right cab may be to use elements of both approaches. This is because it isn't necessarily safe to blindly exclude all the cabs that aren't in the same polygon as the pick-up location. A cab in an adjacent polygon may still be closest in terms of actual driving distance even allowing for the possibility that the cab must get around a river or other obstacle. The key is to consider the entry points between one polygon and another. Figure 9-3 shows how we might take this into account.

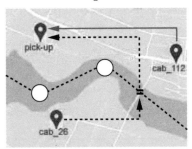

Figure 9-3: Using entry points to connect adjacent areas

The dotted line running across the middle of the figure represents the boundary dividing the area into two polygons: the one north of the river and the one south of the river. The equal sign laid on the bridge marks the entry point where cabs can move from one polygon to the other. For cabs in the polygon bordering that of the pick-up place, the distance to the pick-up place is composed of two intervals: the interval between the cab's current location and the entry point, and the interval between the entry point and the pick-up place.

To find the closest cab, you should therefore determine which polygon each cab is in and use that determination to decide how to calculate the distance from that cab to the pick-up location: either a direct straight-line distance if the cab is in the same polygon as the pick-up location, or the distance by way of the entry point if it's in an adjacent polygon. Here you make that calculation just for cab_26:

```
from shapely.geometry import Point, Polygon
from geopy.distance import distance

coords = [(46.082991, 38.987384), (46.075489, 38.987599), (46.079395,
        38.997684), (46.073822, 39.007297), (46.081741, 39.008842)]
❶ poly = Polygon(coords)
❷ cab_26 = Point(46.073852, 38.991890)
pick_up = Point(46.080074, 38.991289)
entry_point = Point(46.075357, 39.000298)

if cab_26.within(poly):
❸ dist = distance((pick_up.x, pick_up.y), (cab_26.x,cab_26.y)).m
else:
❹ dist = distance((cab_26.x,cab_26.y), (entry_point.x,entry_point.y)).m +
        distance((entry_point.x,entry_point.y), (pick_up.x, pick_up.y)).m

print(round(dist))
```

The script uses both Shapely and geopy. First you define a Shapely Polygon object including the pick-up location, as before ❶. You likewise define Point objects for the cab, the pick-up location, and the entry point ❷. Then you calculate the distance in meters with the help of geopy's distance() function. If the cab is within the polygon, you find the distance directly between the cab and the pick-up location ❸. If not, you first calculate the distance between the cab and the entry point and then the distance between the entry point and the pick-up place, summing them to get the total distance ❹. Here's the result:

```
1544
```

---

**EXERCISE #15: FURTHER IMPROVING THE PICK-UP ALGORITHM**

In the script we just discussed, you processed the location data related to a single cab to determine the distance between this cab and the pick-up place. Modify the script so that it can determine the distances between the pick-up place and each of several cabs. You'll need to group the points representing cabs into a list and then process this list in a loop, using the if/else statement from the preceding script as the loop's body. Then identify the closest cab to the pick-up place.

---

## Combining Spatial and Nonspatial Data

So far in this chapter, you've worked exclusively with spatial data, but it's important to realize that spatial analyses often need to factor in nonspatial data as well. For example, what's the use of knowing that a store is located within 10 miles of your current location if you don't know whether the item you want is currently in stock there? Or, turning back to our taxi example, what's the use of being able to determine the closest cab to a pick-up location if you don't know whether that cab is available or currently serving another order? In this section, we'll examine how to account for nonspatial data as part of a spatial analysis.

### Deriving Nonspatial Attributes

Information about the current availability of cabs could be derived from a dataset containing ride orders. Once an order is assigned to a cab, this information might be placed in an orders data structure, where orders are listed as either open (in process) or closed (completed). According to this scheme, identifying only those orders that are open would tell you which cabs are unavailable to serve a new order. Here's how you could implement this logic in Python:

```python
import pandas as pd
orders = [
    ('order_039', 'open', 'cab_14'),
```

```
        ('order_034', 'open', 'cab_79'),
        ('order_032', 'open', 'cab_104'),
        ('order_026', 'closed', 'cab_79'),
        ('order_021', 'open', 'cab_45'),
        ('order_018', 'closed', 'cab_26'),
        ('order_008', 'closed', 'cab_112')
]

df_orders = pd.DataFrame(orders, columns =['order','status','cab'])
df_orders_open = df_orders[df_orders['status']=='open']
unavailable_list = df_orders_open['cab'].values.tolist()
print(unavailable_list)
```

The orders list of tuples used in this example might be derived from a more complete dataset, such as a collection of all the orders opened within the last two hours, that includes additional information about each order (pick-up location, drop-off location, start time, end time, and so on). For simplicity, here the dataset has already been reduced to just the fields needed for the current task. You convert the list into a DataFrame, then filter it to include only the orders whose status is open. Finally, you convert the DataFrame into a list containing only the values from the cab column. This list of unavailable cabs looks as follows:

```
['cab_14', 'cab_79', 'cab_104', 'cab_45']
```

Armed with this list, you need to check the other cabs and determine which is the closest to the pick-up place. Append this code to the previous script:

```
from geopy.distance import distance
pick_up = 46.083822, 38.967845
cab_26 = 46.073852, 38.991890
cab_112 = 46.078228, 39.003949
cab_104 = 46.071226, 39.004947
cab_14 = 46.004859, 38.095825
cab_79 = 46.088621, 39.033929
cab_45 = 46.141225, 39.124934
cabs = {'cab_26': cab_26, 'cab_112': cab_112, 'cab_14': cab_14,
        'cab_104': cab_104, 'cab_79': cab_79, 'cab_45': cab_45}
dist_list = []

for cab_name, cab_loc in cabs.items():
    if cab_name not in unavailable_list:
        dist = distance(pick_up, cab_loc).m
        dist_list.append((cab_name, round(dist)))

print(dist_list)
print(min(dist_list, key=lambda x: x[1]))
```

For the purposes of the example, you manually define the geo coordinates of the pick-up place and all the cabs as tuples, and you send the coordinates of the cabs to a dictionary, where the keys are the cab names. Then you iterate over the dictionary, and for each cab not in `unavailable_list`, you use geopy to calculate the distance between the cab and the pick-up place. Finally, you print the entire list of available cabs with their distances to the pick-up place, as well as just the closest cab, yielding the following output:

```
[('cab_26', 2165), ('cab_112', 2861)]
('cab_26', 2165)
```

In this case, `cab_26` is the closest available cab.

---

**EXERCISE #16: FILTERING DATA WITH A LIST COMPREHENSION**

In the preceding section, you filtered the orders list down to just a list of unavailable cabs by first converting orders to a DataFrame. Now try generating the `unavailable_list` list without pandas, using a list comprehension instead. With this approach, you can obtain the list of cabs assigned to currently open orders with a single line of code:

```
unavailable_list = [x[2] for x in orders if x[1] == 'open']
```

After this replacement, you won't need to change anything else in the rest of the script.

---

## Joining Spatial and Nonspatial Datasets

In the previous example, you kept the spatial data (each cab's location) and the nonspatial data (which cabs were available) in separate data structures. Sometimes, however, it may be advantageous to combine spatial and nonspatial data in the same structure.

Consider that a cab may need to satisfy some other conditions apart from availability to be assigned to an order. For example, a client may need a cab with a baby seat. To find the right cab, you'll need to rely on a dataset that includes nonspatial information about the cabs as well as each cab's distance from the pick-up location. For the former, you may use a dataset that contains just two columns: the cab name and the presence of a baby seat. You create it here:

```
cabs_list = [
  ('cab_14',1),
  ('cab_79',0),
  ('cab_104',0),
  ('cab_45',1),
  ('cab_26',0),
  ('cab_112',1)
]
```

Cabs with a 1 in the second column have a baby seat. Next you convert the list to a DataFrame. You also create a second DataFrame from dist_list, the list of available cabs and their distances to the pick-up place that you generated in the preceding section:

```
df_cabs = pd.DataFrame(cabs_list, columns =['cab', 'seat'])
df_dist = pd.DataFrame(dist_list, columns =['cab', 'dist'])
```

You now merge these DataFrames based on the cab column:

```
df = pd.merge(df_cabs, df_dist, on='cab', how='inner')
```

You use an inner join, meaning only cabs included in both df_cabs and df_dist make it into the new DataFrame. In practice, since df_dist contains only cabs that are currently available, this excludes unavailable cabs from the result set. The merged DataFrame now includes both spatial data (each cab's distance to the pick-up place) and nonspatial data (whether or not each cab has a baby seat):

```
       cab  seat  dist
0   cab_26     0  2165
1  cab_112     1  2861
```

You convert the DataFrame into a list of tuples, which you then filter, leaving only the rows where the seat field is set to 1:

```
result_list = list(df.itertuples(index=False,name=None))
result_list = [x for x in result_list if x[1] == 1]
```

You use the DataFrame's itertuples() method to convert each row into a tuple, then you wrap the tuples into a list with the list() function.

The final step is to determine the row with the lowest value in the distance field, which is identified by index 2:

```
print(min(result_list, key=lambda x: x[2]))
```

Here's the result:

```
('cab_112', 1, 2861)
```

Compare this to the result shown at the end of the previous section. As you can see, the need for a baby seat led us to choose a different cab for the job.

## Summary

Using the real-world example of a taxi service, this chapter illustrated how you can perform spatial data analyses. To start with, you looked at an example of turning a human-readable address into geo coordinates using Google's Geocoding API and the googlemaps Python library. Then you learned to use a Telegram bot to collect location data from smartphones. Next, you used the geopy and Shapely libraries to perform fundamental geospatial operations, such as measuring the distance between points and determining if points are within a certain area. With the help of these libraries, built-in Python data structures, and pandas DataFrames, you designed an application to identify the best cab for a given pick-up based on various spatial and nonspatial criteria.

# 10

## ANALYZING TIME SERIES DATA

*Time series data,* or *timestamped data,* is a set of data points indexed in chronological order. Common examples include economic indices, weather records, and patient health indicators, all captured over time. This chapter covers techniques for analyzing time series data and extracting meaningful statistics from it using the pandas library. We'll focus on analyzing stock market data, but the same techniques can be applied to all kinds of time series data.

### Regular vs. Irregular Time Series

A time series can be created for any variable that changes over time, and those changes can be recorded either at regular or irregular time intervals. Regular intervals are more common. In finance, for example, it's typical to use a time series to track the price of a stock from one day to the next, as shown here:

```
Date         Closing Price
-----------  -------------
16-FEB-2022  10.26
17-FEB-2022  10.34
18-FEB-2022  10.99
```

As you can see, the `Date` column in this time series contains timestamps, arranged in chronological order, for a sequence of consecutive days. The corresponding data points, often referred to as *observations*, are presented in the `Closing Price` column. Time series of this type are said to be *regular* or *continuous* because the observations are made continuously through time at regular intervals.

Another example of a regular time series would be a collection of latitude and longitude coordinates for a vehicle, recorded every minute, as shown here:

```
Time      Coordinates
-------   ----------------
20:43:00  37.801618, -122.374308
20:44:00  37.796599, -122.379432
20:45:00  37.788443, -122.388526
```

Here the timestamps are times, not dates, but they still proceed in chronological order, minute by minute.

Unlike regular time series, *irregular time series* are used to record sequences of events as they occur or are planned to occur, not at regular intervals. As a simple example, consider the agenda of a conference:

```
Time      Event
-------   ----------------
8:00 AM   Registration
9:00 AM   Morning Sessions
12:10 PM  Lunch
12:30 PM  Afternoon Sessions
```

The timestamps for this series of data points are irregularly distributed, based on the amount of time each event is expected to take.

Irregular time series are commonly used in applications where the data comes unpredictably. For software developers, a typical irregular time series would be a log of errors encountered while running a server or executing an application. It's hard to predict when the errors will occur, and they almost certainly won't happen at regular intervals. To give another example, an application that tracks electricity consumption may use an irregular time series to record anomalies such as bursts and failures that occur randomly.

What regular and irregular time series have in common is that data points in them are listed in chronological order. Indeed, time series analysis hinges on this key feature. Strict chronological order is what allows you to consistently compare events or values within a time series, identifying key statistics and trends.

In the case of stock data, for example, the chronological order lets you track a stock's performance over time. In the case of the minute-by-minute geo coordinates of a vehicle, you might use adjacent pairs of coordinates to calculate the distance driven each minute and then use that distance to compare the vehicle's average speed from one minute to the next. Meanwhile, the chronological order of the conference agenda lets you immediately see the expected duration of each event.

In some cases, the timestamps themselves may not actually be needed to analyze the time series; all that matters is that the records in the series are in chronological order. Consider the following irregular time series of two consecutive error messages your script might return when trying to connect to a MySQL database with the wrong password:

```
_mysql_connector.MySQLInterfaceError: Access denied for user
'root'@'localhost' (using password: YES)
NameError: name 'cursor' is not defined
```

The second error message tells you that the variable named cursor hasn't been defined. However, the root of the problem can be understood only if you look at the preceding error message: since the password was incorrect, no connection could be established to the database, so no cursor object could be created.

Analyzing a sequence of error messages is a common task for programmers, but it's usually done manually, without any coding. For the rest of the chapter, we'll focus on time series with numeric data points, since these can readily be analyzed using Python scripts. In particular, we'll look at how to extract meaningful information from regular time series containing stock market data.

## Common Time Series Analysis Techniques

Suppose you want to analyze a time series of daily closing stock prices for a given stock over a certain period of time. In this section, you'll learn some common techniques to use in your analysis, but first you'll need some stock data.

As you saw in Chapters 3 and 5, you can obtain stock market data within a Python script using the yfinance library. Here, for example, you gather the stock data for the TSLA (Tesla, Inc.) ticker for the last five trading days:

```
import yfinance as yf
ticker = 'TSLA'
tkr = yf.Ticker(ticker)
df = tkr.history(period='5d')
```

The result takes the form of a pandas DataFrame and will look something like the following (your dates and the data returned will vary):

| Date | Open | High | Low | Close | Volume | Dividends | Stock Splits |
|---|---|---|---|---|---|---|---|
| 2022-01-10 | 1000.00 | 1059.09 | 980.00 | 1058.11 | 30605000 | 0 | 0 |
| 2022-01-11 | 1053.67 | 1075.84 | 1038.81 | 1064.40 | 22021100 | 0 | 0 |
| 2022-01-12 | 1078.84 | 1114.83 | 1072.58 | 1106.21 | 27913000 | 0 | 0 |
| 2022-01-13 | 1109.06 | 1115.59 | 1026.54 | 1031.56 | 32403300 | 0 | 0 |
| 2022-01-14 | 1019.88 | 1052.00 | 1013.38 | 1049.60 | 24246600 | 0 | 0 |

As you can see, the DataFrame is indexed by date, meaning the data is a proper, chronologically arranged time series. There are columns for the opening and closing price as well as the day's high and low prices. Meanwhile, the Volume column shows the total number of shares traded that day, and the two rightmost columns provide details about the dividends and splits the company has given to its shareholders.

You likely won't need all of these columns for your analysis. In fact, for now you just need the Close column. Here you print it out as a pandas Series:

```
print(df['Close'])
```

The Series will look similar to the following:

```
Date
2022-01-10    1058.11
2022-01-11    1064.40
2022-01-12    1106.21
2022-01-13    1031.56
2022-01-14    1049.60
```

Now you're ready to begin your time series analysis. We'll focus on two common techniques: calculating percentage changes over time and performing aggregate calculations within a rolling time window. You'll see how these techniques can work together to reveal trends in the data.

### Calculating Percentage Changes

Perhaps the most typical time series analysis technique is to track how much the observed data changes over time. In the case of stock market data, this might involve calculating the percentage change of a stock value over a certain time interval. This way, you can quantify how the stock is performing and develop a short-term investment strategy.

Technically speaking, a percentage change is the difference (expressed as a percent) between values from two different points in time. To calculate such a change, you therefore need to be able to shift data points in time. That is, you shift the older data point forward in time so it aligns with the newer data point; then you can compare the data points and calculate the percentage change.

When a time series is implemented as a pandas Series or DataFrame, you can use the shift() method to shift data points in time by the desired number of periods. Continuing with our TSLA ticker example, you might want to know how much the stock's closing price has changed over a period of two days. In this case, you'd use shift(2) to bring the closing price from two days earlier in line with the closing price for a given day. To get a feel for how shifting works, here you shift the Close column forward two days, save the result as 2DaysShift, and concatenate the result with the original Close column:

```
print(pd.concat([df['Close'], df['Close'].shift(2)], axis=1, keys= ['Close', '2DaysShift']))
```

The output should look something like this:

```
            Close   2DaysShift
Date
2022-01-10  1058.11        NaN
2022-01-11  1064.40        NaN
2022-01-12  1106.21    1058.11
2022-01-13  1031.56    1064.40
2022-01-14  1049.60    1106.21
```

As you can see, the values in the Close column are echoed in the 2DaysShift column, offset by two days. The first two values in 2DaysShift are NaN because you don't have prices from two days earlier for the first two days in the time series.

To find the percentage change between the price from two days earlier and the price for a given day, you could take the difference between the given day's value and the earlier value and divide it by the earlier value:

```
(df['Close'] - df['Close'].shift(2))/ df['Close'].shift(2)
```

In financial analysis, however, it's common to instead divide the new value by the old value and take the natural logarithm of the result. This calculation provides an almost exact approximation of the percentage change when the change is within the range +/– 5 percent, and it remains very close up to +/– 20 percent. Here, you calculate the two-day percentage difference using the natural logarithm and store the result as a new column called 2daysRise in the df DataFrame:

```
import numpy as np
df['2daysRise'] = np.log(df['Close'] / df['Close'].shift(2))
```

You obtain a day's closing price and divide it by the closing price two trading days earlier, accessed using shift(2). Then you use NumPy's log() function to take the natural logarithm of the result. Now you can print the Close and 2daysRise columns of the DataFrame:

```
print(df[['Close','2daysRise']])
```

The outputted time series will look similar to the following:

```
            Close   2daysRise
Date
2022-01-10  1058.11        NaN
2022-01-11  1064.40        NaN
2022-01-12  1106.21   0.044455
2022-01-13  1031.56  -0.031339
2022-01-14  1049.60  -0.052530
```

The 2daysRise column shows the percentage change of the stock compared to two days earlier. Once again, the first two values in the column are NaN because you don't have prices from two days earlier for the first two days in the time series.

## Rolling Window Calculations

Another common time series analysis technique is to compare each value with the average value over *n* periods. This is called a *rolling window calculation*: you create a time window of a fixed size and perform an aggregate calculation on the values within that time window as it moves, or *rolls*, across the time series. In the case of stock data, you might use a rolling window calculation to find the average closing price of the two previous days, then compare the current day's closing price with that average. This would give you a sense of the stock price's stability over time.

Every pandas object has a rolling() method for looking at a rolling window of values. Here, you use it in combination with shift() and mean() to find the average Tesla stock price for the previous two days:

```
df['2daysAvg'] = df['Close'].shift(1).rolling(2).mean()
print(df[['Close', '2daysAvg']])
```

In the first line, you use shift(1) to shift the data points in the series by one day. You do this because you want to exclude the current day's price when calculating an average to be compared with it. Next, you form the rolling window with rolling(2), indicating that you want to draw on two consecutive rows when you make your calculations. Finally, you invoke the mean() method to calculate an average for each pair of consecutive rows covered by the rolling window. You store the results in a new column called 2daysAvg, which you print, along with the Close column. The resulting DataFrame will look something like this:

```
            Close  2daysAvg
Date
2022-01-10  1058.11      NaN
2022-01-11  1064.40      NaN
2022-01-12  1106.21  1061.26
2022-01-13  1031.56  1085.30
2022-01-14  1049.60  1068.89
```

The prices in the 2daysAvg column are averages of the two previous trading days. For example, the value assigned to 2022-01-12 is the average of the prices on 2022-01-10 and 2022-01-11.

### Calculating the Percentage Change of a Rolling Average

Given a rolling average of the previous two days' closing prices, the next logical step is to calculate the percentage change between each day's price and its associated rolling average. Here you perform that calculation, once again using the natural logarithm to approximate the percentage change:

```
df['2daysAvgRise'] = np.log(df['Close'] / df['2daysAvg'])
print(df[['Close','2daysRise','2daysAvgRise']])
```

You store the results in a new column called 2daysAvgRise. Then you print the Close, 2daysRise, and 2daysAvgRise columns together. The output will look similar to this:

|            | Close   | 2daysRise | 2daysAvgRise |
|------------|---------|-----------|--------------|
| Date       |         |           |              |
| 2022-01-10 | 1058.11 | NaN       | NaN          |
| 2022-01-11 | 1064.40 | NaN       | NaN          |
| 2022-01-12 | 1106.21 | 0.044455  | 0.041492     |
| 2022-01-13 | 1031.56 | -0.031339 | -0.050793    |
| 2022-01-14 | 1049.60 | -0.052530 | -0.018202    |

For this particular time series, both of the newly created metrics, 2daysRise and 2daysAvgRise, show both negative and positive values. This indicates that the stock's closing price was volatile throughout the period of observation. Of course, your own results might reveal a different trend.

## Multivariate Time Series

A *multivariate time series* is a time series with more than one variable that changes over time. When you first obtained the Tesla stock data through the yfinance library, for example, it came as a multivariate time series, since it included not just the stock's closing price but also the opening price, high and low prices, and several other data points for each day. In this case, the multivariate time series tracked multiple features of the same object, an individual stock. Other multivariate time series may track the same feature of several different objects, such as the closing prices of multiple stocks gathered for the same period of time.

In the following script, you create this second type of a multivariate time series, obtaining five days' worth of stock data for multiple tickers:

```
import pandas as pd
import yfinance as yf
❶ stocks = pd.DataFrame()
❷ tickers = ['MSFT','TSLA','GM','AAPL','ORCL','AMZN']
```

```
❸ for ticker in tickers:
       tkr = yf.Ticker(ticker)
       hist = tkr.history(period='5d')
❹  hist = pd.DataFrame(hist[['Close']].rename(columns={'Close': ticker}))
❺  if stocks.empty:
    ❻  stocks = hist
       else:
    ❼  stocks = stocks.join(hist)
```

You first define the stocks DataFrame ❶, where you'll accumulate the closing prices for multiple tickers. Then you define a list of tickers ❷ and iterate over the list ❸, using the yfinance library to obtain the last five days of data for each ticker. Within the loop, you reduce the hist DataFrame returned by yfinance to a single-column DataFrame containing the closing prices of the given stock, along with the corresponding timestamps as the index ❹. You then check if the stocks DataFrame is empty ❺. If it is, it's your first time through the loop, so you initialize the stocks DataFrame with the hist DataFrame ❻. On subsequent iterations, stocks won't be empty, so you join the current hist DataFrame to the stocks DataFrame, adding another ticker's closing prices to the dataset ❼. The if/else structure is needed because you can't perform a join operation on an empty DataFrame.

The resulting stocks DataFrame will look similar to the following:

```
                MSFT     TSLA     GM     AAPL    ORCL     AMZN
Date
2022-01-10    314.26  1058.11  61.07  172.19   89.27  3229.71
2022-01-11    314.98  1064.40  61.45  175.08   88.48  3307.23
2022-01-12    318.26  1106.21  61.02  175.52   88.30  3304.13
2022-01-13    304.79  1031.56  61.77  172.19   87.79  3224.28
2022-01-14    310.20  1049.60  61.09  173.07   87.69  3242.76
```

You have a multivariate time series, with the different columns showing the closing prices of different stocks, all across the same span of time.

## Processing Multivariate Time Series

Processing multivariate time series is similar to working with single-variable time series except that you have to deal with several variables within each row. Therefore, your calculations often occur inside a loop iterating over the columns in the series. For example, suppose you want to filter the stocks DataFrame, weeding out the tickers whose prices dropped more than some threshold (say, 3 percent) below the previous day's price at least once in the given period. Here you iterate over the columns and analyze the data for each ticker to determine which stocks should be kept in the DataFrame:

```
❶ stocks_to_keep = []
❷ for i in stocks.columns:
       if stocks[stocks[i]/stocks[i].shift(1)< .97].empty:
           stocks_to_keep.append(i)
   print(stocks_to_keep)
```

First, you create a list to accumulate the column names you want to keep ❶. Then you iterate over the columns of the stocks DataFrame ❷, determining whether each column contains any values that are more than 3 percent lower than the value in the previous row. Specifically, you use the [] operator to filter the DataFrame and the shift() method to compare each day's closing price to that of the previous day. If a column doesn't contain any values that meet the filtering condition (that is, if the filtered column is empty), you append the column name to the stocks_to_keep list.

Given the stocks DataFrame shown previously, the resulting stocks_to_keep list will look as follows:

```
['GM', 'AAPL', 'ORCL', 'AMZN']
```

As you can see, TSLA and MSFT aren't in the list, because they contained one or more values that fell more than 3 percent below the previous day's closing price. Of course, your own results will vary; you might end up with an empty list or a list that includes all the tickers. In those cases, try experimenting with the filtering threshold. If the list is empty, try decreasing the threshold from 0.97 to 0.96 or lower. In contrast, if the list includes all the tickers, try increasing the threshold.

Here you print the stocks DataFrame so that it includes only the columns from the stocks_to_keep list:

```
print(stocks[stocks_to_keep])
```

In my case, the output looks like this:

```
               GM    AAPL    ORCL     AMZN
Date
2022-01-10  61.07  172.19  89.27  3229.71
2022-01-11  61.45  175.08  88.48  3307.23
2022-01-12  61.02  175.52  88.30  3304.13
2022-01-13  61.77  172.19  87.79  3224.28
2022-01-14  61.09  173.07  87.69  3242.76
```

As expected, the TSLA and MSFT columns have been filtered out because they contain one or more values that exceed the 3 percent threshold of volatility.

## Analyzing Dependencies Between Variables

One common task when analyzing multivariate time series is to identify relationships between different variables in the dataset. These relationships may or may not exist. For example, there's likely some degree of dependency between a stock's opening and closing prices since on a given day the closing price rarely differs from the opening price by more than a few percent. On the other hand, you may not find a dependency between the closing prices of two stocks from different sectors of the economy.

In this section, we'll look at some techniques for verifying the existence of a relationship between time series variables. To demonstrate, we'll examine whether there's a dependency between the change in a stock's price and its sales volume. To start with, run the following script to obtain a month's worth of stock data for your analysis:

```
import yfinance as yf
import numpy as np
ticker = 'TSLA'
tkr = yf.Ticker(ticker)
df = tkr.history(period='1mo')
```

As you've already seen, yfinance generates a multivariate time series in the form of a DataFrame with many columns. For the purpose of this example, you only need two of them: Close and Volume. Here, you reduce the DataFrame accordingly and change the Close column's name to Price:

```
df = df[['Close','Volume']].rename(columns={'Close': 'Price'})
```

To determine if there's a relationship between the Price and Volume columns, you should calculate the percentage change in each column from day to day. Here you calculate the daily percentage change in the Price column using shift(1) and NumPy's log() function, as discussed previously, and store the result in a new priceRise column:

```
df['priceRise'] = np.log(df['Price'] / df['Price'].shift(1))
```

You use the same technique to create a volumeRise column, which shows the percentage change in volume compared to the previous day:

```
df['volumeRise'] = np.log(df['Volume'] / df['Volume'].shift(1))
```

As noted earlier, the natural logarithm provides a close approximation of the percentage change within a range of +/− 20 percent. While some values in the volumeRise column may well exceed this range, you still can use log() here because a high degree of accuracy isn't required in this example; stock market analysis is typically more focused on predicting trends than finding exact values.

If you now print the df DataFrame, it will look something like this:

| Date | Price | Volume | priceRise | volumeRise |
|---|---|---|---|---|
| 2021-12-15 | 975.98 | 25056400 | NaN | NaN |
| 2021-12-16 | 926.91 | 27590500 | -0.051585 | 0.096342 |
| 2021-12-17 | 932.57 | 33479100 | 0.006077 | 0.193450 |
| 2021-12-20 | 899.94 | 18826700 | -0.035616 | -0.575645 |
| 2021-12-21 | 938.53 | 23839300 | 0.041987 | 0.236059 |
| 2021-12-22 | 1008.86 | 31211400 | 0.072271 | 0.269448 |
| 2021-12-23 | 1067.00 | 30904400 | 0.056020 | -0.009885 |
| 2021-12-27 | 1093.93 | 23715300 | 0.024935 | -0.264778 |

| 2021-12-28 | 1088.46 | 20108000 | -0.005013 | -0.165003 |
|---|---|---|---|---|
| 2021-12-29 | 1086.18 | 18718000 | -0.002097 | -0.071632 |
| 2021-12-30 | 1070.33 | 15680300 | -0.014700 | -0.177080 |
| 2021-12-31 | 1056.78 | 13528700 | -0.012750 | -0.147592 |
| 2022-01-03 | 1199.78 | 34643800 | 0.126912 | 0.940305 |
| 2022-01-04 | 1149.58 | 33416100 | -0.042733 | -0.036081 |
| 2022-01-05 | 1088.11 | 26706600 | -0.054954 | -0.224127 |
| 2022-01-06 | 1064.69 | 30112200 | -0.021758 | 0.120020 |
| 2022-01-07 | 1026.95 | 27919000 | -0.036090 | -0.075623 |
| 2022-01-10 | 1058.11 | 30605000 | 0.029891 | 0.091856 |
| 2022-01-11 | 1064.40 | 22021100 | 0.005918 | -0.329162 |
| 2022-01-12 | 1106.21 | 27913000 | 0.038537 | 0.237091 |
| 2022-01-13 | 1031.56 | 32403300 | -0.069876 | 0.149168 |
| 2022-01-14 | 1049.60 | 24246600 | 0.017346 | -0.289984 |

If there were a dependency between price and volume, you would expect above-average changes in price (that is, increased volatility) to correlate with above-average changes in volume. To see if this is the case, you should set some threshold for the priceRise column and view only those rows where the percentage change in price is above that threshold. Looking through the values in the priceRise column in this particular output, for example, you might choose a 5 percent threshold. Another dataset may suggest another threshold, such as 3 or 7 percent. The idea is that only a few records should cross the threshold, so as a general rule, the more volatile the stock, the higher the threshold should be.

Here you print just those rows where priceRise exceeds the threshold:

```
print(df[abs(df['priceRise']) > .05])
```

You use the abs() function to get the absolute value of a percentage change so that, for example, both 0.06 and -0.06 satisfy the condition specified here. Given the sample data shown previously, you end up with the following:

| | Price | Volume | priceRise | volumeRise |
|---|---|---|---|---|
| Date | | | | |
| 2021-12-16 | 926.91 | 27590500 | -0.051585 | 0.096342 |
| 2021-12-22 | 1008.86 | 31211400 | 0.072271 | 0.269448 |
| 2021-12-23 | 1067.00 | 30904400 | 0.056020 | -0.009885 |
| 2022-01-03 | 1199.78 | 34643800 | 0.126912 | 0.940305 |
| 2022-01-05 | 1088.11 | 26706600 | -0.054954 | -0.224127 |
| 2022-01-13 | 1031.56 | 32403300 | -0.069876 | 0.149168 |

Next, you calculate the average volume change over the entire series:

```
print(df['volumeRise'].mean().round(4))
```

For this particular series, the result is the following:

```
-0.0016
```

Finally, you calculate the average volume change for just those rows with above-average changes in price. If the result is greater than the average volume change across the entire series, you'll know there's a connection between increased volatility and increased volume:

```
print(df[abs(df['priceRise']) > .05]['volumeRise'].mean().round(4))
```

This is what you get for this particular series:

```
0.2035
```

As you can see, the average volume change calculated over the filtered series is much higher than the average volume change calculated over the entire series. This suggests there may be a positive correlation between price volatility and sales volume volatility.

---

**EXERCISE #17: ADDING MORE METRICS TO ANALYZE DEPENDENCIES**

Continuing with the DataFrame from the previous section, you may notice that although there's likely a connection between the priceRise and volumeRise columns, it isn't completely straightforward. For example, on 2022-12-16 the price dropped approximately 5 percent and the sales volume rose 10 percent, but almost the same price drop on 2022-01-05 came with a 22 percent drop in sales volume.

To understand these discrepancies, you need to look at more metrics that could correlate with sales volumes. For example, it would be interesting to look at a rolling window calculation showing the total sales volume over the two previous days. The assumption is that if a day's volume of sales exceeds (or is almost equal to) the sum of the volume for the last two days, then most likely you shouldn't expect further growth in sales volume the next day. That is, the rolling window calculation may help you predict trends in sales volume.

To test if this assumption is true, first add a volumeSum column to the DataFrame to accommodate the rolling window calculation:

```
df['volumeSum'] = df['Volume'].shift(1).rolling(2).sum().fillna(0).astype(int)
```

You shift the data points by one day to exclude the current day's volume from the sum being calculated. Then, you create a two-day rolling window and use sum() to calculate the total sales volume within that window. The values in the new column are floats by default, but you convert them to integers with astype(). Before you can do this conversion, you have to replace NaN values with zeros, which you do with the fillna() method.

Now, with the volumeSum metric in hand, you might want to look again at the most volatile days in your series:

```
print(df[abs(df['priceRise']) > .05].replace(0, np.nan).dropna())
```

For the sample data used here, here again are the days when the price changed by more than 5 percent compared to the previous day, now with the volumeSum column added:

|  | Price | Volume | priceRise | volumeRise | volumeSum |
|---|---|---|---|---|---|
| Date |  |  |  |  |  |
| 2021-12-22 | 1008.86 | 31211400 | 0.072271 | 0.269448 | 42666000 |
| 2021-12-23 | 1067.00 | 30904400 | 0.056020 | -0.009885 | 55050700 |
| 2022-01-03 | 1199.78 | 34643800 | 0.126912 | 0.940305 | 29209000 |
| 2022-01-05 | 1088.11 | 26706600 | -0.054954 | -0.224127 | 68059900 |
| 2022-01-13 | 1031.56 | 32403300 | -0.069876 | 0.149168 | 49934100 |

The figures in the volumeSum column suggest that a lower total sales volume over the two previous days is correlated with a higher potential for either growth or decline in sales volume today, and vice versa. Look, for example, at the figures for 2022-01-03: the volumeRise value for this day is the highest in the result set, while the volumeSum value is the lowest. In fact, the sales volume for this day is almost equal to the sales volume sum over the previous two days (2021-12-30 and 2021-12-31), thus showing significant growth.

Recall, however, that the original assumption was that on days like this one, where the sales volume exceeds (or roughly matches) the sum of the volume for the last two days, we shouldn't expect further growth in volume the following day. To confirm this, you can add a column showing the next day's sales volume:

```
df['nextVolume'] = df['Volume'].shift(-1).fillna(0).astype(int)
print(df[abs(df['priceRise']) > .05].replace(0, np.nan).dropna())
```

You create the nextVolume column by shifting Volume by -1 units. That is, you move the next day's volume backward in time to align with the current day. Here's the output:

|  | Price | Volume | priceRise | volumeRise | volumeSum | nextVolume |
|---|---|---|---|---|---|---|
| Date |  |  |  |  |  |  |
| 2021-12-22 | 1008.86 | 31211400 | 0.072271 | 0.269448 | 42666000 | 30904400 |
| 2021-12-23 | 1067.00 | 30904400 | 0.056020 | -0.009885 | 55050700 | 23715300 |
| 2022-01-03 | 1199.78 | 34643800 | 0.126912 | 0.940305 | 29209000 | 33416100 |
| 2022-01-05 | 1088.11 | 26706600 | -0.054954 | -0.224127 | 68059900 | 30112200 |
| 2022-01-13 | 1031.56 | 32403300 | -0.069876 | 0.149168 | 49934100 | 24246600 |

As you can see, the assumption is true for 2022-01-03: nextVolume is less than Volume. However, you may need more metrics for your analysis to be accurate. Try adding another metric that sums up the values of priceRise for the previous two days. If it shows a positive value, this means the prices generally were in an uptrend for the last two days. A negative value indicates falling prices. Use this new metric along with the already existing priceRise and volumeSum metrics to figure out how they together may affect the values in the volumeRise column.

# Summary

As you learned in this chapter, a time series is a dataset organized in chronological order, where one or more variables change over time. Taking stock market data as an example, you looked at some techniques for using pandas to analyze time series data in order to derive useful statistics from it. You learned to shift data points in a time series in order to calculate changes over time. You also learned to perform rolling window calculations, or aggregations within a fixed-size time interval that moves across the whole series. Together, these techniques help you make judgments about trends in the data. Finally, you looked at methods for identifying dependencies between different variables in a multivariate time series.

# 11

## GAINING INSIGHTS FROM DATA

Companies generate vast amounts of data every day in the form of raw facts, figures, and events, but what does all that data really tell you? To extract knowledge and gain insight from the data, you need to transform, analyze, and visualize it. In other words, you need to turn the raw data into meaningful information that you can use to make decisions, answer questions, and solve problems.

Consider the case of a supermarket that collects large volumes of customer transaction data. Analysts at the supermarket may be interested in studying this data to gain insight into customers' buying preferences. In particular, they may want to perform a *market basket analysis*, a data mining technique that analyzes transactions and identifies items that are commonly purchased together. Armed with this knowledge, the supermarket could make more informed business decisions—for instance, about the layout of items in the store, or about how to bundle items together into discounts.

In this chapter, we'll explore this example in detail, examining how to gain insights from transaction data by performing a market basket analysis with Python. You'll learn how to use the mlxtend library and the Apriori algorithm to identify items that are commonly purchased together, and you'll see how that knowledge can be leveraged to make smart business decisions.

Although identifying buyer preferences will be the focus of this chapter, this isn't the only application for a market basket analysis. The technique is also used in domains such as telecommunications, web usage mining, banking, and health care. In web usage mining, for example, a market basket analysis can determine where the user of a web page will likely go next and generate associations of pages frequently visited together.

## Association Rules

A market basket analysis is about measuring the strength of the relationships between objects based on their co-occurrence in the same transactions. The relationships between objects are represented as *association rules*, which are denoted as follows:

```
X -> Y
```

X and Y, referred to as the *antecedent* and *consequent* of the rule, respectively, represent distinct *itemsets*, or groups of one or more items from the transaction data being mined. For example, an association rule that describes a relationship between the items *curd* and *sour cream* would be denoted like so:

```
curd -> sour cream
```

In this case, curd is the antecedent and sour cream is the consequent. The rule is asserting that people who buy curd are also likely to buy sour cream.

By itself, an association rule such as this doesn't actually tell you very much. The key to a successful market basket analysis is to use the transaction data to evaluate the strength of association rules based on various metrics. To demonstrate, we'll take a simple example. Suppose we have 100 customer transactions, 25 of which contain curd and 30 of which contain sour cream. Of those 30 transactions that contain sour cream, 20 transactions also contain curd. Table 11-1 summarizes these figures.

**Table 11-1:** Transaction Figures for Curd and Sour Cream

|              | Curd | Sour cream | Curd and sour cream | Total |
|--------------|------|------------|---------------------|-------|
| **Transactions** | 25 | 30 | 20 | 100 |

Given this transaction data, we can evaluate the strength of the association rule curd `-> sour cream` using metrics such as support, confidence, and lift. These metrics will help us gauge whether or not there truly is an association between curd and sour cream.

## Support

*Support* is the ratio of transactions that include one or more items to the total number of transactions. For example, the support for curd in the sample transaction data can be calculated as follows:

```
support(curd) = curd/total = 25/100 = 0.25
```

In the context of an association rule, support is the ratio of transactions that include both the antecedent and consequent to the total number of transactions. The support of the curd `-> sour cream` association rule is therefore:

```
support(curd -> sour cream) = (curd & sour cream)/total = 20/100 = 0.2
```

The support metric falls in the range of 0 to 1, and it tells you what percent of the time an itemset appears in a transaction. In this case, we can see that 20 percent of transactions included both curd and sour cream. Support is symmetric for any given association rule; that is, the support for curd `-> sour cream` is the same as the support for sour cream `-> curd`.

## Confidence

The *confidence* of an association rule is the ratio of transactions where both the antecedent and consequent are bought to transactions where the antecedent is bought. In other words, confidence measures what share of transactions containing the antecedent also contain the consequent. The confidence for the curd `-> sour cream` association rule can be calculated as follows:

```
confidence(curd -> sour cream) = (curd & sour cream)/curd = 20/25 = 0.8
```

You can interpret this as meaning that if a customer purchased curd, there's an 80 percent likelihood that they also purchased sour cream.

Like support, confidence falls within a range of 0 to 1, but unlike support, confidence isn't symmetric. That means the confidence for the rule curd `-> sour cream` may be different from the confidence for the rule sour cream `-> curd`, as shown here:

```
confidence(sour cream -> curd) = (curd & sour cream)/sour cream = 20/30 = 0.66
```

In this case, you get a lower confidence value when the antecedent and consequent of the association rule are reversed. This tells you it's less likely that someone buying sour cream will also buy curd than it is that someone buying curd will also buy sour cream.

### Lift

*Lift* assesses the strength of an association rule compared to the random co-occurrence of the items that appear in the rule. The lift of the association rule `curd -> sour cream` is the ratio of the observed support for `curd -> sour cream` to that expected if curd and sour cream were independent of each other. This can be calculated as follows:

```
lift(sour cream -> curd) = support(curd & sour cream)/(support(curd)*support(sour cream))
                         = 0.2/(0.25*0.3) = 2.66
```

Lift values are symmetric—if you swap the antecedent and consequent, the lift remains the same. The possible values for lift range from 0 to infinity, and the larger the lift ratio, the stronger the association. In particular, a lift ratio larger than 1 indicates that the relationship between the antecedent and consequent is stronger than would be expected if they were independent, meaning the two items are often bought together. A lift ratio equal to 1 indicates no correlation between the antecedent and consequent. A lift ratio less than 1 tells you that there's a negative correlation between the antecedent and consequent, meaning they're unlikely to be purchased together. In this case, you can interpret the lift ratio of 2.66 as meaning that when a customer buys curd, there's a 166 percent increase in expectation that they will also purchase sour cream.

## The Apriori Algorithm

You've learned what association rules are and seen some metrics for evaluating their strength, but how do you actually generate association rules for a market basket analysis? One way is to use the *Apriori algorithm*, an automated process for analyzing transaction data. In general terms, the algorithm consists of two steps:

1.  Identify all the *frequent itemsets*, or groups of one or more items that appear in many transactions, in the dataset. The algorithm does this by finding all the items or groups of items whose support value exceeds a certain threshold.

2.  Generate association rules for these frequent itemsets by considering all possible binary partitions of each itemset (that is, all divisions of the itemset into an antecedent group and a consequent group) and calculating a set of association metrics for each partition.

Once the association rules have been generated, you can evaluate them based on the metrics discussed in the previous section.

Several third-party Python libraries come with implementations of the Apriori algorithm. One is the mlxtend library. Short for *machine learning extensions*, mlxtend includes tools for carrying out a number of common data science tasks. In this section, we'll walk through an example market basket analysis using mlxtend's Apriori algorithm implementation. But first, install the mlxtend library with pip, as follows:

```
$ pip install mlxtend
```

NOTE *For more information about mlxtend, consult the library's documentation at* http://rasbt.github.io/mlxtend.

## Creating a Transaction Dataset

To conduct your market basket analysis, you need some sample transaction data. For simplicity, you can use just a few transactions, defined as a list of lists, as shown here:

```
transactions = [
  ['curd', 'sour cream'], ['curd', 'orange', 'sour cream'],
  ['bread', 'cheese', 'butter'], ['bread', 'butter'], ['bread', 'milk'],
  ['apple', 'orange', 'pear'], ['bread', 'milk', 'eggs'], ['tea', 'lemon'],
  ['curd', 'sour cream', 'apple'], ['eggs', 'wheat flour', 'milk'],
  ['pasta', 'cheese'], ['bread', 'cheese'], ['pasta', 'olive oil', 'cheese'],
  ['curd', 'jam'], ['bread', 'cheese', 'butter'],
  ['bread', 'sour cream', 'butter'], ['strawberry', 'sour cream'],
  ['curd', 'sour cream'], ['bread', 'coffee'], ['onion', 'garlic']
]
```

Each inner list contains the itemset for a single transaction, with the whole transactions list containing 20 transactions in total. To maintain the quantitative proportions defined in the original curd/sour cream example, the dataset contains five transactions with curd, six transactions with sour cream, and four that contain both curd and sour cream.

To run the transaction data through mlxtend's Apriori algorithm, you need to transform it into a *one-hot encoded Boolean array*, a structure where each column represents an item that can be purchased, each row represents a transaction, and each value is either True or False (True if the transaction included that particular item or False if not). Here you perform the necessary transformation using mlxtend's TransactionEncoder object:

```
import pandas as pd
from mlxtend.preprocessing import TransactionEncoder

❶ encoder = TransactionEncoder()
❷ encoded_array = encoder.fit(transactions).transform(transactions)
❸ df_itemsets = pd.DataFrame(encoded_array, columns=encoder.columns_)
```

You create a TransactionEncoder object ❶ and use it to transform the transactions list of lists into a one-hot encoded Boolean array called encoded_array ❷. Then you convert the array into a pandas DataFrame called df_itemsets ❸, a fragment of which is shown here:

|   | apple | bread | butter | cheese | coffee | curd | eggs | ... |
|---|-------|-------|--------|--------|--------|------|------|-----|
| 0 | False | False | False  | False  | False  | True | False | ... |

```
1    False  False   False   False   False   True   False  ...
2    False  True    True    True    False  False   False  ...
3    False  True    True    False   False  False   False  ...
4    False  True    False   False   False  False   False  ...
5    True   False   False   False   False  False   False  ...
6    False  True    False   False   False  False   True   ...
--snip--

[20 rows x 20 columns]
```

The DataFrame consists of 20 rows and 20 columns, where the rows represent the transactions and the columns represent the items. To confirm that the original list of lists included 20 transactions drawing on 20 possible items, use the following code:

```
print('Number of transactions: ', len(transactions))
print('Number of unique items: ', len(set(sum(transactions, []))))
```

In both cases, you should get 20.

## Identifying Frequent Itemsets

Now that the transaction data is in a usable format, you can use mlxtend's apriori() function to identify all the frequent itemsets in the transaction data—that is, all the items or groups of items with a high enough support metric. Here's how:

```
from mlxtend.frequent_patterns import apriori
frequent_itemsets = apriori(df_itemsets, min_support=0.1, use_colnames=True)
```

You import the apriori() function from the mlxtend.frequent_patterns module. Then you call the function, passing the DataFrame containing the transaction data as the first parameter. You also set the min_support parameter to 0.1 to return the itemsets with at least 10 percent support. (Remember, the support metric indicates what percentage of the transactions an item or group of items occurs in.) You set use_colnames to True to identify the columns included in each itemset by name (such as curd or sour cream) rather than by index number. As a result, apriori() returns the following DataFrame:

```
    support           itemsets
0    0.10             (apple)
1    0.40             (bread)
2    0.20            (butter)
3    0.25            (cheese)
4    0.25              (curd)
5    0.10              (eggs)
6    0.15              (milk)
7    0.10            (orange)
8    0.10             (pasta)
9    0.30        (sour cream)
10   0.20     (bread, butter)
```

| | | | |
|---|---|---|---|
| 11 | 0.15 | (bread, cheese) | |
| 12 | 0.10 | (bread, milk) | |
| 13 | 0.10 | (cheese, butter) | |
| 14 | 0.10 | (pasta, cheese) | |
| 15 | 0.20 | (sour cream, curd) | |
| 16 | 0.10 | (milk, eggs) | |
| 17 | 0.10 | (bread, cheese, butter) | |

As noted earlier, an itemset can consist of one or more items, and indeed, apriori() has returned several single-item itemsets. Ultimately, mlxtend will omit these single-item itemsets when it formulates association rules, but it will nevertheless need data on *all* the frequent itemsets (including those with one item) to successfully generate the rules. Still, as a matter of interest, you may wish at this point to view only those itemsets with multiple items. To do so, first add a length column to the frequent_itemsets DataFrame, as follows:

```
frequent_itemsets['length'] = frequent_itemsets['itemsets'].apply(lambda itemset: len(itemset))
```

Then, use pandas's select syntax to filter the DataFrame to just those rows with a length field of 2 or more:

```
print(frequent_itemsets[frequent_itemsets['length'] >= 2])
```

You'll see the following result, without any of the single-item itemsets:

| | | | |
|---|---|---|---|
| 10 | 0.20 | (bread, butter) | 2 |
| 11 | 0.15 | (bread, cheese) | 2 |
| 12 | 0.10 | (bread, milk) | 2 |
| 13 | 0.10 | (cheese, butter) | 2 |
| 14 | 0.10 | (pasta, cheese) | 2 |
| 15 | 0.20 | (sour cream, curd) | 2 |
| 16 | 0.10 | (milk, eggs) | 2 |
| 17 | 0.10 | (bread, cheese, butter) | 3 |

To reiterate, however, mlxtend requires information on all the frequent itemsets when generating association rules. Therefore, make sure you don't actually remove any rows from the original frequent_itemsets DataFrame.

## Generating Association Rules

You've identified all the itemsets that meet the desired support threshold. The second step of the Apriori algorithm is to generate association rules for those itemsets. For this, you use the association_rules() function from mlxtend's frequent_patterns module:

```
from mlxtend.frequent_patterns import association_rules
rules = association_rules(frequent_itemsets, metric="confidence", min_threshold=0.5)
```

Here you invoke the association_rules() function, passing in the frequent_itemsets DataFrame as the first parameter. You also choose a metric for evaluating the rules and set a threshold value for that metric.

Specifically, you say that the function should only return those association rules with a confidence metric of 0.5 or more. As noted in the previous section, the function will automatically skip generating rules for single-member itemsets.

The association_rules() function returns the rules in the form of a DataFrame, where each row represents a single association rule. The DataFrame has columns for the antecedents, consequents, and various metrics, including support, confidence, and lift. Here, you print a selection of the columns:

```
print(rules.iloc[:,0:7])
```

You'll see the following output:

| | antecedents | consequents | antecedent sup. | consequent sup. | support | confidence | lift |
|---|---|---|---|---|---|---|---|
| 0 | (bread) | (butter) | 0.40 | 0.20 | 0.20 | 0.500000 | 2.500000 |
| 1 | (butter) | (bread) | 0.20 | 0.40 | 0.20 | 1.000000 | 2.500000 |
| 2 | (cheese) | (bread) | 0.25 | 0.40 | 0.15 | 0.600000 | 1.500000 |
| 3 | (milk) | (bread) | 0.15 | 0.40 | 0.10 | 0.666667 | 1.666667 |
| 4 | (butter) | (cheese) | 0.20 | 0.25 | 0.10 | 0.500000 | 2.000000 |
| 5 | (pasta) | (cheese) | 0.10 | 0.25 | 0.10 | 1.000000 | 4.000000 |
| 6 | (sour cream) | (curd) | 0.30 | 0.25 | 0.20 | 0.666667 | 2.666667 |
| 7 | (curd) | (sour cream) | 0.25 | 0.30 | 0.20 | 0.800000 | 2.666667 |
| 8 | (milk) | (eggs) | 0.15 | 0.10 | 0.10 | 0.666667 | 6.666667 |
| 9 | (eggs) | (milk) | 0.10 | 0.15 | 0.10 | 1.000000 | 6.666667 |
| 10 | (bread, cheese) | (butter) | 0.15 | 0.20 | 0.10 | 0.666667 | 3.333333 |
| 11 | (bread, butter) | (cheese) | 0.20 | 0.25 | 0.10 | 0.500000 | 2.000000 |
| 12 | (cheese, butter) | (bread) | 0.10 | 0.40 | 0.10 | 1.000000 | 2.500000 |
| 13 | (butter) | (bread, cheese) | 0.20 | 0.15 | 0.10 | 0.500000 | 3.333333 |

```
[14 rows x 7 columns]
```

Looking over these rules, some may seem redundant. For example, there's both a bread -> butter rule and a butter -> bread rule. Likewise, there are several rules based on the (bread, cheese, butter) itemset. In part, this is because, as noted earlier in the chapter, confidence isn't symmetric; if you swap the antecedent and consequent in a rule, the confidence value can change. Additionally, for a three-member itemset, the lift can change depending on which items are part of the antecedent and which are part of the consequent. Thus, (bread, cheese) -> butter has a different lift than (bread, butter) -> cheese.

## Visualizing Association Rules

As you learned in Chapter 8, visualization is a simple yet powerful technique for analyzing data. In the context of a market basket analysis, visualization provides a convenient way to evaluate the strength of a set of association rules by viewing the metrics for different antecedent/consequent pairs. In this section, you'll use Matplotlib to visualize the association rules you generated in the previous section as an annotated heatmap.

A *heatmap* is a grid-like plot where cells are color-coded to indicate their value. In this example, you'll create a heatmap showing the lift metric of the various association rules. You'll arrange all the antecedents along the y-axis and the consequents along the x-axis, and fill in the area where a rule's antecedent and consequent intersect with a color to indicate that rule's lift value. The darker the color, the higher the lift.

**NOTE** *We're visualizing the lift in this example because it's a popular metric for evaluating association rules. However, you might opt to visualize a different metric instead, such as confidence.*

To create the visualization, you first make an empty DataFrame, into which you copy the antecedents, consequents, and lift columns of the rules DataFrame created earlier:

```
rules_plot = pd.DataFrame()
rules_plot['antecedents']= rules['antecedents'].apply(lambda x: ','.join(list(x)))
rules_plot['consequents']= rules['consequents'].apply(lambda x: ','.join(list(x)))
rules_plot['lift']= rules['lift'].apply(lambda x: round(x, 2))
```

You use lambda functions to convert the values of the antecedents and consequents columns from the rules DataFrame into strings, which will make it easier to use them as labels in the visualization. Originally the values were frozensets, immutable versions of Python sets. You use another lambda function to round the lift values to two decimal places.

Next, you need to transform the newly created rules_plot DataFrame into a matrix that will be used for creating the heatmap, with the consequents arranged horizontally and the antecedents arranged vertically. For that, you can reshape rules_plot so that the unique values in the antecedents column form the index and the unique values in the consequents column become the new columns, while the values of the lift column are used for populating the reshaped DataFrame's values. You use the rules_plot DataFrame's pivot() method for this, as follows:

```
pivot = rules_plot.pivot(index = 'antecedents', columns = 'consequents', values= 'lift')
```

You specify the antecedents and consequents columns to form axes of the resulting pivot DataFrame and draw on the lift column for the values. If you print pivot, it will look like this:

| consequents<br>antecedents | bread | butter | cheese | cheese,bread | curd | eggs | milk | sour cream |
|---|---|---|---|---|---|---|---|---|
| bread | NaN | 2.50 | NaN | NaN | NaN | NaN | NaN | NaN |
| bread,butter | NaN | NaN | 2.0 | NaN | NaN | NaN | NaN | NaN |
| butter | 2.50 | NaN | 2.0 | 3.33 | NaN | NaN | NaN | NaN |
| cheese | 1.50 | NaN | NaN | NaN | NaN | NaN | NaN | NaN |
| cheese,bread | NaN | 3.33 | NaN | NaN | NaN | NaN | NaN | NaN |
| cheese,butter | 2.50 | NaN | NaN | NaN | NaN | NaN | NaN | NaN |
| curd | NaN | NaN | NaN | NaN | NaN | NaN | NaN | 2.67 |
| eggs | NaN | NaN | NaN | NaN | NaN | NaN | 6.67 | NaN |

| | | | | | | | | | |
|---|---|---|---|---|---|---|---|---|---|
| milk | 1.67 | NaN | NaN | | NaN | NaN | 6.67 | NaN | NaN |
| pasta | NaN | NaN | 4.0 | | NaN | NaN | NaN | NaN | NaN |
| sour cream | NaN | NaN | NaN | | NaN | 2.67 | NaN | NaN | NaN |

This DataFrame contains everything you need to build your heatmap: the values of the index (the antecedents) will become the y-axis labels, the names of the columns (the consequents) will become the x-axis labels, and the grid of numbers and NaNs will become the values for the plot. (In this context, a NaN indicates no association rule was generated for that antecedent/consequent pair.) Here, you extract these components into separate variables:

```
antecedents = list(pivot.index.values)
consequents = list(pivot.columns)
import numpy as np
pivot = pivot.to_numpy()
```

Now you have the y-axis labels in the antecedents list, the x-axis labels in the consequents list, and the values for the plot in the pivot NumPy array. You use all these components in the following script to build the heatmap with Matplotlib:

```
   import matplotlib
   import matplotlib.pyplot as plt
   import numpy as np
   fig, ax = plt.subplots()
❶ im = ax.imshow(pivot, cmap = 'Reds')
   ax.set_xticks(np.arange(len(consequents)))
   ax.set_yticks(np.arange(len(antecedents)))
   ax.set_xticklabels(consequents)
   ax.set_yticklabels(antecedents)
❷ plt.setp(ax.get_xticklabels(), rotation=45, ha="right",
           rotation_mode="anchor")
❸ for i in range(len(antecedents)):
       for j in range(len(consequents)):
         ❹ if not np.isnan(pivot[i, j]):
           ❺ text = ax.text(j, i, pivot[i, j], ha="center", va="center")
   ax.set_title("Lift metric for frequent itemsets")
   fig.tight_layout()
   plt.show()
```

The key points of plotting with Matplotlib were covered in Chapter 8. Here, we'll only consider the lines specific to this particular example. The imshow() method converts the data from the pivot array into a color-coded 2D image ❶. With the method's cmap parameter, you specify how to map the numeric values from the array to colors. Matplotlib has a number of built-in color mappings you can choose from, including the Reds mapping used here.

After creating the axis labels, you use the setp() method to rotate the x-axis labels by 45 degrees ❷. This helps fit the labels within the horizontal space allotted. Then, you loop over the data in the pivot array ❸ and create text annotations for each square in the heatmap using the text() method ❺. The first two parameters, j and i, are the x- and y-coordinates for the label. The next parameter, pivot[i, j], is the text of the label, and the remaining parameters set the label's justification. Before calling the text() method, you use an if statement to filter out the antecedent/consequent pairs without any lift data ❹. Otherwise, a NaN label would appear in each empty square of the heatmap.

Figure 11-1 shows the resulting visualization.

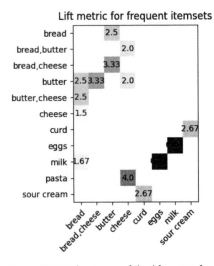

Figure 11-1: A heatmap of the lift metric for the sample association rules

The heatmap helps you immediately see which association rules have the highest lift values based on the darkness of the shading. Looking at this visualization, you can state with a high degree of certainty that a customer who buys milk is also likely to buy eggs. Similarly, you can be pretty sure that a customer who buys pasta will also buy cheese. Other associations, such as butter with cheese, also exist, but as you can see, they aren't backed as strongly by the lift metric.

The heatmap also illustrates how the lift metric is symmetric. Look, for example, at the values of the bread -> butter and butter -> bread rules. They're the same. You may notice, however, that some antecedent/consequent pairs in the plot don't have a symmetric lift value. For example, the lift for the cheese -> bread rule is shown as 1.5, but there isn't a lift value for bread -> cheese on the plot. This is because when you originally generated the association rules with mlxtend's association_rules() function, you set a 50 percent confidence threshold. This excluded many potential association rules, including bread -> cheese, which has a 37.5 percent confidence rating compared to the 60 percent confidence rating of cheese -> bread. Thus, no data for a bread -> cheese rule was available to plot.

## Gaining Actionable Insights from Association Rules

Using the Apriori algorithm, you identified the frequent itemsets in a sample batch of transaction data, and you generated association rules based on those itemsets. These rules tell you, in essence, how likely it is that a customer will buy one product if they've bought another, and by visualizing the rules' lift metrics on a heatmap, you saw which rules were particularly convincing. The next logical question to consider is how a business could actually benefit from this information.

In this section, we'll look at two different ways a business could derive useful insights from a collection of association rules. We'll examine how to generate product recommendations based on the items a customer has purchased and how to efficiently plan discounts based around frequent itemsets. Both of these applications have the potential to increase revenue for the business while also delivering a better experience for customers.

### Generating Recommendations

After an item has appeared in a customer's basket, which item is likely to be added next? Of course, you can't say for sure, but you can make a prediction based on the association rules mined from your transaction data. The results of this prediction can form the basis for a set of recommendations of items that are frequently bought together with the item currently in the basket. Retailers commonly use such recommendations to show customers other items they may want to purchase.

Perhaps the most natural way to generate recommendations of this type is to look at all the association rules where the item currently in the basket acts as the antecedent. Then, you identify the strongest rules—perhaps the three rules with the highest confidence values—and extract their consequents. The following example illustrates how to do this for the item *butter*. You start by finding the rules where *butter* is the antecedent, using the pandas library's filtering features:

```
butter_antecedent = rules[rules['antecedents'] == {'butter'}][['consequents','confidence']]
        .sort_values('confidence', ascending = False)
```

Here you sort the rules by the confidence column so that the rules with the highest confidence rating appear at the beginning of the butter_antecedent DataFrame. Next you use a list comprehension to extract the top three consequents:

```
butter_consequents = [list(item) for item in butter_antecedent.iloc[0:3,]['consequents']]
```

In this list comprehension, you loop over the consequents column in the butter_antecedent DataFrame, picking up the first three values. Based on the butter_consequents list, you can generate a recommendation:

```
item = 'butter'
print('Items frequently bought together with', item, 'are:', butter_consequents)
```

The recommendation will look as follows:

```
Items frequently bought together with butter are: [['bread'], ['cheese'], ['cheese', 'bread']]
```

This indicates that customers who buy butter also often buy either bread or cheese, or both.

### Planning Discounts Based on Association Rules

The association rules generated for frequent itemsets can also be used for choosing which products to discount. Ideally, you should have a discounted item in each significant group of products to satisfy as many customers as possible. In other words, you should choose a single item to be discounted in each frequent itemset.

To accomplish this, the first thing you need is a set of frequent itemsets to work on. Unfortunately, the rules DataFrame generated earlier by the association_rules() function has columns for antecedents and consequents but not for the rules' complete itemsets. You therefore need to create an itemsets column by merging the antecedents and consequents columns, as shown here:

```
from functools import reduce
rules['itemsets'] = rules[['antecedents', 'consequents']].apply(lambda x:
                 reduce(frozenset.union, x), axis=1)
```

You use the reduce() function from Python's functools module to apply the frozenset.union() method to the values of the antecedents and consequents columns. This combines the separate frozensets from these columns into a single one.

To see what you have as a result, you might print the newly created itemsets column along with the antecedents and consequents columns:

```
print(rules[['antecedents','consequents','itemsets']])
```

The output will look as follows:

|    | antecedents | consequents | itemsets |
|----|-------------|-------------|----------|
| 0  | (butter) | (bread) | (butter, bread) |
| 1  | (bread) | (butter) | (butter, bread) |
| 2  | (cheese) | (bread) | (bread, cheese) |
| 3  | (milk) | (bread) | (milk, bread) |
| 4  | (butter) | (cheese) | (butter, cheese) |
| 5  | (pasta) | (cheese) | (pasta, cheese) |
| 6  | (sour cream) | (curd) | (sour cream, curd) |
| 7  | (curd) | (sour cream) | (sour cream, curd) |
| 8  | (milk) | (eggs) | (milk, eggs) |
| 9  | (eggs) | (milk) | (milk, eggs) |
| 10 | (butter, cheese) | (bread) | (bread, butter, cheese) |
| 11 | (butter, bread) | (cheese) | (butter, cheese, bread) |
| 12 | (bread, cheese) | (butter) | (bread, butter, cheese) |
| 13 | (butter) | (bread, cheese) | (butter, cheese, bread) |

Notice that there are some duplicates in the new `itemsets` column. As discussed earlier, the same itemset may form more than one association rule, since the order of items influences some rule metrics. The order of items in an itemset doesn't matter for the current task, however, so you can safely remove duplicate itemsets, as shown here:

```
rules.drop_duplicates(subset=['itemsets'], keep='first', inplace=True)
```

You use the DataFrame's `drop_duplicates()` method for this, specifying to look for duplicates in the `itemsets` column. You keep the first row within a set of duplicates, and by setting `inplace` to `True`, you delete the duplicate rows from the existing DataFrame rather than creating a new DataFrame with the duplicates removed.

If you now print out the `itemsets` column:

```
print(rules['itemsets'])
```

you'll only see the following:

```
0               (bread, butter)
2               (bread, cheese)
3                 (bread, milk)
4              (butter, cheese)
5               (cheese, pasta)
6            (curd, sour cream)
8                  (milk, eggs)
10      (bread, cheese, butter)
```

Next, you choose one item from each itemset to be discounted:

```
  discounted = []
  others = []
❶ for itemset in rules['itemsets']:
❷   for i, item in enumerate(itemset):
❸     if item not in others:
❹       discounted.append(item)
         itemset = set(itemset)
         itemset.discard(item)
❺       others.extend(itemset)
         break
❻     if i == len(itemset)-1:
         discounted.append(item)
         itemset = set(itemset)
         itemset.discard(item)
         others.extend(itemset)
  print(discounted)
```

You first create the `discounted` list to accumulate the items being chosen for discount and the `others` list to receive the items in an itemset that aren't chosen for discount. Then you iterate over each itemset ❶ and each item in it ❷. You look for an item not already included in the `others` list, since such an item would either not be in any of the preceding itemsets or have already been chosen as the discounted item for a preceding itemset, meaning it would be efficient to choose it as this itemset's discounted item too ❸. You send the chosen item to the discounted list ❹, then send the remaining items of the itemset to the others list ❺. If you've iterated over all the items in an itemset and failed to find an item that isn't included in the others list, you choose the last item in the itemset and send it to the discounted list ❻.

The resulting discounted list will vary, since the Python frozensets representing the itemsets are unordered, but it will look something like the following:

```
['bread', 'bread', 'bread', 'cheese', 'pasta', 'curd', 'eggs', 'bread']
```

Compare the result with the itemsets column shown earlier, and you'll see that each itemset has one discounted item in it. Moreover, you've distributed the discounts very efficiently, so the actual number of discounted items is significantly less than the number of itemsets. You can see this by removing the duplicates from the discounted list:

```
print(list(set(discounted)))
```

As the output shows, even though there are eight itemsets, you've only had to discount five items:

```
['cheese', 'eggs', 'bread', 'pasta', 'curd']
```

Thus, you've managed to discount one item in each itemset (a significant benefit for many customers) without actually having to discount many items (a significant benefit for the business).

---

**EXERCISE #18: MINING REAL TRANSACTION DATA**

In this chapter, you've worked with a sample dataset containing just 20 transactions. Now it's finally time to get your hands dirty with a big dataset. In this exercise, you'll work to derive frequent itemsets from a real collection of more than half a million purchased items. This dataset can be found in the UCI Machine Learning Repository at *https://archive.ics.uci.edu/ml/ datasets/online+retail*.

You'll need to download the *Online Retail.xlsx* file to your machine, or use the direct link *https://archive.ics.uci.edu/ml/machine-learning-databases/00352/Online%20Retail.xlsx* to access the file. Before you can read this Excel file into a pandas DataFrame for further processing, however, you'll need to install the openpyxl library. This library, which enables you to manipulate Excel files from within Python scripts, can be installed with pip as follows:

```
$ pip install openpyxl
```

*(continued)*

After that, use openpyxl to load the dataset into a DataFrame:

```
import pandas as pd
df_retail = pd.read_excel('path/to/Online Retail.xlsx', index_col=0,
engine='openpyxl')
```

Depending on your machine, the loading process may take several minutes to complete. Then, to make sure that the load has been successful, check the number of rows in the `df_retail` DataFrame and output the first few rows:

```
print('The number of instances: ', len(df_retail))
print(df_retail.head())
```

The output should look as follows:

```
The number of instances:  541909

          StockCode              Description  Quantity InvoiceDate UnitPrice Country
InvoiceNo
536365       85123A  WHITE HANGING HEART T-LIG...      6  2010-12-01      2.55      UK
536365        71053       WHITE METAL LANTERN         6  2010-12-01      3.39      UK
536365       84406B  CREAM CUPID HEARTS COAT...        8  2010-12-01      2.75      UK
536365       84029G    KNITTED UNION FLAG HOT...        6  2010-12-01      3.39      UK
536365       84029E    RED WOOLLY HOTTIE WHITE...       6  2010-12-01      3.39      UK

[5 rows x 7 columns]
```

Real data like this can be messy, so at this point you need to do some cleanup to prepare the data for further processing. To start with, you need to remove all the rows that have a NaN in the Description field. This field contains the item names, so having NaNs would skew the process of identifying frequent itemsets:

```
df_retail = df_retail.dropna(subset=['Description'])
```

To check if this has worked, output the length of the updated `df_retail` DataFrame:

```
print(len(df_retail))
```

You'll see 540455, indicating that there are now 1,454 fewer rows in the DataFrame.

To further cleanse the data, make sure to explicitly cast the Description values to the str data type:

```
df_retail = df_retail.astype({"Description":'str'})
```

Now you're ready to transform the dataset into a format that can be processed with mlxtend. First, group the data into transactions using the `InvoiceNo` column and transform the DataFrame into a list of lists, where each list contains the itemset assigned to a transaction:

```
trans = df_retail.groupby(['InvoiceNo'])['Description'].apply(list).to_list()
```

You now can learn the number of actual transactions represented in the dataset:

```
print(len(trans))
```

You should get 24446.

The next steps in the analysis were discussed in detail earlier in the chapter. To sum up, you'll need to do the following:

1. Transform the `trans` list of lists into a one-hot encoded Boolean array using mlxtend's `TransactionEncoder` object.

2. Generate frequent itemsets with the `apriori()` function (for this example, use `min_support=0.025`).

3. Generate association rules with the `association_rules()` function (for this example, use `metric="confidence"`, `min_threshold=0.3`).

Once you're done, you can print the generated rules:

```
print(rules.iloc[:,0:7])
```

The output should look similar to the following:

|  | antecedents | consequents | ...confidence | lift |
|---|---|---|---|---|
| 0 | (ALARM CLOCK BAKELI...) | (ALARM CLOCK BAKELIKE GREEN) ... | 0.5975 | 14.5942 |
| 1 | (ALARM CLOCK BAKELI...) | (ALARM CLOCK BAKELIKE RED) ... | 0.6453 | 14.5942 |
| 2 | (GREEN REGENCY TEACUP AND...) | (PINK REGENCY TEACUP AND...) ... | 0.6092 | 18.5945 |
| 3 | (PINK REGENCY TEACUP AND...) | (GREEN REGENCY TEACUP AND...) ... | 0.8039 | 18.5945 |
| 4 | (GREEN REGENCY TEACUP AND...) | (ROSES REGENCY TEACUP AND...) ... | 0.7417 | 16.1894 |
| 5 | (ROSES REGENCY TEACUP AND...) | (GREEN REGENCY TEACUP AND...) ... | 0.7000 | 16.1894 |
| 6 | (JUMBO BAG PINK POLKADOT) | (JUMBO BAG RED RETROSPOT) ... | 0.6766 | 7.7481 |
| 7 | (JUMBO BAG RED RETROSPOT) | (JUMBO BAG PINK POLKADOT) ... | 0.3901 | 7.7481 |
| 8 | (JUMBO SHOPPER VINTAGE RED...) | (JUMBO BAG RED RETROSPOT) ... | 0.5754 | 6.5883 |
| 9 | (JUMBO BAG RED RET...) | (JUMBO SHOPPER VINTAGE RED...) ... | 0.3199 | 6.5883 |
| 10 | (JUMBO STORAGE BAG SUKI) | (JUMBO BAG RED RETROSPOT) ... | 0.6103 | 6.9882 |
| 11 | (JUMBO BAG RED RE...) | (JUMBO STORAGE BAG...) ... | 0.3433 | 6.9882 |
| 12 | (LUNCH BAG BLACK SKULL.) | (LUNCH BAG RED RETROSPOT) ... | 0.5003 | 7.6119 |
| 13 | (LUNCH BAG RED RETROSPOT) | (LUNCH BAG BLACK SKULL) ... | 0.4032 | 7.6119 |
| 14 | (LUNCH BAG PINK POLKADOT) | (LUNCH BAG RED RETROSPOT) ... | 0.5522 | 8.4009 |
| 15 | (LUNCH BAG RED RETROSPOT) | (LUNCH BAG PINK POLKADOT) ... | 0.3814 | 8.4009 |
| 16 | (PINK REGENCY TEACUP AND...) | (ROSES REGENCY TEACUP AND...) ... | 0.7665 | 16.7311 |
| 17 | (ROSES REGENCY TEACUP AND...) | (PINK REGENCY TEACUP AND...) ... | 0.5482 | 16.7311 |

*(continued)*

> To generate a larger or smaller collection of association rules, try experimenting with the `min_support` parameter passed to the `apriori()` function as well as the `metric` and `threshold` parameters passed to the `association_rules()` function.

## Summary

As you've seen, performing a market basket analysis is a valuable way to extract useful information from large amounts of transaction data. In this chapter, you learned how to use the Apriori algorithm to mine transaction data for association rules, and you saw how to evaluate those rules along different metrics. In this way, you were able to gain insight about what items are commonly purchased together. You used that knowledge to make product recommendations to customers and to efficiently plan discounts.

# 12

## MACHINE LEARNING FOR DATA ANALYSIS

*Machine learning* is a method of data analysis where applications leverage existing data to discover patterns and make decisions, without being explicitly programmed to do so. In other words, the applications learn for themselves, independent of human interference. A robust data analysis technique, machine learning is used in many fields, including but not limited to classification, clustering, predictive analytics, learning associations, anomaly detection, image analysis, and natural language processing.

This chapter provides an overview of some fundamental machine learning concepts, then explores two machine learning examples in depth. First we'll perform a sentiment analysis, developing a model to predict the number of stars (from one to five) associated with a product review. After that, we'll develop another model to predict changes in the price of a stock.

# Why Machine Learning?

Machine learning lets computers perform tasks that would be difficult, if not impossible, using conventional programming techniques. For instance, imagine you need to build an image-processing application that can distinguish between different types of animals based on submitted photos. In this hypothetical scenario, you already have a code library that can identify the edges of an object (such as an animal) in an image. In this way, you can transform the animal shown in a photo into a characteristic set of lines. But how can you programmatically distinguish between the lines representing two different animals—say, a cat and a dog?

A traditional programming approach would be to manually craft rules that map every characteristic line combination to an animal. Unfortunately, this solution would require a huge amount of code, and it could completely fail when a new photo is submitted whose edges don't fit one of the manually defined rules. In contrast, applications built on machine learning algorithms don't rely on predefined logic but instead hinge on the application's ability to automatically learn from previously seen data. Thus, a machine learning–based photo-tagging application would look for patterns in the line combinations derived from previous photos and then make predictions about the animals in new photos based on probability statistics.

# Types of Machine Learning

Data scientists distinguish between several types of machine learning. The two most common are supervised learning and unsupervised learning. In this chapter we'll primarily be concerned with supervised learning, but this section provides a brief overview of both types.

## Supervised Learning

*Supervised learning* uses a labeled dataset (referred to as a *training set*) to teach a model to yield the desired output when given new, previously unseen data. Technically, supervised learning is the technique of inferring a function that maps an input to an output based on the training set. You've already seen an example of supervised learning in Chapter 3, where we used a set of example product reviews to train a model to predict whether new product reviews were positive or negative.

The input data for a supervised learning algorithm can represent characteristics of real-world objects or events. For example, you might use the characteristics of homes for sale (square footage, number of bedrooms and bathrooms, and so on) as input for an algorithm designed to predict home values. These values would be the output of the algorithm. You'd train the algorithm with a collection of input-output pairs, consisting of the characteristics of various homes and their associated values, then feed it the characteristics of new homes and receive those new homes' estimated values as output.

Other supervised learning algorithms are designed to work not with characteristics but with *observational data*: data gathered through observing an activity or behavior. As an example, consider a time series produced by the sensors monitoring noise levels at an airport. This observational noise level data might be submitted to a machine learning algorithm, along with information such as the time of day and day of the week, so that the algorithm can learn to predict the noise levels in the coming hours. In this example, the times and days of the week are the input, and the noise levels are the output. In other words, the algorithm would be designed to predict future observational data.

---

### INPUT AND OUTPUT IN MACHINE LEARNING

In the world of programming, *input* typically refers to data that a function, script, or application receives. The input is then used to generate *output*, which is data that the function, script, or application returns. In the context of supervised machine learning, however, *input* and *output* have slightly different meanings. When a machine learning model is being trained, it receives *pairs* of input and output data, such as product reviews (input) and their associated classifications as positive or negative (output). Then, once the model has been trained, new input values are provided alone, and the model generates appropriate output values based on what it has learned from the example input-output pairs.

A machine learning model's input can consist of one or more variables, which are referred to as *independent variables* or *features*. Meanwhile, the output is typically a single variable known as a *target* or *dependent variable*, so called because the output *depends* on the input.

---

Both the home value predictions and the noise level predictions are examples of *regression*, a common supervised learning technique for predicting continuous values. The other common supervised learning technique is *classification*, where the model assigns one of a finite number of class labels to each input. Distinguishing between favorable and unfavorable product reviews is an example of classification, as are other *sentiment analysis* applications, where text fragments are identified as being either positive or negative. We'll explore an example of sentiment analysis later in this chapter.

## Unsupervised Learning

*Unsupervised learning* is a machine learning technique in which there's no training stage. You only give the application input data, without any corresponding output values to learn from. In that sense, unsupervised machine learning models have to work on their own, discovering hidden patterns in the input data.

A great example of unsupervised learning is *association analysis*, where a machine learning application identifies items within a set that have an affinity for each other. In Chapter 11, you performed an association analysis on a set of transaction data, identifying items commonly purchased together. You used the Apriori algorithm, which doesn't require example output data to learn from; instead, it takes all the transaction data as an input and searches the transactions for frequent itemsets, thus representing learning with no training.

## How Machine Learning Works

A typical machine learning pipeline relies on three major components:

- Data to learn from
- A statistical model to apply to the data
- New, previously unseen data to process

The following sections take a closer look at each of these components.

### Data to Learn From

Machine learning is based on the idea that computer systems can learn, so any machine learning algorithm requires data to learn from. As we've already discussed, the nature of this data varies depending on whether the machine learning model is supervised or unsupervised. In the case of supervised machine learning, the data to learn from takes the form of input-output pairs that train the model to later predict outputs based on new inputs. In unsupervised learning, on the other hand, the model receives only input data, which it mines for patterns in order to produce output.

While all machine learning applications require data to learn from, the requisite format of this data may vary from algorithm to algorithm. Many algorithms learn from a dataset organized as a table, in which the rows represent various instances, such as perhaps individual objects or particular moments in time, and the columns represent attributes pertaining to those instances. A classic example is the Iris dataset (*https://archive.ics.uci.edu/ml/ datasets/Iris*). It has 150 rows, each of which contains observations about a different specimen of iris. Here are the first four rows of the dataset:

| sepal length | sepal width | petal length | petal width | species |
|---|---|---|---|---|
| 5.1 | 3.5 | 1.4 | 0.2 | Iris-setosa |
| 4.9 | 3.0 | 1.4 | 0.2 | Iris-setosa |
| 4.7 | 3.2 | 1.3 | 0.2 | Iris-setosa |
| 4.6 | 3.1 | 1.5 | 0.2 | Iris-setosa |

The first four columns represent different attributes, or features, of the specimens. The fifth column contains a label for each instance: the iris's exact species name. If you trained a classification model with this dataset, you'd use the values in the first four columns as the independent variables, or input, while the fifth column would be the dependent variable, or output. After learning from this data, ideally the model would be able to classify new iris specimens by species.

Other machine learning algorithms learn from non-tabular data. For example, the Apriori algorithm used for association analysis, which we discussed in the previous chapter, takes a set of transactions (or baskets) of different sizes as input data. Here's a simple example of such a transaction set:

```
(butter, cheese)
(cheese, pasta, bread, milk)
(milk, cheese, eggs, bread, butter)
(bread, cheese, butter)
```

Beyond the question of how the machine learning data is structured, the type of data used also varies from algorithm to algorithm. As the previous examples illustrate, some machine learning algorithms work with numeric or textual data. There are also algorithms designed to work with photo, video, or audio data.

## A Statistical Model

Whatever data format the machine learning algorithm requires, the input data must be transformed in such a way that it can be analyzed to produce outputs. This is where a *statistical model* comes into play: statistics are used to create a representation of the data so the algorithm can identify relationships between variables, discover insights, make predictions about new data, generate recommendations, and so on. Statistical models lie at the heart of any machine learning algorithm.

For example, the Apriori algorithm uses the support metric as a statistical model to find frequent itemsets. (As discussed in Chapter 11, support is the percentage of transactions that include an itemset.) In particular, the algorithm identifies every possible itemset and calculates the corresponding support metric, then selects only those itemsets with a sufficiently high support. Here's a simple example illustrating how the algorithm works behind the scenes:

```
Itemset          Support
--------------   -------
butter, cheese   0.75
bread, cheese    0.75
milk, bread      0.50
bread, butter    0.50
```

This example shows only two-item itemsets. In fact, after calculating the support for every possible two-item itemset, the Apriori algorithm moves on to analyzing every three-item itemset, four-item itemset, and so on. Then the algorithm uses the support values for the itemsets of all sizes to generate a list of frequent itemsets.

## Previously Unseen Data

In supervised machine learning, once you've trained a model on example data, you can apply it to new, previously unseen data. Before doing so, however, you might want to evaluate the model, which is why it's common practice to split the initial dataset into training and testing sets. The former is the data the model learns from, and the latter becomes previously unseen data for testing purposes.

The testing data still has both input and output, but only the input is shown to the model. Then the real output is compared to the output suggested by the model to assess the accuracy of its predictions. Once you've made sure the model's accuracy is acceptable, you can use fresh input data to do predictive analysis.

In the case of unsupervised learning, there is no distinction between data to learn from and previously unseen data. All the data is essentially previously unseen, and the model tries to learn from it by analyzing its underlying features.

# A Sentiment Analysis Example: Classifying Product Reviews

Now that we've reviewed the basics of machine learning, you're ready to conduct a sample sentiment analysis. As explained previously, this natural language processing technique allows you to programmatically determine whether a piece of writing is positive or negative. (More categories, such as neutral, very positive, or very negative, are also possibilities in some applications.) In essence, sentiment analysis is a form of classification, a supervised machine learning technique that sorts data into discrete categories.

In Chapter 3, you used scikit-learn to perform a basic sentiment analysis on a set of product reviews from Amazon. You trained a model to identify whether reviews were good or bad. In this section, you'll expand on the work you did in that chapter. You'll obtain an actual set of product reviews directly from Amazon and use it to train a classification model. The goal of the model is to predict the star ratings of reviews, on a one to five scale. Thus, the model will sort reviews into five possible categories, rather than just two.

## Obtaining Product Reviews

The first step in building the model is to download a set of actual product reviews from Amazon. One easy way to do this is to use Amazon Reviews Exporter, a Google Chrome browser extension that downloads an Amazon product's reviews as a CSV file. You can install this extension in your Chrome browser with one click from this page: *https://chrome.google.com/webstore/detail/ amazon-reviews-exporter-c/njlppnciolcibljfdobcefcngiampidm.*

With the extension installed, open an Amazon product page in Chrome. For this example, we'll use the Amazon page for No Starch Press's *Python Crash Course* by Eric Matthes (*https://www.amazon.com/Python-Crash-Course-2nd -Edition/dp/1593279280*), which at the time of this writing has 445 reviews. To download the book's reviews, find and click the Amazon Reviews Exporter button in your Chrome toolbar.

Once you have the reviews in a CSV file, you can read them into a pandas DataFrame as follows:

```
import pandas as pd
df = pd.read_csv('reviews.csv')
```

Before proceeding, you might want to look at the total number of reviews and the first few reviews loaded in the DataFrame:

```
print('The number of reviews: ', len(df))
print(df[['title', 'rating']].head(10))
```

The output should look something like this:

```
The number of reviews:  445
                                             title  rating
0  Great inner content! Not that great outer qual...     4
1                             Very enjoyable read       5
2                             The updated preface      5
3  Good for beginner but does not go too far or deep   4
4                             Worth Every Penny!       5
5                             Easy to understand       5
6                          Great book for python.      5
7              Not bad, but some disappointment       4
8  Truely for the person that doesn't know how to...   3
9         Easy to Follow, Good Intro for Self Learner  5
```

This view shows only the title and rating fields for each record. We'll treat the review titles as the independent variable in the model (that is, the input) and the ratings as the dependent variable (the output). Notice that we're ignoring the full text of each review and focusing just on the titles. This seems reasonable for the purposes of training a model for sentiment classification, since the title typically represents a summary of the reviewer's feelings about the product. By contrast, the full review text often includes other nonemotional information, like a description of the book's contents.

## Cleansing the Data

Before you can process real-world data, it almost always requires cleansing. In this particular example, you'll need to filter out reviews that aren't written in English. For that, you'll need a way to programmatically determine the language of each review. There are several Python libraries with language-detection capabilities; we'll use google_trans_new.

### Installing google_trans_new

Use pip to install the google_trans_new library, as follows:

```
$ pip install google_trans_new
```

Before going any further, make sure google_trans_new has fixed the known bug that raises a JSONDecodeError exception during language detection. For that, run the following test in a Python session:

```
$ from google_trans_new import google_translator
$ detector = google_translator()
$ detector.detect('Good')
```

If this test runs without an error, you're ready to proceed. If it raises a JSONDecodeError exception, you'll need to make some small changes to the library's source code in *google_trans_new.py*. Locate the file with pip:

```
$ pip show google_trans_new
```

The command will show some basic information about the library, including the location of its source code on your local machine. Go to that location, and open *google_trans_new.py* in a text editor. Then find lines 151 and 233, which will look like this:

```
response = (decoded_line + ']')
```

and change them to:

```
response = decoded_line
```

Save the changes, restart your Python session, and rerun the test. It should now correctly identify *good* as an English-language word:

```
$ from google_trans_new import google_translator
$ detector = google_translator()
$ detector.detect('Good')
['en', 'english']
```

NOTE *For more information about google_trans_new, visit* https://pypi.org/project/google-trans-new.

### Removing Non-English Reviews

Now you're ready to detect the language of each review and filter out the reviews that aren't in English. In the following code, you use the google _translator module from google_trans_new to determine the language of each review title, and you store the language in a new column of the DataFrame. It may take a while to detect the language of a large number of samples, so be patient when you run the code:

```
from google_trans_new import google_translator
detector = google_translator()
df['lang'] = df['title'].apply(lambda x: detector.detect(x)[0])
```

You first create a google_translator object, then use a lambda expression to apply the object's detect() method to each review title. You save the results to a new column called lang. Here you print that column, along with title and rating:

```
print(df[['title', 'rating', 'lang']])
```

The output will look similar to the following:

|   | title | rating | lang |
|---|---|---|---|
| 0 | Great inner content! Not that great outer qual... | 4 | en |
| 1 | Very enjoyable read | 5 | en |
| 2 | The updated preface | 5 | en |
| 3 | Good for beginner but does not go too far or deep | 4 | en |
| 4 | Worth Every Penny! | 5 | en |
| --snip-- | | | |
| 440 | Not bad | 1 | en |
| 441 | Good | 5 | en |
| 442 | Super | 5 | en |
| 443 | 内容はとても良い、作りは× | 4 | ja |
| 444 | 非常实用 | 5 | zh-CN |

Your next step is to filter the dataset, keeping only those reviews that are written in English:

```
df = df[df['lang'] == 'en']
```

This operation should reduce the total number of rows in the dataset. To verify that it worked, count the number of rows in the updated DataFrame:

```
print(len(df))
```

The row count should be less than it was originally because all the non-English reviews have been removed.

## Splitting and Transforming the Data

Before you go any further, you need to split the reviews into a training set for developing the model and a testing set for evaluating its accuracy. You also need to transform the natural language of the review titles into numerical data that the model can understand. As you saw in "Transforming Text into Numerical Feature Vectors" in Chapter 3, the bag of words (BoW) technique can be used for that purpose; to review how it works, refer back to that section.

The following code uses scikit-learn to both split and transform the data. The code follows the same format used in Chapter 3:

```
from sklearn.model_selection import train_test_split
from sklearn.feature_extraction.text import CountVectorizer
reviews = df['title'].values
ratings = df['rating'].values
❶ reviews_train, reviews_test, y_train, y_test = train_test_split(reviews,
               ratings, test_size=0.2, random_state=1000)
```

```
  vectorizer = CountVectorizer()
  vectorizer.fit(reviews_train)
❷ x_train = vectorizer.transform(reviews_train)
  x_test = vectorizer.transform(reviews_test)
```

To recap, scikit-learn's train_test_split() function randomly splits the data into a training set and a testing set ❶, and the library's CountVectorizer class has methods for transforming text data into numerical feature vectors ❷. The code generates the following structures, implementing the training and testing sets as NumPy arrays and their corresponding feature vectors as SciPy sparse matrices:

**reviews_train**  An array containing the review titles chosen for training

**reviews_test**  An array containing the review titles chosen for testing

**y_train**  An array containing the star ratings corresponding to the reviews in reviews_train

**y_test**  An array containing the star ratings corresponding to the reviews in reviews_test

**x_train**  A matrix containing the set of feature vectors for the review titles found in the reviews_train array

**x_test**  A matrix containing the set of feature vectors for the review titles found in the reviews_test array

We're most interested in x_train and x_test, the numerical feature vectors scikit-learn has generated from the review titles using the BoW technique. Each of these matrices should include one row per review headline, with this row representing the headline's numerical feature vector. To check the number of rows in the matrix generated from the reviews_train array, use:

```
print(len(x_train.toarray()))
```

The resulting number should be 80 percent of the total number of English-language reviews, since you split the data into training and testing sets using the 80/20 pattern. The x_test matrix should contain the other 20 percent of the feature vectors, which you can verify with:

```
print(len(x_test.toarray()))
```

You might also want to check the length of the feature vectors in the training matrix:

```
print(len(x_train.toarray()[0]))
```

You print the length of just the first row in the matrix, but each row's length is the same. The result may look as follows:

442

This means that 442 unique words occur in the training set's review titles. This collection of words is called the *vocabulary dictionary* of the dataset.

If you're curious, here's how to print the entire matrix:

```
print(x_train.toarray())
```

The result will look something like this:

```
[[0 0 0 ... 1 0 0]
 [0 0 0 ... 0 0 0]
 [0 0 0 ... 0 0 0]
 --snip--
 [0 0 0 ... 0 0 0]
 [0 0 0 ... 0 0 0]
 [0 0 0 ... 0 0 0]]
```

Each column of the matrix corresponds to one of the words in the dataset's vocabulary dictionary, and the numbers tell you how many times each word appears in any given review title. As you can see, the matrix consists mostly of zeros. This is to be expected: the average review title in the example set consists of just 5 to 10 words, but the vocabulary dictionary of the entire set consists of 442 words, meaning that in a typical row, only 5 to 10 elements out of 442 will be set to 1 or higher. Nevertheless, this representation of the example data is exactly what you need to train a classification model for sentiment analysis.

## Training the Model

Now you're ready to train your model. In particular, you need to train a *classifier*, a machine learning model that sorts data into categories, so that it can predict the number of stars of a review. For that, you can use scikit-learn's LogisticRegression classifier:

```
from sklearn.linear_model import LogisticRegression
classifier = LogisticRegression()
classifier.fit(x_train, y_train)
```

You import the LogisticRegression class and create a classifier object. Then you train the classifier by passing it the x_train matrix (the feature vectors of the review titles in the training set) and the y_train array (the corresponding star ratings).

## Evaluating the Model

Now that the model has been trained, you can use the x_test matrix to evaluate its accuracy, comparing the model's predicted ratings to the actual ratings in the y_test array. In Chapter 3, you used the classifier object's score() method to evaluate its accuracy. Here you'll use a different evaluation method, one that allows for more precision:

```
  import numpy as np
❶ predicted = classifier.predict(x_test)
```

```
accuracy = ❷ np.mean(❸ predicted == y_test)
print("Accuracy:", round(accuracy,2))
```

You use the classifier's `predict()` method to predict ratings based on the x_test feature vectors ❶. Then you test for equivalency between the model's predictions and the actual star ratings ❸. The result of this comparison is a Boolean array, where `True` and `False` indicate accurate and inaccurate predictions. By taking the arithmetic mean of the array ❷, you get an overall accuracy rating for the model. (For the purposes of calculating the mean, each `True` is treated as a 1 and each `False` as a 0.) Printing the result should give you something like:

```
Accuracy: 0.68
```

This indicates that the model is 68 percent accurate, meaning that on average approximately 7 out of 10 predictions are correct. To get a more fine-grained understanding of the model's accuracy, however, you need to use other scikit-learn features to examine more specific metrics. For example, you can study the model's *confusion matrix*, a grid that compares predicted classifications with actual classifications. A confusion matrix can help reveal the model's accuracy within each individual class, as well as show whether the model is likely to confuse two classes (mislabel one class as another). You can create the confusion matrix for your classification model as follows:

```
from sklearn import metrics
print(metrics.confusion_matrix(y_test, predicted, labels = [1,2,3,4,5]))
```

You import scikit-learn's `metrics` module, then use the `confusion_matrix()` method to generate the matrix. You pass the method the actual ratings of the test set (`y_test`), the ratings predicted by your model (`predicted`), and the labels corresponding to those ratings. The matrix will look something like this:

```
[[ 0,  0,  0,  1,  7],
 [ 0,  0,  1,  0,  1],
 [ 0,  0,  0,  4,  3],
 [ 0,  0,  0,  1,  6],
 [ 0,  0,  0,  3, 54]]
```

Here, the rows correspond to actual ratings, and the columns correspond to predicted ratings. For example, looking at the numbers in the first row tells you the test set contained eight actual one-star ratings, one of which was predicted to be a four-star rating and seven of which were predicted to be five-star ratings.

The main diagonal of the confusion matrix (top left to bottom right) shows the number of correct predictions for each rating level. Examining this diagonal, you can see that the model made 54 correct predictions for five-star reviews and only 1 correct prediction for four-star reviews. No one-, two-, or three-star reviews were correctly identified. Overall, out of a test set of 81 reviews, 55 were correctly predicted.

This outcome raises a number of questions. For one, why does the model only work well for five-star reviews? The problem could be that the example dataset has only five-star reviews in sufficient quantity. To check if this is the case, you might count the rows in each rating group:

```
print(df.groupby('rating').size())
```

You group the original DataFrame containing both the training and testing data by the rating column and use the size() method to get the number of entries in each group. The output might look something like this:

```
rating
1     25
2     15
3     23
4     51
5    290
```

As you can see, this count confirms our hypothesis: there are far more five-star reviews than any other rating, suggesting the model didn't have enough data to effectively learn the features of reviews with four stars or lower.

To further explore the accuracy of the model, you might also want to look at its main classification metrics, comparing the y_test and predicted arrays. You can do this with the help of the classification_report() function found in scikit-learn's metrics module:

```
print(metrics.classification_report(y_test, predicted, labels = [1,2,3,4,5]))
```

The generated report will look something like this:

|  | precision | recall | f1-score | support |
|---|---|---|---|---|
| 1 | 0.00 | 0.00 | 0.00 | 8 |
| 2 | 0.00 | 0.00 | 0.00 | 2 |
| 3 | 0.00 | 0.00 | 0.00 | 7 |
| 4 | 0.11 | 0.14 | 0.12 | 7 |
| 5 | 0.76 | 0.95 | 0.84 | 57 |
| accuracy |  |  | 0.68 | 81 |
| macro avg | 0.17 | 0.22 | 0.19 | 81 |
| weighted avg | 0.54 | 0.68 | 0.60 | 81 |

This report shows the summary of the main classification metrics for each class of reviews. Here, we'll focus on support and recall; for more information about the other metrics in the report, see *https://scikit-learn.org/ stable/modules/generated/sklearn.metrics.classification_report.html#sklearn.metrics .classification_report*.

The support metric shows the number of reviews for each class of ratings. In particular, it reveals that the reviews are distributed extremely unevenly across rating groups, with the test set exhibiting the same tendency as the entire dataset. Of the total of 81 reviews, there are 57 five-star reviews and only 2 two-star reviews.

Recall shows the ratio of correctly predicted reviews to all the reviews with a certain rating. For example, the recall metric for five-star reviews is 0.95, meaning the model was 95 percent accurate at predicting five-star reviews, while the same metric for four-star reviews is just 0.14. Since the reviews with the other ratings don't have any correct predictions, the weighted average recall for the whole test set is shown to be 0.68 at the bottom of the report. This is the same accuracy rating you got near the start of this section.

Taking into consideration all these points, you can reasonably conclude that the problem is that the example set you're using has a highly unequal number of reviews in each rating group.

---

### EXERCISE #19: EXPANDING THE EXAMPLE SET

As you just learned, the overall accuracy of a classification model can be misleading if you have an unequal number of instances of each class in the dataset. Try expanding your dataset by downloading more Amazon reviews. Aim to have a roughly equal and sufficiently large number of instances of each star rating (say, 500 per group). Then retrain your model and test it again to see if its accuracy improves.

---

## Predicting Stock Trends

To further explore how machine learning can be applied to data analysis, next we'll create a model for predicting stock market trends. For simplicity, we'll create another classification model: one that predicts whether the price of a stock tomorrow will be higher, lower, or the same as it is today. A more sophisticated model might instead use regression to predict the actual price of a stock from day to day.

**WARNING** *The model discussed here is for example purposes only, not for real use. Real-world machine learning models used for stock trading are typically much more complex. Any attempt to use this book's model to make actual stock trades may lead to losses, for which neither the author nor the publisher will be responsible.*

Compared to this chapter's sentiment analysis example, our stock prediction model (and indeed, many models that involve nontextual data) raises a new question: how do we decide what data to use as the model's features, or inputs? For the sentiment analysis model, you used the feature vectors generated from the text of the review headlines via the BoW technique. The content of such a vector firmly depends on the content of the corresponding text. In this sense, the content of the vector is predefined, being formed from the features extracted from the corresponding text in accordance with a certain rule.

By contrast, when your model involves nontextual data such as stock prices, it's often up to you to decide on, and perhaps even calculate, the set of features to be used as the input data for the model. Percentage change in price since the previous day, average price over the past week, and total trading volume over the two preceding days? Perhaps. Percentage change in price since two days ago, average price over the past month, and change in volume since yesterday? Could be. Financial analysts use all sorts of metrics such as these, in different combinations, as input data for their stock prediction models.

In Chapter 10, you learned how to derive metrics from stock market data by calculating percentage changes over time, rolling window averages, and the like. We'll revisit some of these techniques later in this section to generate the features for our prediction model. But first, we need to obtain some data.

## Getting Data

To train your model, you'll need a year's worth of data for an individual stock. For the purpose of this example, we'll use Apple (AAPL). Here, you use the yfinance library to obtain the company's stock data for the last year:

```
import yfinance as yf
tkr = yf.Ticker('AAPL')
hist = tkr.history(period="1y")
```

You'll use the resulting hist DataFrame to derive metrics about the stock, such as the day-to-day percentage change of the price, and feed those metrics to your model. However, you can reasonably assume that there are also external factors (that is, information that can't be derived from the stock data itself) that influence Apple's stock price. For example, the overall performance of the wider stock market might affect the performance of an individual stock. Thus, it would be interesting to also take into account data about a broader stock market index as part of your model.

One of the most well-known stock market indexes is the S&P 500. It measures the stock performance of 500 large companies. As you saw in Chapter 4, you can obtain S&P 500 data in Python via the pandas-datareader library. Here you use the library's get_data_stooq() method to retrieve one year's worth of S&P 500 data from the Stooq website:

```
import pandas_datareader.data as pdr
from datetime import date, timedelta
end = date.today()
❶ start = end - timedelta(days=365)
❷ index_data = pdr.get_data_stooq('^SPX', start, end)
```

Using Python's datetime module, you define the start and end dates of your query relative to the current date ❶. Then you call the get_data_stooq() method, using '^SPX' to request S&P 500 data, and store the result in the index_data DataFrame ❷.

Now that you have both Apple stock figures and S&P 500 index figures for the same one-year time period, you can combine the data into a single DataFrame:

```
df = hist.join(index_data, rsuffix = '_idx')
```

The DataFrames being joined have columns with the same names. To avoid overlap, you use the `rsuffix` parameter. It instructs the `join()` method to add the suffix `'_idx'` to all the column names from the `index_data` DataFrame.

For our purposes, you'll only be interested in the daily closing prices and trading volumes for both Apple and the S&P 500. Here you filter the DataFrame to just those columns:

```
df = df[['Close','Volume','Close_idx','Volume_idx']]
```

If you now print the `df` DataFrame, you should see something like this:

```
                 Close      Volume  Close_idx  Volume_idx
Date
2021-01-15  126.361000  111598500    3768.25  2741656357
2021-01-19  127.046791   90757300    3798.91  2485142099
2021-01-20  131.221039  104319500    3851.85  2350471631
2021-01-21  136.031403  120150900    3853.07  2591055660
2021-01-22  138.217926  114459400    3841.47  2290691535
--snip--
2022-01-10  172.190002  106765600    4670.29  2668776356
2022-01-11  175.080002   76138300    4713.07  2238558923
2022-01-12  175.529999   74805200    4726.35  2122392627
2022-01-13  172.190002   84505800    4659.03  2392404427
2022-01-14  173.070007   80355000    4662.85  2520603472
```

The DataFrame contains a continuous multivariate time series. The next step is to derive features from the data that can be used as input for the machine learning model.

### Deriving Features from Continuous Data

You want to train your model on information about the changes in price and volume from day to day. As you learned in Chapter 10, you calculate percentage changes in continuous time series data by shifting data points in time, bringing past data points in line with present data points for the purposes of comparison. In the following code, you use `shift(1)` to calculate the percentage change of each DataFrame column from one day to the next, saving the results in a new batch of columns:

```
import numpy as np
df['priceRise'] = np.log(df['Close'] / df['Close'].shift(1))
df['volumeRise'] = np.log(df['Volume'] / df['Volume'].shift(1))
df['priceRise_idx'] = np.log(df['Close_idx'] / df['Close_idx'].shift(1))
df['volumeRise_idx'] = np.log(df['Volume_idx'] / df['Volume_idx'].shift(1))
df = df.dropna()
```

For each of the four columns, you divide each data point by the data point from the day before, then take the natural logarithm of the result. Remember, the natural logarithm provides a close approximation of the percentage change. You end up with several new columns:

**priceRise**  The percentage change of Apple's stock price from one day to the next

**volumeRise**  The percentage change of Apple's trading volume from one day to the next

**priceRise_idx**  The percentage change of the S&P 500 index price from one day to the next

**volumeRise_idx**  The percentage change of trading volume for the S&P 500 from one day to the next

You can now filter the DataFrame again to only include the new columns:

```
df = df[['priceRise','volumeRise','priceRise_idx','volumeRise_idx']]
```

The contents of the DataFrame will now look similar to the following:

| Date | priceRise | volumeRise | priceRise_idx | volumeRise_idx |
|---|---|---|---|---|
| 2021-01-19 | 0.005413 | -0.206719 | 0.008103 | -0.098232 |
| 2021-01-20 | 0.032328 | 0.139269 | 0.013839 | -0.055714 |
| 2021-01-21 | 0.036003 | 0.141290 | 0.000317 | 0.097449 |
| 2021-01-22 | 0.015946 | -0.048528 | -0.003015 | -0.123212 |
| 2021-01-25 | 0.027308 | 0.319914 | 0.003609 | 0.199500 |
| --snip-- | | | | |
| 2022-01-10 | 0.000116 | 0.209566 | -0.001442 | 0.100199 |
| 2022-01-11 | 0.016644 | -0.338084 | 0.009118 | -0.175788 |
| 2022-01-12 | 0.002567 | -0.017664 | 0.002814 | -0.053288 |
| 2022-01-13 | -0.019211 | 0.121933 | -0.014346 | 0.119755 |
| 2022-01-14 | 0.005098 | -0.050366 | 0.000820 | 0.052199 |

These columns will become the features, or independent variables, for the model.

## Generating the Output Variable

The next step is to generate the output variable (also called the target or dependent variable) for the existing dataset. This variable should convey what happens with the stock's price on the next day: does it go up, go down, or stay the same? You can find this out by looking at the next day's priceRise column, which you access through df['priceRise'].shift(-1). The negative shift moves future values backward in time. Based on this shift, you can generate a new column with a -1 if the price goes down, a 0 if the price stays the same, or a 1 if the price goes up. Here's how:

```
❶ conditions = [
    (df['priceRise'].shift(-1) > 0.01),
    (df['priceRise'].shift(-1)< -0.01)
]
```

```
❷ choices = [1, -1]
   df['Pred'] = ❸ np.select(conditions, choices, default=0)
```

The algorithm implemented here assumes the following:

1. A price increase of more than 1 percent in relation to the next day is regarded as a rise (1).
2. A price decrease by more than 1 percent in relation to the next day is regarded as a fall (-1).
3. The rest is regarded as stagnation (0).

To implement the algorithm, you define a conditions list that checks the data according to points 1 and 2 ❶ as well as a choices list with the values 1 and -1 to indicate a rise or fall in price ❷. Then you feed the two lists to NumPy's select() function ❸, which builds an array by selecting values from choices based on the values in conditions. If neither condition is satisfied, a default value of 0 is assigned, satisfying point 3. You store the array in a new DataFrame column, Pred, that you can use as the output for training and testing your model. Essentially, -1, 0, and 1 are now the possible classes that the model can choose from when classifying new data.

## Training and Evaluating the Model

To train your model, scikit-learn requires that you present the input and output data in separate NumPy arrays. You generate the arrays from the df DataFrame here:

```
features = df[['priceRise','volumeRise','priceRise_idx','volumeRise_idx']].to_numpy()
features = np.around(features, decimals=2)
target = df['Pred'].to_numpy()
```

The features array now contains the four independent variables (the input), and the target array contains the one dependent variable (the output). Next, you can split the data into training and testing sets and train the model:

```
from sklearn.model_selection import train_test_split
rows_train, rows_test, y_train, y_test = train_test_split(features, target, test_size=0.2)
from sklearn.linear_model import LogisticRegression
clf = LogisticRegression()
clf.fit(rows_train, y_train)
```

Just as you did in the sentiment analysis example earlier in the chapter, you use scikit-learn's train_test_split() function to divide the dataset according to the 80/20 pattern, and you use the LogisticRegression classifier to train the model. Next, you pass the testing portion of the dataset to the classifier's score() method to evaluate its accuracy:

```
print(clf.score(rows_test, y_test))
```

The result might look as follows:

```
0.6274509803921569
```

This indicates the model accurately predicted the next day's trajectory of Apple stock about 62 percent of the time. Of course, you may get a different figure.

---

**EXERCISE #20: EXPERIMENTING WITH DIFFERENT STOCKS AND NEW METRICS**

Continuing with the preceding example, experiment with different stocks and think up new metrics derived from the stock data to use as additional independent variables, trying to improve the model's accuracy. You might want to use some of the metrics derived in Chapter 10.

---

## Summary

In this chapter you learned how some data analysis tasks, such as classification, can be accomplished with machine learning, a method that enables computer systems to learn from historical data or past experience. In particular, you looked at how machine learning algorithms can be used for the NLP task of sentiment analysis. You converted text data from Amazon product reviews into machine-readable numerical feature vectors, then trained a model to classify reviews according to their star ratings. You also learned how to generate features based on numerical stock market data, and you used those features to train a model to predict changes in a stock's price.

There are many possibilities for combining machine learning, statistical methods, public APIs, and the capabilities of data structures available in Python. This book has shown you some of those possibilities, covering a variety of topics, and hopefully has given you the inspiration to find many new innovative solutions.

# INDEX

itemsets, 176
itertuples() method, 159

## J

joining two DataFrames, 122
join() method, 47–48, 112, 118, 208
JSON, 4, 31, 61, 70
json.dump() method, 32
json.dumps() method, 46
json.load() method, 32, 61
json.loads() method, 66
json module, 61
json_normalize() method, 68, 70

## K

key-value method, 8
key-value pairs, 28, 88, 112
key-value store, 89

## L

LAG() function, 85
lambda function, 31, 152
last-in, first-out (LIFO), 20
left join, 48
len() function, 19
lift, 178
line charts, 128
line graphs, 128
linewidth parameter, 135
list, 16, 96, 110
list comprehension, 13, 23, 158, 186
list() function, 159
list.index() method, 17
list.insert() method, 17
list object methods, 16
list of dictionaries, 29
list of tuples, 27, 96–97, 150
location coordinates, 5
location data, 5
loc property, 42
logistic regression, 55
LogisticRegression classifier, 203, 210

## M

machine learning, 53, 193
    extensions (mlxtend), 178
many-to-many join, 52, 125

market basket analysis, 175
matching table, 125
Matplotlib, 127, 131
matplotlib.pyplot module, 131
mean() function, 52
mean() method, 52
merge() method, 47, 51, 98–99, 112,
        118, 126
min() function, 152
mlxtend library, 178
MongoClient() constructor, 91
MongoDB, 90
mset() method, 89
MultiIndex, 101
    keys, 103
multilevel index, 100
multivariate time series, 167
MySQL, 74–75
MySQL Connector/Python driver, 79
MySQL database, 163
mysql> prompt, 79, 85

## N

named entity recognition (NER), 11
NaN, 48, 124–125, 165, 184, 190
natural language processing (NLP),
        3, 21
    with Python and spaCy, 27
News API, 10, 66
nlp pipeline, 22
nltk.sentiment package, 11
None entry, 115
nonrelational databases, 74, 88
nonspatial attributes, 156
NoSQL, 8
    database, 88
NOT NULL, 78
np.amax(), 40
np.average(), 40
np.median(), 40
numerical data, 3
NumPy, 37
numpy.append() function, 117
NumPy array, 38, 210
numpy.concatenate() function, 116
NumPy's amax() function, 40
NumPy statistical functions, 39

*More no-nonsense books from*  **NO STARCH PRESS**

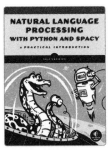

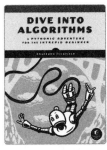

Never before has the world relied so heavily on the Internet to stay connected and informed. That makes the Electronic Frontier Foundation's mission—to ensure that technology supports freedom, justice, and innovation for all people—more urgent than ever.

For over 30 years, EFF has fought for tech users through activism, in the courts, and by developing software to overcome obstacles to your privacy, security, and free expression. This dedication empowers all of us through darkness. With your help we can navigate toward a brighter digital future.